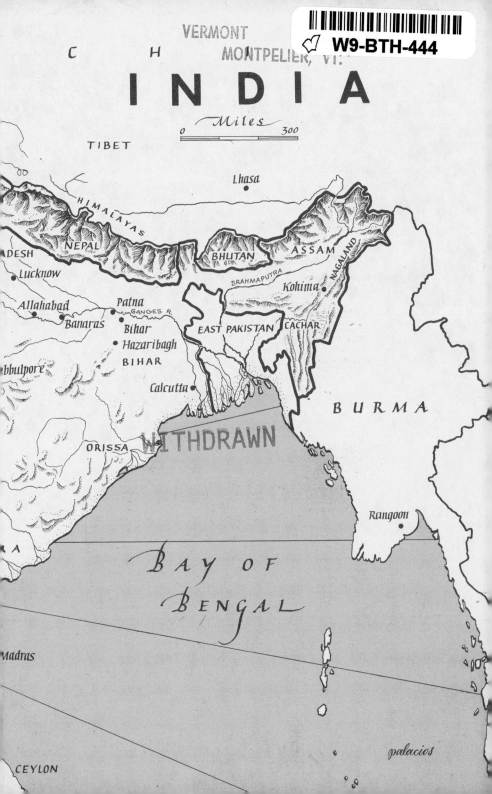

I N D I A

Miles

0   300

C   H

TIBET

Lhasa

HIMALAYAS

NEPAL

BHUTAN

ASSAM

NAGALAND

ADESH

Lucknow

BRAHMAPUTRA

Kohima

Allahabad

Patna

GANGES R.

Banaras

Bihar

EAST PAKISTAN

CACHAR

Hazaribagh

BIHAR

bbulpore

Calcutta

BURMA

ORISSA

WITHDRAWN

Rangoon

RA

B A Y   O F

B E N G A L

Madras

palacios

CEYLON

AFTER NEHRU, WHO?

After Nehru, Who?

by **WELLES HANGEN**

HARCOURT, BRACE & WORLD, INC.　NEW YORK

To My Mother

PREFACE

EVER SINCE I first went overseas as a news correspondent in 1948, I have been fascinated by the question that is the title of this book. Long before I came to India, I sought the answer from every Indian I knew in Cairo, Moscow, and other capitals where I was stationed. Since 1959 I have had the opportunity to pursue my quest in India itself with people of all castes, classes, and political complexions. The result is this book.

One argument I advanced in urging the National Broadcasting Company to set up a news bureau in New Delhi was that the Nehru period was drawing to a close and that India was entering a fateful hour of decision. NBC was quick to see the point and assigned me as its first full-time correspondent in India.

When I arrived in India, I met many people who said that the question of Jawaharlal Nehru's successor was irrelevant. They had a touching faith in Nehru's durability and preferred to close their eyes to the future. Others I talked to were willing to concede that the Prime Minister was mortal,

but they insisted that the situation after Nehru would be
so radically different that there was no point in trying to
assay the prospects and performance of the present contenders for his position.

Both these judgments struck me as counsels of despair. I
could not believe that the Indian political scene was uniquely
impervious to every technique of observation and analysis
used with profit in other countries. Today I am more than
ever convinced that it is not only possible, but essential, that
an effort be made to delineate the personalities who now
show most promise of being able to succeed Nehru or to
exert decisive influence on the Indian scene after his passing.
To say that no attempt should be made to assess those now
vying for the premiership because new leaders may supplant
them is like forbidding the study of presently known chemi-
cal elements lest new and more important elements may some
day be discovered. New personalities will of course enter
Indian politics, but unless they are dropped from the sky,
they will reflect much the same environment that has shaped
the lives of the eight Indians whom I have tried to portray
in this book. In fact, younger leaders will probably hold
similar views and show the same attitudes as one or more of
the subjects of this book. Therefore, I think it would be a
fatal mistake for Americans or anyone else to suspend political judgment because it is not possible to predict with certainty what will happen after Nehru. Indeed, who can predict what will happen to India even while Nehru remains?
Political probabilities have never been mathematically calculated in a country like India.

One reason for the reluctance to conceive of India without
Nehru is the astonishing ignorance, even in India, about the
likely inheritors of his power. There is the mistaken notion
that only Nehru stands between India and leaderless chaos.
Soon after I arrived in India, I set out to test the validity of
this idea. I visited every major Indian city and almost all the
states. I interviewed hundreds of politicians and others interested in Indian politics. I talked to India's urbane philosopher-
President, Sarvepalli Radhakrishnan, and to untouchables
in the slums of Bombay. My conclusion was that gifted leader-

ship is available but little known even in India. This book
is an effort to chart the political and personal contour lines
of this leadership. The seven men and one woman who impressed me as the most significant or potentially most significant public personalities in India today are described in
the chapters that follow.

I have made no attempt to be all-inclusive. I have deliberately tried to get away from the standard approach of analyz-
ing India in terms of its problems. My approach to the country
is through eight of its leading political or military figures.
Some weighty economic and sociological issues are slighted
or ignored in favor of what I regard as the compelling aspects
of these eight Indians and the country they aspire to lead. I
think the personal approach is particularly valid in depicting
India because personalities transcend programs, parties, platforms, and policies in India today. Myron Weiner and other
students of Indian politics have adduced abundant evidence
to support this conclusion.

Besides being politically important, each of the subjects of
this book is a vital and challenging human being. I venture
to hope that even the reader who has no special interest in
India or foreign affairs as such may be interested in meeting
these eight Indians through my eyes. I have found these individuals my most rewarding experience in India.

One thing that surprised me when I started gathering material for this book was the dearth of published matter about
anyone except Nehru and Gandhi. There was almost nothing
available about most of the leading contenders to succeed
Nehru. For this reason I have relied primarily on my eight
subjects themselves—what they have told me and others in
recent years. My thanks go to each of my principal subjects
for giving me many hours of their time since I came to India.
All have been exceedingly generous and co-operative. Their
frankness has enabled me to understand their outlook and
personality in a way that no amount of academic research
could have done. My gratitude has not, of course, deterred
me from including unfavorable facts or pronouncing critical
judgment on each of the potential Nehru heirs. If, as Gandhi
said, God is truth, it would be sacrilegious to do otherwise.

I trust that all my Indian friends, including the eight re-markable subjects of this book, will credit my sincerity in this.

Besides the chosen eight, I am deeply indebted to many others in India, America, and Britain. It is not possible to name everyone who has shared in some way in the making of this book. I am particularly grateful to Paul Grimes, former New York *Times* correspondent in India, and to Chanchal Sarkar, a Delhi editor of the *Statesman,* who read portions of the manuscript and offered many valuable suggestions. They bear no responsibility for whatever factual errors remain or for editorial judgments expressed in these pages. Of the many Indian newspapermen who contributed their knowledge and perspective to this book, I want particularly to mention Sri Mulgaokar, of the Hindustan *Times;* Prem Bhatia, of the *Times of India;* and Frank Moraes, D. R. Mankekar, and C. L. Suri, of the *Indian Express.* Other Indians who were exceed-ingly helpful, and I deem it a privilege to thank, were Mrs. Vijaya Lakshmi Pandit, C. D. Deshmukh, Rajkumari Amrit Kaur, Dr. Ram Subhag Singh, General K. S. Thimayya (ret.), U. N. Dhebar, G. D. Birla, Hardit Singh Malik, Purshottam Trikumdas, J. J. Singh, Rafik Zakaria, K. M. Panikkar, Mrs. Kusum Nair, Mrs. Rajen Nehru, Mrs. Violet Alva, Minoo R. Masani, V. Viswanathan, L. P. Singh, C. D. Pande, Mahesh Saran, and Sadiq Ali. Among the foreign community in India, my gratitude goes to U.S. Ambassador John Kenneth Gal-braith, Albert A. Lakeland, Jr., Craig Baxter, Horace J. Davis, Miss Jane Abel, Myron Weiner, Donald Kerr, Douglas Ens-minger, and Everett M. Woodman (who has since left India to become president of Colby Junior College for Women, in New London, New Hampshire) for their advice and helpful-ness. In England I was fortunate in having the sympathetic assistance of Mrs. Harold Laski, Reginald Sorensen, M.P., John Strachey, M.P., Sir Penderel Moon, Michael Edwardes, Mrs. John Bonham, and a number of others who had served in India or knew the subjects of this book when they were in England.

I have found the following books particularly useful and have occasionally drawn upon them: *India Today,* by Frank Moraes (Macmillan, 1960), *Communism in India,* by Gene D.

Overstreet and Marshall Windmiller (University of California Press, 1959), and *Leadership and Political Institutions in India,* edited by Richard L. Park and Irene Tinker (Princeton University Press, 1959), particularly the chapters "Business Organization and Leadership in India Today," by Helen B. Lamb, and "Dynamics of Socialist Leadership in India," by Thomas A. Rusch.

I am happy to acknowledge the assistance I received from the Government of India's Press Information Bureau and from Captain G. S. Pablay, of the Defense Ministry, in obtaining photographs for this book. My thanks are also due to Girja Kumar, chief librarian of Sapru House, and to R. D. Pradhan, private secretary to the Chief Minister of Maharashtra, both of whom provided valuable facilities and background material. Special mention is due my able and devoted office manager, P. K. Khanna, who pursued the most elusive data with tireless persistence.

Through the laborious process of researching and writing this book, the National Broadcasting Company has been exceptionally helpful and indulgent. I am beholden to William R. McAndrew, executive vice president for news, who cheerfully allowed me to take a leave of absence from the network to finish the writing, and to Leonard Allen, the manager of news, who followed my difficulties with understanding and sympathy.

The worst tribulations of this book were borne by my wife with such even-tempered grace and unfailing sagacity that I feel I should list her as a coauthor. In many ways she is. Her enthusiasm for the idea behind this book kept mine aflame, and her critical comments on each successive draft of the manuscript saved me from the sin of complacency. Whatever sins do appear in these pages must be charged solely to me.

No one can write, or even think, about India without a certain feeling of awe. What presumption to dream of measuring the infinite! At the risk of being doubly presumptuous, I find solace in the words that Victor Hugo wrote at the opening of *Les Misérables:*

"As long as there exists by reason of law or custom, a social order that artificially creates hells on earth and complicates a destiny that is divine . . . books like this cannot be useless."

WELLES HANGEN

New Delhi
November 1962

CONTENTS

xiii

LIST OF ILLUSTRATIONS

AFTER NEHRU, WHO?

INTRODUCTION

GERTRUDE STEIN SAID that the United States was the oldest country in the world because it entered the twentieth century first. By her reckoning India will be one of the youngest. It will be born in its twentieth-century incarnation some time after the year 2000. Today India is a nation in the fetal stage fighting for life in the womb of history.

The struggle for existence is not new for India. It was chronicled even before the Aryans from the north flooded the plains of Hindustan some 4,500 years ago, setting a pattern of invasion and subjugation to be repeated each time India was reborn. The difference now is that if India is subjugated in its present preincarnation, even the Hindu Law of Karma may not be able to contrive a rebirth in freedom. Modern techniques of suppression coupled with old habits of submission are not likely to give the country a second chance in our time. And if India, the largest body of uncoerced humanity on earth today, were energized as well as enslaved, a calamity of incalculable consequences would have befallen the world.

Attention must therefore be paid to this country and its people. One may harden his heart but not close his mind to the fate of a nation with twice as many inhabitants as Western Europe.

It is fashionable in the West, especially in the United States, to say that India is important because it is competing with Communist China for the mind of Asia. India represents democracy; China, totalitarianism. Each, it is said, is striving desperately to outdistance the other in the race for "development" and higher living standards. The outcome will supposedly decide the future of representative government not only in Asia but perhaps in the rest of the underdeveloped world. In such an apocalyptic struggle India assumes transcendent importance. According to proponents of this view, the United States and other Western democracies must give India unstinting support, including massive economic assistance, to enable it to conduct its epic defense of freedom.

I have met many Americans and some Europeans who accept this Wagnerian vision of Asian colossi in collision. I have yet to meet an Asian outside India who does. The reason is simple. Anyone familiar with Asia knows that India has never been acknowledged as leader or pace-setter of the continent, least of all now in the heyday of Asian nationalisms. The Chinese feel even more contempt for the Indians than for other foreigners. The Japanese might as well live in Europe or America for all the affinity they feel for Mother India. Ceylon, Burma, Nepal, Bhutan, and Sikkim are suspicious of Indian intentions or fearful of being swamped by India's expanding population. They have little affection for their giant neighbor. You need only utter the word "Kashmir" to gauge a Pakistani's reaction to India.

I lived for a number of years in the Middle East, but I cannot remember one Arab or Iranian or Turk who thought his country's future would be affected, let alone decided, by what happened to parliamentary government in India. In the Far East and southeast Asia, China may be the focus of fear, but India is certainly not the wellspring of hope.

It is not what happens in India that will shape the rest of

Asia in the next decade; it is what happens in the individual
Asian countries themselves. Democrats in Korea, Thailand,
and Syria will receive no sudden accretion of strength because
democratic India's growth rate has finally caught up with
China's. The problem for Asian democrats—as for Asian
despots—has little to do with what happens in India or China.
It has everything to do with local conditions in each Asian
country. There is no convenient mold into which all the
countries of the largest continent can be neatly fitted. Their
politics, like their coffee, is brewed at home. The external
forces able to change the local blend are the great powers,
primarily the United States, China, and the Soviet Union.
Impoverished, overburdened India, unable even to assure
street lighting in New Delhi, is no beacon for the rest of Asia.
India may boast a parliament; it also has the lowest standard
of living and the lowest per capita income anywhere in non-
Communist Asia outside Pakistan.

If Asia is hostile or indifferent to India, India returns the
compliment. Even educated Indians are surprisingly ignorant
about their continent. Indian diplomats resist being posted to
Asian capitals; Indian students want to attend European or
American universities; Indian businessmen prefer to trade
with the West; Indian scholars know more about English
Chartists than they do about Asian nationalists, and Indian
customs officials give fellow Asians the hardest time of all.
Nehru discovered India after he was thirty, but he still has
not discovered the rest of Asia except in his speeches.

If India is not the beacon and bellwether of Asia, does it
follow that India is unimportant and that the West can
safely ignore it? I believe not. India is important for itself,
simply because it is too big to ignore. More than one seventh
of the human race, or more than the combined population of
Africa and South America, lives in India today. One out of
every three people in the emergent countries of the non-
Communist world is an Indian. As the London *Economist*
says, "A third of the problem to be solved lies within India's
boundaries." Moreover, India's 443 million people (at latest
count) are increasing their numbers by seven or eight million
a year, adding the equivalent of another New York City every

twelve months. From 1951 to 1961 the number of Indians in India rose by seventy-seven million, more than the population of Brazil. By 1981 India is expected to have 630 million citizens.

The birth rate is relatively static, but the death rate has been halved since 1901 and, even more important, infant mortality has sunk from 232 per 1,000 live births in that year to ninety-eight today. In 1931 life expectancy in India was only twenty-three; now it is estimated to be forty-five.

To my way of thinking, such a volcanic eruption of humanity hardly needs to solicit the world's attention by its political example. India compels by sheer magnitude. A few statistics may be of interest. If the government allotted less than a yard and a half more cloth to every person in the country, the entire export surplus would disappear. If every Indian were to consume just one ounce more of rice or wheat a day, every grain warehouse in the country would be emptied and India's stockpile of American wheat and rice would be dissipated in less than a year. There are as many students in school in India as there are people in France. Nehru often talks about India's having entered the bicycle age, but he does not often mention that it will take a little over 400 years at current rates of output to produce one bicycle for everyone living in India today.

India's geographical dimensions are equally staggering. The country is two thirds the size of Europe (excluding Russia) and more than one third as large as the United States. Thirteen Britains could be comfortably spread over India's broad face. You can travel by train for eight days and nights without ever changing direction and still you will not have traversed the length or breadth of India. From north to south and from east to west, India measures about 2,000 miles each way—the distance from New York to Mexico City.

You don't have to travel 2,000 miles in India to retrace several millenniums of history. You can cover a thousand years in a few hundred miles. You go by plane and train and bus and ricksha and bullock cart. You pass cotton fields planted with irradiated seed and irrigated by the Persian wheel. Crated machine tools from Russia and the West move on the backs of groaning coolies clad in nothing but a loincloth. Peasant women wearing silver bangles and carrying naked children balance stacks of bricks on their heads as they toil to build an air-conditioned office building.

The landscape changes even more than the people, because there is a sameness about the face of poverty everywhere. I remember in 1961 going from the torrid, sun-parched plains of northern India to the eroded upland of the Deccan, in the south; then to the delightful Nilgiris (Blue Hills), in Madras state, where the red-coated master of the hunt completes a landscape that might have been lifted from Sussex. Like all cool places in India, the Nilgiris are an interlude that passes too quickly. My next stop was Coimbatore, the new textile city that grew up out of cotton fields. Finally, Kerala, India's stepchild and the country's largest exporter of pepper and educated brains.

If you go west to east, you start from Bombay, that sultry queen of Indian cities, where everything in the country seems to begin. You make a kind of arc passing through the slightly more prosperous farmland of Gujarat, past the old textile mills of Ahmedabad and into the strange world of Rajasthan, with the old Rajput forts on the hills looking as if they had been copied from the Rhineland or the Scottish Highlands. Old Delhi is dusty and New Delhi is neuter and the plains go on forever. Misery's chief milestone is the eastern part of sprawling Uttar Pradesh (what the British called the United Provinces), where the peasants live in the ground like animals and remind you of descriptions of French serfs before 1789. The coal and steel towns of Bihar and West Bengal are as raw, grimy, and impersonal as anything Karl Marx ever saw. And he certainly never saw anything like the nightmare city of Calcutta, where the pavements are the biggest housing project. And at last you find another of those cool interludes in the tea gardens of Assam. You're weary but you still have not seen much of India—nothing of divided Kashmir or the bustling Punjab or the proud city of Madras or the naked primitiveness of Orissa and Andhra, in the southeast.

At least the statistics are now comprehensible. You understand why India speaks 845 languages and dialects, why more than 300 castes and subcastes hold society in their vicelike grip, and why fifteen semiautonomous Indian states (with a sixteenth in formation) compete savagely for a larger share of the purse. You have seen enough untouchables to believe the government when it says that India's outcastes alone outnumber the two most populous African countries combined. Who thinks of India as a tribal country? Yet its thirty million tribal people, many just emerging from the Late Stone Age, exceed the total population of California and Texas.

Such are a few of the dimensions of the sprawling, clay-footed colossus that stretches from the Karakoram Mountains in the north to Kanyakumari (Cape Comorin) in the south and from the Great Indian Desert in the west to the jungles of Burma in the east.

Whenever I am back in America, people ask me if India will succeed. I am always hard put to answer. To say that India is a logical impossibility is to speak of a fact that (as Tagore might have said) is too apparent to be completely true. But to answer, "Yes, India will succeed," is like predicting that the Ganges will succeed. The truth about India and the Ganges seems to be that they will neither succeed nor fail; they will endure. For India this is no mean accomplishment. Whether India endures under democratic or authoritarian institutions is the vital question. It really concerns only India, unless the country were again subjugated by a foreign conqueror (which seems unlikely) or a native Indian authoritarianism could succeed in mobilizing and activizing India's vast human resources. India, like China, could then become a threat to its neighbors and the world. Barring full-scale invasion or the catastrophe of world war, I have always felt that the answer to the question of how India will endure in the years ahead does not lie in Washington or Moscow or Peking, but in India itself. India's leaders must ultimately decide the fate of their country. The foremost Indian leader of his generation, Pandit Jawaharlal Nehru, is now in his seventies. Before very long he must relinquish the responsibilities he has carried so many years. A new generation, now waiting in the wings, will come on stage. This book is an attempt to sketch the human and ideological contours of some outstanding members of the new generation as well as of several influential holdovers from the old.

Most books about India are neatly compartmentalized into chapters on the country's political, economic, and social problems. There is usually no more than a fleeting glance at some of the leaders who will have to wrestle with these problems in what Selig Harrison calls India's "most dangerous decades." I have chosen a different approach. I shall try to depict India in terms of the ideas and experiences of eight Indians whom I consider interesting, important, and representative. One of the eight may or may not be India's next prime minister, but each of them stands for something in Indian life that will, I believe, endure with India itself. Each of the eight commands some following. Each, it seems to me, is a living refutation of the widely accepted notion (not only outside India) that Nehru is the sole leader who can pilot India, that after he leaves, the ship of state will be like a derelict in a typhoon. One thing that has struck me since I first came to India in 1959 is that Nehru is indispensable only so long as Indians believe he is. There is no real vacuum of leadership in India, only a vacuum of recognition. Scholars are fond of saying that Nehru is the last of the charismatic leaders who can unite India by personal and emotional appeal. This is true but not necessarily tragic. India cannot always be held together by the prestige of those who went to jail under the British. Nehru is no more irreplaceable today than Franklin D. Roosevelt was in 1945. One reason that Nehru appears indispensable is the gulf that sets him apart from his fellow countrymen. As Philip Deane has said, Nehru is still ruling a mentally foreign country. His tools are the obsolete doctrines of English Fabian socialism. Unable to communicate with most of his colleagues, the Prime Minister has tended to take all important questions in his own hands. One of his cabinet ministers calls Nehru India's biggest banyan tree, in whose deep shade not a blade of grass grows. The shade extends far beyond the central government offices in New Delhi. I sometimes feel that Nehru stunts everyone else in the country. The new mantra seems to be, "There is no thought but Nehru's." If squatters' huts obstruct New

Delhi traffic, if two states quarrel over the price of electricity, or if Calcutta's garbage starts piling higher than usual, Nehru is asked to find the answer or at least to sanction an answer found by lesser mortals. If a parade or a Boy Scout jamboree is to be held in the capital, the Prime Minister's advice is earnestly solicited. Indians have come to assume that Nehru must attend all ground-breakings, lay all cornerstones, cut all ribbons, inaugurate or close all conferences, send messages of encouragement to all worthy organizations, scold all wrongdoers, and uplift all those who are sorely tried.

Much of his time is spent in receiving foreign dignitaries at the airport and even (as when President Dwight D. Eisenhower visited Delhi) in getting out of his car to clear a path for them through enthusiastic crowds.

Nehru is prime minister, minister of external affairs (including Commonwealth affairs), defense minister, head of the Atomic Energy Department, chairman of the Planning Commission, majority leader in both houses of Parliament, and *de facto* head of the eight-million-member Congress party, which has ruled India since independence. Nehru is beloved by India's masses and intelligentsia as an aristocrat who sacrificed wealth and position to spend more than ten years in British jails during the long struggle for freedom. He is the universally revered "political heir" of Mohandas Karamchand Gandhi, the apostle of nonviolent resistance to British rule. The Mahatma ("great soul") differed with Nehru on many issues but recognized that the best way to moderate his radical socialism was to make Nehru leader of Congress * and the country. Nehru has run India's central or Union government since 1946, when he was named operating head of the interim administration under the British before India and Pakistan were given formal independence on August 15, 1947. He has been a kind of benevolent mogul, eschewing compulsion but reserving all important decisions for himself. He has mo-

---

* Whenever I use the term "Congress" or "Congress party" in this book, I refer to the Indian National Congress, the political movement founded in 1885 that spearheaded the demand for Indian independence from Britain. Similarly, the term "Congressman" always refers to a member of the party, not a legislator.

nopolized authority in New Delhi not for its own sake, but
because he has always been convinced of his own pre-eminent
wisdom. At the same time he has meticulously nurtured India's imported parliamentary institutions, seemingly in hopes
they might someday be a check on the ambitions of an un-
benevolent despot.

Many people in India who concede that Nehru can now
be replaced have told me that only he could have held the
country together in the early years after the partition of British India. I have never been able to accept this idea. Sardar
Vallabhbhai Patel, deputy prime minister in Nehru's first
cabinet and chief architect of the integration of India's 555
princely states with the rest of the country, enjoyed virtually
equal status with Nehru. I feel that Patel could have ruled
successfully until his death in December 1950. By that time
more than three years had elapsed since the monstrous slaughter and forcible transfers of population that accompanied the
withdrawal of British power from the subcontinent. India had
found an uneasy peace by December 1950. Congress party stalwarts like the late Maulana Abul Kalam Azad, then education
minister, and Pandit Govind Ballabh Pant, later Union home
minister, could have carried on after Patel if there had been
no Nehru. The Indian Army, the Civil Service, and the Congress party all antedate Nehru. I think their vested interest in
maintaining Indian unity would have been as effectively asserted in the early years as it is likely to be after Nehru goes.

The historical fact, however, is that Nehru was there and
that he enjoyed unchallenged supremacy in the Congress party
after Patel's death. He became the party spokesman on domestic policy as he was already its authority on foreign affairs.
The difference was that in foreign policy Nehru could put his
conception of Indian nonalignment into practice. Whatever
misgivings conservative Indian Congressmen may have felt, the
Prime Minister could walk a tightrope between the two power
blocs, befriending each and extracting aid from each. He could
keep India in the Commonwealth and simultaneously preach
anticolonialism in Africa and Asia. He could conclude the now
repudiated agreement with Communist China espousing *Panch
Sheel*, or the "five principles of peaceful coexistence," and

recognize Peking's authority over India's historic buffer, Tibet, without evoking more than a murmur from skeptics in his own party until the Tibetan revolt broke out in March 1959.

On the domestic front, however, Nehru's socialism collided from the beginning with the conservative majority in the Congress party. He can enunciate party policy and push through high-sounding resolutions on land reform, state-owned industry, co-operative farming, and a "socialistic pattern of society." But the resolutions remain largely on paper because the powerful landowners and business and professional interests who dominate the Congress party in the state capitals can usually frustrate Nehru's dreams by what one Delhi editor calls their "masterly inactivity."

To understand this impasse you must understand the Congress party, the most important and baffling political phenomenon in India today. It is a huge, amorphous, crumbling coalition of conflicting regional, linguistic, caste, and political interests. Once bound together in pursuit of independence from British rule, party members are now united in little but their self-interest. The president and theoretical head of the party at the time of writing is Damodaram Sanjivayya, a youthful untouchable who was chief minister of the south Indian state of Andhra. In fact, the Congress president is completely overshadowed by Nehru, assisted in party matters by Nehru's daughter, Mrs. Indira Gandhi (no relative of the Mahatma), and the present Union Home Minister, Lal Bahadur Shastri. But to think Congress has a single head is a gross misreading of political anatomy. Like some of the Hindu deities, the party actually has many heads.

Real power at the Center (as Indians call New Delhi) lies with Nehru. In states where the Congress party is not at odds with itself, the chief minister usually dominates. He controls the Congress majority in the provincial legislature as well as the state party organization. The chief minister dispenses patronage, runs the state government, and oversees the police. In practice he decides how law and order are to be maintained in the state and how far directives from Delhi are to be implemented. No law passed by the central Parliament can be really effective in a state without the chief minister's concurrence. By going to the Union government in Delhi, Indian politicians often lose their grass-roots support. A capable chief minister like Kamaraj K. Nadar, of Madras, can maintain a powerful political machine in his state and simultaneously influence the Center.

In most states the Congress party tends to be conservative, or at least pragmatic. The rank and file, made up of small landowners, merchants, and government servants, are as suspicious of change as any Bombay textile magnate or Assam tea planter. They dare not openly oppose Nehru's brand of socialism, but, as I pointed out, they can often thwart its application in their own areas. Land reform is delayed, then evaded. Village co-operatives are set up—on paper—and promptly forgotten or taken over by the local moneylender or landlord. The same fate often awaits the village panchayats, or councils, that Nehru has sought to revive as a means of stimulating local self-government and decentralizing authority. They become the mouthpiece of local officials or of the dominant caste in the village. Nehru preaches against communalism,* and none in Congress will dissent. But Congress is increasingly a Hindu organization with a few tame Moslems, Sikhs, and Christians available for display purposes. Brahman Congressmen in the villages are as zealous as any of their caste brothers in excluding untouchables (dubbed *Harijans*, or "children of God," by Gandhi) from the village well, the temple, and even the cremation ground. The sanctimonious, khaddar-clad rural Congressman often does more to enflame communal passions than avowed extremists. In parts of India the Congressman's white Gandhi cap and mouthing of Gandhian precepts about love of one's fellow man have become symbols of hypocrisy.

What is called the Right Wing of the Congress party is a disparate collection of big businessmen, landlords, petty traders, and a scattering of professional men. Among them are free enterprisers, advocates of a mixed economy, and "Gandhian socialists" who champion village industry. Not surprisingly,

---

* A catchall term widely used in India to denote any sectarian appeal or allegiance based on caste or religion. The term usually refers to Hindu-Moslem friction although it is also applied to differences between the Hindu majority and India's Sikh and Christian minorities.

there is no recognized leader of the Right Wing. In the central cabinet, Finance Minister Morarji Desai is generally considered the leading Right Wing spokesman although he denies he is a conservative and calls himself a socialist. He has many challengers for the Right Wing following. The only cement that holds the Congress Right Wing together is its fear of the Left Wing.

The Congress Leftists, who are a minority, preach socialism and secularism. Nehru is in the Left Wing but not of it. He tries to dissociate himself in public from all factions, although his sympathies are unmistakable. The socialism propounded by the Congress Left Wing includes an expanding "public sector" and nationalization of industries where monopoly control exists. It is also interpreted to mean achievement of Nehru's goal of "voluntary collective farming," or collectivization by majority vote of the cultivators. The Congress Left Wing demands a strong central government and controls on prices, profits, and incomes. It wants the state to take a stronger line against caste survivals and other divisive tendencies in the country. In foreign policy the Congress Leftists would pursue Nehru's version of nonalignment with an even more pronounced pro-Soviet bias.

Like the Right Wing, the Congress Leftists lack an all-India leader capable of taking over from Nehru. In recent years they have gravitated toward Krishna Menon and Mrs. Indira Gandhi, but a cohesive group with loyalty to anyone but Nehru has yet to emerge.

For his part, Nehru shelters and protects the Congress Left Wing, not only because it mirrors his ideas, but because he has an old Fabian socialist's horror of Right Wing reaction. I will never forget his pounding the table in anger when I asked him at a news conference in March 1962 whether he considered Right Wing parties a more serious threat to India than the Communists. "Right Wing parties are always the greatest threat," he boomed. "I think nothing can be worse than the Right Wing, because the Right Wing means going back to an ancient world, feudalism and all that. I can't stand a feudalist conception of India. It means ignorance, decay, stagnation, and all that goes to the death of a nation."

As long as he lives, Nehru will be emotionally inclined toward the Congress Left Wing, although he may not always support it in practice. When he goes, the Left will be on its own, faced by the Rightist majority.

It would be a grave error, however, to conclude that all or even most divisions in the Congress party are on policy or ideological questions. The real cause of trouble is personal rivalries and factional antagonism based on caste, language, region, or the age-old craving of the "outs" to get in. In Madhya Pradesh, in central India, group infighting has crippled Congress and endangered its control of the state. In Rajasthan and Mysore, caste feuds for control of the local Congress party have made opposition gains possible. Nehru and his chief lieutenants have repeatedly had to intervene to settle group squabbles that threatened to destroy Congress in the states. Many Congressmen privately predict that the party will split after Nehru. A Right-Left cleavage would be the ostensible reason for the breakup of the party. But in fact, the cloak of ideology is likely to be used to conceal a straight factional split based on personal rivalry. Once disintegration began, Congress might well splinter into a number of state-based parties appealing to a caste or regional electorate. A genuine two-party system is not yet in sight for India.

As long as Congress maintains a precarious unity, the most important organized opposition (despite Nehru's table-thumping answer to my question) is clearly the Indian Communist party. The Communist party majority treads the "parliamentary" road to power prescribed by Soviet ideologists since the Twentieth Party Congress in 1956. A small but vocal minority of Indian comrades demands "direct action" of the kind that brought the Chinese Communists to power. This basic split is reflected in every facet of Indian Communism. The "Rightist" faction succeeded (with on-the-spot help from Soviet theoretician Mikhail A. Suslov) in getting the party's Vijayawada congress in 1961 to endorse co-operation with "all democratic, secular and progressive forces" in the Congress party and outside. This "popular-front" line calls for infiltrating Congress in hopes of neutralizing the conservatives and capturing the Left Wing after Nehru. But the Communists' own Left Wingers reject these tactics and insist on an all-out drive to unseat Congress, which they regard as hopelessly lost to bourgeois reaction. Instead of a popular front, the Communist Left raises the slogan of "alternative government."

The party was demoralized and disrupted by Communist China's open attack on India in October 1962. Seven state councils of the party quickly denounced Peking and declared their solidarity with the Nehru government. The Communist organ *New Age* followed suit with a front-page editorial flatly accusing the Chinese of violating India's "territorial integrity" and calling on all "patriotic Indians" to rally to the country's defense. This truly amazing Communist document appeared the same day that *Pravda* warned the Indian comrades against "chauvinist tendencies" and admonished them to support Peking's three-point "peace" plan, which Nehru had already turned down. Only a handful of extreme Left Wing Indian Communists refused to follow the line laid down by *New Age*.

The same factional struggle had all but paralyzed the leadership of Indian Communism long before the Chinese attacked. At the meeting of the party's 110-member National Council (Central Committee) in April 1962, an untenable compromise was reached to avoid a walkout by the Leftist faction. The new position of party chairman was created for the veteran "Rightist" Shripad Amrit Dange, while the Left-leaning former chief minister of the Communist government in Kerala, E. M. S. Namboodripad, was elected general secretary of the party. This two-headed executive was part of an expanded nine-member inner politburo, or "secretariat," in which the Leftists enjoyed a five-to-four majority. However, in the Central Executive, or full politburo, the "Rightist," or pro-Soviet, wing dominated. In the National Council neither faction could command a stable majority until the Chinese attack gave the "Rightists" the ascendancy. The bitter intriguing and infighting left the Indian Communists leaderless and divided at the national level.

Neither Namboodripad nor Dange, the party's two top office-holders, can be sure of winning majority support in the party on any key issue. Neither has a national following. Dange, who was the party's leader in the lower house of Parliament for many years, was defeated in 1962 for re-election from his home constituency in Bombay. Namboodripad no longer controls even the Kerala unit of the Communist party. No younger Communist leaders of national stature are in sight.

The party's ambiguous stand during the years before the Chinese attack in October 1962 made it the target of intense national indignation when the Himalayan front burst into flames. Communist headquarters in Delhi was invaded by thousands of demonstrators, who made a bonfire of party literature and set fire to the offices. Communist speakers were forcibly prevented from addressing progovernment rallies. A number of party workers were beaten up. The National Council (Central Committee) met in emergency session soon after the Chinese attack and passed an epochal resolution condemning Peking as an aggressor, refuting Chinese charges that Nehru is an "imperialist," and pledging full support to the Prime Minister in the struggle to recover Indian territory. In an even more astonishing departure from Communist dogma, the Indian comrades endorsed the purchase of American and other Western arms to bolster India's defenses. The effect of the resolution was to set the Indian party at odds with every other Communist party in the world. Indian Communists had explicitly taken issue with both Moscow (which reluctantly supported the Chinese) and Peking. The immediate result of the changed situation was to drive three "pro-Chinese" leaders out of the party Secretariat, thereby giving Dange and the "nationalists" an iron grip on the party. The eclipse of the Leftists was complete when Indian police began rounding them up under emergency regulations empowering the government to suspend civil rights during wartime.

Even before the denouement of October 1962 the party's equivocations on Tibet and the border dispute with China had cost it heavily in prestige and membership, which declined to 178,000 by early 1962—a drop of 40,000 in four years. Namboodripad is reputed to have said that as many as half of those who carry party cards are "completely nonfunctioning." The Indian Communists have admitted publicly that party propaganda and political work is often ineffective and disorganized. The All-India Students' Federation, one of the oldest Communist-front organizations, was dissolved in the fall of 1961. The Communist-dominated All-India Trade Union Congress (AITUC) has steadily lost members.

Factionalism has plagued the Indian Communist party ever since it was founded in 1922. The present disarray is likely to continue at least as long as the Moscow-Peking rift. The Indian Communists long regarded Krishna Menon as their only hope in the early post-Nehru period. They campaigned to re-elect him to Parliament in 1962 and would probably support him if he made a bid for power after Nehru. For this reason I have included Menon in this book rather than any of the Communist party leaders.

Despite their debacle on the all-India level, the Communists have managed to retain and even slightly improve their position as the leading opposition party by exploiting caste and regional grievances in such states as Kerala and Andhra. Communist votes in those states are primarily an expression of caste consciousness coupled with social protest. The Communist party in both places has become closely identified with low-caste Hindu laborers and untouchables. In Kerala the Communists are also active among impoverished Roman Catholic peasants. Unemployment and high prices may prompt other castes and non-Hindus to vote Communist, but the party's real strength is its identification with specific depressed groups. There is a fair chance that the Communists may recapture Kerala, which they ruled in 1957 to 1959 for twenty-eight months.

At the state level the Communists are less vulnerable on such national issues as their attitude toward China. Moreover, since the state Communist organization is usually controlled by one faction of the party or the other, the effect of dissension in the leadership is less noticeable there. The upshot is that state units of the Communist party now frequently defy the National Council and the high command in New Delhi. The party shows signs of becoming state-based. As long as they are reduced to playing on local caste antipathies, the Communists cannot hope to wield decisive power on a national scale in India. But it would be foolish to underestimate their potential. The leadership rift may not last forever. Meanwhile, class consciousness is beginning to displace caste feelings among India's growing industrial proletariat. Defeat in war or economic collapse could make possible a Communist take-over in India, but my impression is that this danger is generally exaggerated in the West.

Apart from the Communist party, there is now no effective Left Wing opposition to Congress. The Praja (People's) Socialist party (PSP), descendant of the old socialist group in Congress, has been deserted by three of its four principal founders. It was routed in the 1962 election. Jayaprakash Narayan, one of the deserters, has repudiated party politics but still commands a sizable following in the Hindi-speaking areas of north and central India. I have devoted a somewhat long chapter to him, not because I think his prospects for succeeding Nehru are good (in fact, they are very poor), but because I think his career is a fascinating example of the power of Indian reality to subdue the most ardent revolutionary. The only other non-Communist group on the Left is the Socialist party, a small radical splinter group headed by that most cantankerous of all Indian politicians, Dr. Ram Manohar Lohia.

To the Right of Congress the thunder is loud but not yet dangerous. The party that worries Nehru most is the Bharatiya Jan Sangh (Indian People's party), the standard-bearer of Hindu traditionalism, which now ranks second only to Congress in Bihar and Madhya Pradesh. In the country as a whole, however, the Jan Sangh won only 6.1 per cent of the vote in the 1962 elections. The party denies it is anti-Moslem, but its leaders never tire of denouncing Pakistan and casting doubt on the loyalty of India's fifty million Moslems. The sinister side of the Jan Sangh is its undercover association with the Rashtriya Swayamsevak Sangh (RSS), or National Volunteer Association, the militant Hindu organization, one of whose members assassinated Gandhi. Many Indians fear that the Jan Sangh, the RSS, and kindred organizations of Hindu extremists may try to unleash anti-Moslem pogroms immediately after Nehru dies.

The irony is that the advent of a form of democracy and the end of total stagnation in rural India have aroused the very forces of obscurantism that Nehru most dreads. When there were no economic opportunities in the village, there was no competition. Now a few openings exist, and the struggle for them is waged with every mildewed weapon of caste and religious prejudice. The worst fanatics are not unlettered coolies from the rice paddies; they are half-educated youths who lounge around teashops or on street corners spoiling for trouble. Economic depression or political turmoil would swell the ranks of such idlers and heighten the danger of communal outbursts. In the short run the Jan Sangh and the RSS would benefit more than the Communists from such a situation, because the Right Wing Hindu groups could exploit anti-Moslem sentiment more effectively. A proletarian revolution is much less likely under present conditions than a communal reaction led by disgruntled petty-bourgeois elements and Hindu extremists in the countryside. Such a reaction would be violent but short-lived. For this reason I regard the Communists as the most serious long-term threat.

I considered including one of the Jan Sangh leaders in this book, but decided against it because no one in the party has yet achieved national standing or even clear political definition. Professor Balraj Madhok, of Delhi, formerly the party's most articulate spokesman in Parliament, was defeated in the 1962 election. A. B. Vajpayee, another Jan Sangh leader in Parliament, failed to keep his seat in the Lok Sabha, or lower house, although he was later returned to the upper chamber, the Rajya Sabha. To an even greater extent than the Communists, the Jan Sangh is a state-based party. Its strength is nominal outside the Hindi-speaking areas and among pockets of Hindu refugees from Pakistan. The Jan Sangh has no national leadership, but its revivalist program does have an appeal in the northern and central states. It reflects the inevitable reaction to the Westernizing and modernizing influences that have impinged on India with increasing effect since independence. Many Right Wing Congressmen in the states find Jan Sangh ideas congenial. The Jan Sangh organ betrayed surprising sympathy for Finance Minister Morarji Desai in July 1962 when it denounced suggestions that Indira Gandhi was her father's logical successor. The party obviously prefers Desai to any other Congress candidate for the premiership.

The Jan Sangh's relationship to the Congress Right Wing is roughly equivalent to the Communists' position vis-à-vis the Congress Left Wing.

The only other Rightist party of national importance is the Swatantra (Freedom) party, founded in 1959 by Chakravarti Rajagopalachari, of Madras, a wily octogenarian Brahman who worked with Gandhi and Nehru before independence and was governor-general (the only Indian to hold the office) when India became a republic in 1950. Rajaji, as he is known in India, later broke with Nehru on the issue of increasing statism, or "permit raj." He founded Swatantra on a platform promising free enterprise and opposing co-operative farming and central planning. The party is closer to the British Tories or the American Republicans than any other Indian political group is, but its membership is curiously mixed: disgruntled former Congressmen, former landlords, recalcitrant former civil servants, some big businessmen, a handful of princes-turned-politician, and some other traditional leaders. The comely Maharani of Jaipur was elected to Parliament in 1962 on the Swatantra ticket. She and other members of former ruling houses enabled Swatantra to become the leading opposition party in Rajasthan and Gujarat, where traditional peasant loyalties are still strong. With due respect to the Maharani, I fear Swatantra's blue bloods are a wasting political asset. Nowhere in the 1962 election did the party's laissez-faire economics strike a responsive chord among voters. This did not surprise me, because I have never seen hungry men clamoring to make sure that the well-fed are relieved of the burden of government controls. Nevertheless, many conservative Congressmen secretly share Swatantra's abhorrence of socialism, and several large Indian business houses prudently contribute to both Congress and Swatantra. Rajaji admits that he has been disappointed by the party's performance. Swatantra is often described as a party of the future, but I doubt that the future will ever materialize for it unless it finds younger leaders and a popular issue.

Everything I have seen in India since 1959 leads me to accept the conclusion of one opposition leader, who says that India has a "government without an alternative." There is no alternative to Congress even though the party's leaders may expose

the country to mortal danger by their negligency (as was demonstrated at the time of the Chinese attack in October 1962).
No matter how enfeebled he becomes, Nehru can remain
prime minister as long as he wants the job. Even after he goes,
Congress can still dominate Indian politics provided it does
not split. If a nonparty leader like Narayan were called in to
take the reins, the call could only come from Congress. A take-
over by the Army is unlikely as long as economic conditions
are no worse and there is some prospect of improvement. To
be on the safe side, I have included one army leader in my
eight profiles. Except for Narayan, all the rest are members
of the Congress party.

I often wonder why anyone would want to be prime minister
of India. What could be more difficult than running the
world's most populous democracy by a combination of per-
suasion, pressure, and pugnacity? The pay is modest (only
1,600 rupees, or $340, a month after taxes), satisfactions are
few, and there is no security. The burdens that come to rest on
the shoulders of India's prime minister dwarf the Himalayas.
Those somber mountains no longer protect India from the
most awesome threat to its independent existence today—
Chinese Communist expansionism. The Himalayan struggle
may wax hot or cold over the years but India must henceforth
live with the fact of Chinese hostility. The hot phase that began with the Chinese attack on October 20, 1962, melted many
differences and divisions in the Indian polity, including the
Congress party. But the national and party unity generated in
the first heat of conflict was more apparent than real. Nothing
has been done to arrest the slow disintegration of Congress.

Next to the Chinese dragon in the Himalayas, the most
urgent problem facing Nehru's successor, whoever he is, will
be people. I have already cited the population statistics. The
only statistic that India can offer in rebuttal is the $100
million allocated in the third five-year plan (1961-1966) for
birth control, or "family planning," as it is delicately referred to in Delhi. Under present conditions of more than 75-
per-cent illiteracy, the government could as well teach Sanskrit
to every peasant as persuade him to forgo the only truly pleas-
urable and productive activity in his life. In rural India today,

children, especially sons, are the highest status symbol. The farmer regards children as an economic asset.

The multiplication of such hungry assets has eaten into the real gains expected from what the *Economist* calls "the world's biggest essay in human improvement." Per capita income, according to the government, rose about 17 per cent, to the equivalent of $69.30 at current prices, in the decade ending in 1960-1961. Even this modest increase is misleading. Surveys of consumer spending show that three quarters of the low-income groups report that their earnings have remained unchanged. Only 10 per cent have improved their position. The number of unemployed continues to rise faster than new job opportunities. The second five-year plan (which was stretched out to six years) was supposed to create eight million new nonfarm jobs. In fact, it created no more than six and a half million. Even if all targets of the current third five-year plan are attained on schedule (now highly doubtful), the pool of jobless will be around ten million at the end of the plan—one million more than at the beginning. Such calculations obscure the fact that no one really knows how many Indians are unemployed or underemployed. Professor P. C. Mahalonobis, head of the Indian Statistical Institute and one of the framers of the second five-year plan, has estimated that besides the totally unemployed, some twenty million Indians have work for one hour a day or less, another twenty-seven million work less than two hours a day, and forty-five million for less than four hours a day. Whether waste of human resources on such a gigantic scale can be overcome without labor direction and other coercive methods has yet to be demonstrated.

The enormity of India's problem is illustrated by the simple fact that by the end of the fifth five-year plan, in 1976, assuming that all goals are achieved on time, per capita income in India will be about $112 a year in current prices—less than Ceylon's per capita income today and about the same as Egypt's. The Indian figure will be two thirds of Ghana's per capita income today and less than one third the present Yugoslav level.

Such comparisons indicate that Nehru's successors can count themselves successful if India achieves anything above normal subsistence levels. Nevertheless, a phalanx of Indian planners and Western friends of India talks glibly today of "take-off" at the end of the fourth or fifth plan to the cherished stage of "self-generating growth." When this day dawns, it is said, India's need for "extraordinary" outside assistance will end, Asian democracy will have been redeemed, and men of good will everywhere can breathe a sigh of relief.

How India can achieve such wonders by democratic means when its per capita income will not even have reached the level of Ceylon or Ghana today has never been explained. Even if considerable resources had not been diverted to military expenditure beginning in October 1962, India's need for aid would probably have increased, rather than diminished, throughout the 1960's and 1970's, because imports for maintence of its productive plant were rising faster than earnings from exports or such things as tourism. Foreign gifts or long-term loans will be required if India's economy is not to go into reverse. Even the United States, which started from a much higher level than India, continued to import large amounts of capital throughout the nineteenth century. The chimera of self-generating growth is, I am afraid, fated to remain always just beyond the end of the "next" five-year plan. Despite all the talk about take-off, India's bullock-cart economy will be earth-bound for the better part of a generation.

Does this mean that almost $5 billion of American aid to India since 1951 has been wasted and that further help should be discontinued? My answer would be an emphatic no. American loans and grants, especially surplus foodstuffs provided under Public Law 480, have helped maintain stable government and an open society in India by enabling the Nehru government to keep pace with the population increase and raise living standards slightly. Emergency shipments of American arms after the Chinese attack in October 1962 improved the Indian Army's fighting capabilities and boosted its morale after a series of reverses on the Himalayan frontier. America's contribution to expanding Indian power production and modernizing the rail system has been indispensable to the industrialization program that has so diversified India's output. Without large-scale Western assistance, India would either have continued to stagnate economically or have been obliged to lean heavily on the Soviet bloc. Such dependence could hardly have been without political consequences for the fledgling Indian republic. From this standpoint I think American aid to India can be said to have been reasonably effective. The cumulative totals are astronomic, but yearly allocations at the current rate of about $500 million amount to less than one eightieth of the annual budget of the U.S. Defense Department. As Barbara Ward has pointed out, even if the West were to give India as much as $2.25 billion a year (more than twice the current amount), it would still not exceed two fifths of 1 per cent of the combined national incomes of the aid-giving countries. The largest item in American aid is surplus farm commodities, whose book value has little relation to what they would fetch on the open market; they are far more of a burden in an American warehouse than in the stomach of a hungry Indian peasant.

Such considerations do not detract from the continuing generosity the United States has shown India. Nehru's grudging acknowledgment of American help has been far less generous than could reasonably be expected. The Indian government talks about its forever dwindling foreign-exchange reserves as if the future depended on them. The fact is that India's own reserves are no longer of much importance. The economy would collapse tomorrow if it were not for the steady input of large amounts of Western, mainly American, aid. Nor could India have possibly re-equipped its Army after the Chinese attack in October 1962 without large-scale American arms aid provided without any hope of eventual dollar payment.

I think a good deal of anguish could be taken out of the aid debate if the United States recognized that its loans and grants will not soon make India self-supporting, nor will they earn much official gratitude in New Delhi. If all goes well, India's need for outright grant aid may taper off in the next fifteen years, but long-term loans at low interest will still be required. If all does not go well, and Indian democracy dies in its cradle, Washington would, of course, have to review its policy. It would probably help even a totalitarian India if it were not Communist. After all, it has helped many other undemocratic governments around the world, and its investment in India is larger than anywhere else.

But to return to Nehru's harried successor (whoever he is), sitting behind the boomerang-shaped desk in New Delhi's South Block office building, it is apparent that Chinese expansionism, population, living standards, and foreign aid will be only some of the more immediate problems on his desk. He will also have to grapple with what Indians call "fissiparous tendencies"—the divisive forces unleashed by caste hatreds, religious fanaticism, regional animosities, and linguistic particularisms. But behind and beyond all these pressing matters, there is something more fundamental. Unless the value system of Indian society undergoes a peaceful but thoroughgoing revolution, problems of production and reproduction will remain unsolved. The tragedy of India is not poverty, but the mentality that accepts, even condones, poverty. The need is not so much machinery, as motivation.

The most perceptive thing I have read about India is a little book called *Blossoms in the Dust*, by Kusum Nair, an Indian lady of the fourth estate. She was commissioned by the Indian government to tour the country to gather material for a book on the accomplishments of the community-development program. She wrote a book, but not the one the government expected. She found that the root cause of stagnation is not material, but mental—the stagnant mentality of most Indian peasants. Planners in Delhi and Washington may assume that everyone living at or near subsistence level is bent on improving his life. Indeed, the argument runs, the poor man's "expectations" have now been aroused to such fever pitch that he may well take the law into his own hands or turn to totalitarian panaceas unless his wants are satisfied by an indulgent democratic government. No one who has seen even a part of the Indian landscape at close range can accept such a theory. The problem in rural India is not rising expectations; it is static expectations or none at all. Kusum Nair had to plead with many south Indian peasants to persuade them even to imagine how much land they would need to support their families. The horizons of most were so narrow that they could not visualize anything substantially better than what they had. She talked to thousands of peasants who had refused to take up irrigation water flowing near their fields or to adopt improved seeds and better methods of cultivation offered by government extension workers. It was not that the peasants were unaware of the increased yields and higher income they would derive from such improvements. But they were reluctant to risk money or make the extra effort required. Many peasants who have taken the plunge and succeeded in augmenting their earnings squander them on nonessentials or look for easier work in town. The Indian village and its inhabitants are all too often lost in what Tagore called "the dreary desert sand of dead habit." The material resources for a better life do not automatically stimulate a desire for it in the caste-ridden Indian countryside. Some groups, of course, want more and are willing to work for it. But, as Kusum Nair says, "The upper level they are prepared to strive for is limited and it is the floor generally that is bottomless. This does not mean that the desired standard is always fixed at subsistence level. . . . It may be considerably more than the minimum necessary to breed and survive. But whatever the level, it tends to be static, with a ceiling rather than a floor, and it is socially determined. Generally, the lower the level, the more static the aspirations tend to be."

The disease of static aspirations is not confined to India, but it is endemic among the 82 per cent of India's people who live in its 550,000 villages.

It is often said that the townspeople and urban intelligentsia should provide the impetus lacking in the countryside. The difficulty is that there are 500 or 1,000 years between the ordinary Indian village and a town of any size. If the floor of aspiration is bottomless in the village, the towns suffer from another evil: there is no ceiling on cupidity. The banya, or merchant, and the urban *nouveaux riches* are often as blinded by greed as the villagers are by tradition. Social conscience finds poor soil in India. The new technical and professional intelligentsia, many of whom have studied abroad and married outside their caste, may breathe fresh air into the dank recesses of Indian society. They may escape the egotism and suspicion that so often nullify collective action by educated Indians. Communist China has stifled its intelligentsia with the professed aim of mobilizing the masses. Nehru has failed to draw strength in adequate measure from either class. Long years of alien rule in India have stultified the will and corroded the outlook to a degree that democracy finds hard to undo.

If Nehru's heirs are to succeed in any but a purely chronological sense, they must tap new sources of strength in Indian society. It will not suffice to inveigh against caste and superstition, as Nehru has done; they will have to find a democratic way of destroying the old rigidities. To instill that sense of urgency that no traditional society can have, the new generation of leaders must appeal to a new generation of followers— to the young engineer working for 400 rupees ($80) a month in the Bihar coal fields, to the Bengali newspaperman just back from a Nieman at Harvard, and to the agricultural graduate who is not afraid to soil his hands. Through them India may one day attain that "heaven of freedom" envisioned by Tagore, "Where the mind is without fear and the head is held high."

Morarji Desai

IF I WERE TOLD at the unlikely hour of five o'clock tomorrow morning in New Delhi to find the man most likely to succeed Nehru as prime minister of India, I would go to Number One Willingdon Crescent. There I would enter the high sandstone gate, pass a sleepy guard, and ring the doorbell of a rambling one-story mansion covered with peeling yellow paint and streaked by the monsoon. If I were admitted—which is unlikely at that hour—I would go to a stifling bedroom, where I would find the object of my quest doing yoga exercises in bed. Morarji Ranchhodji Desai, India's puritanical prophet of solvency and salvation, would already be well launched on another day's crusade.

The Finance Minister of the Indian government is a man of medium height and spare build. He looks younger than his sixty-six years. His head is close-shaven, his face is smooth, and his eyes are steady behind flesh-colored glasses. He moves with youthful agility. His sleeveless outer vest, diaper-like dhoti, and white Gandhi cap are always spotless and unwrinkled. His appearance and manner remind me of a fastidious professor of mathematics rather than of an Indian politician who regards himself as Nehru's logical heir. His voice is low and a bit weary, as if he were forever fated to teach first truths to a class of retarded pupils.

His professorial exterior is no clue to the complex and commanding personality of the man who balances the books of the world's most populous democracy and now ranks second only to Nehru in the cabinet hierarchy. Morarji Desai, moralist, policeman, and incorruptible administrator, is the first choice of Indian conservatives and many moderates to be the next prime minister. In matters of policy he is autocratic and overbearing, but he answers India's craving for strong leadership. His dietary taboos and personal asceticism may be nothing but faddism, but they conform to the Indian ideal of renunciation. His prescriptions for India may reflect no theoretical profundity, but they are pragmatic and contain a sufficient admixture of morality and revivalism to appeal to the Indian taste for politics flavored with religion.

No Indian leader has collected more sobriquets than Desai. He is called the Congress party monk, the man behind the iron mask, and the lotus with the steel stem. He is compared to Cromwell and Sir Stafford Cripps. I never knew Cromwell or Sir Stafford Cripps, but my impression is that these comparisons are misleading. There is, I admit, a mortuary coldness about Desai's public image, especially his stern little homilies on hardships to come for India. But the man himself is not cold except when he wishes to be. His smile is engaging. The words that sound bigoted or heartless in cold print are the persuasive voice of reason when you hear them from his lips. He enjoys a joke (even about liquor) and can laugh. There is a gentleness and apparent humility about him that never come through the harsh filter of newspaper pictures and the texts of his speeches. Whereas Krishna Menon is abusive and Nehru often petulant in Parliament, Desai is restrained. In the face of bitter opposition taunts, his rebuttals seem to be more in sorrow than in anger. Like a good preacher, he never closes the door against the repentant. Nearing the end of the seventh decade of his life, he is no crank, whatever his eccentricities, and no blinkered bigot, however much he cherishes his brand of Hinduism. Of him a critical Indian weekly once wrote: "His judgment may be in error; his calculation may be faulty; he may be unknowingly influenced by a hundred concealed infirmities of the human mind. But his conscience must be clear. And that is why Mr. Desai, who does not seduce our affections, extorts our respect. He has the virtue of unyielding constancy."

The West calls Desai a conservative. The Communists call him a reactionary. And he calls himself a Gandhian and a socialist. In fact, he fits none of these standard political classifications. He has told me more than once that there is no place for conservatives in a country where 440 out of 443 million people earn less than the equivalent of $600 a year. He has no nostalgia for the old order in India and no fear of change, so the Communists are obviously wrong when they call him a reactionary. As for being a Gandhian, the Mahatma's cardinal tenet was nonviolence, which Desai has always eschewed in favor of the big stick when it comes to protecting lives and property. And, finally, if socialism means anything in a country like India, it means state ownership of the principal means of production. But Desai has seen the red ink on the balance sheets of far too many Indian government enterprises to have any illusions about the blessings of nationalization. I remember him sitting behind his big desk in his North Block office in New Delhi telling me earnestly, "When every person cultivates sufficient courage and discretion to see that he is not exploited, then we can get the perfect society." That prescription ought to qualify him for the title of India's most rugged individualist. He calls nationalization a "great burden" and favors a fair return on capital "so long as it is earned honestly and through enterprise." He says that the essence of a socialist pattern of society is an "atmosphere of social justice."

No board of directors in New York or London should conclude from such sentiments that Desai is the answer to their prayers. He is that rare species of politician, one who commits himself to no one. He is no one's mouthpiece. He is not even committed to an ideology. I have always considered him at heart an administrator and a policeman. His criterion is efficiency, and his framework is legality. Nothing else really matters except where Hindu morality impinges, as in the case of prohibition. But in larger issues he is increasingly inclined to apply purely pragmatic standards of judgment. The same might be said of S. K. Patil, the minister of food and agriculture. The difference is that whereas Indian business might support both Patil and Desai, it realizes it can never have Desai in its pocket. It is true that the Finance Minister has been close for many years to G. D. Birla and other Indian industrialists. But he has never been their stooge. Similarly, his fiscal sobriety and sturdy dependability have made him popular in London and Washington without identifying him in Indian eyes as a man of the West. Although Nehru originally brought him to Delhi, Desai has now worked his own passage to the Center and is no longer beholden to the Prime Minister.

If Desai does become prime minister of India, he will be ruthless with dishonest businessmen while giving considerable scope to legitimate private enterprise. He would also encourage the investment of foreign private capital in India. He has none of Nehru's deep-seated suspicion of the "private sector" and his revulsion at the profit motive. India's state-owned industry would be maintained and expanded, but not necessarily at the expense of private operators. If private capital was forthcoming, Desai's inclination would be to let it do the job. Since coming to Delhi he knows only too well the limitations of India's creaking and archaic government machine. Though he is not a conservative in the Western sense of that term, he is a conservative about methods. He absolutely rejects revolutionary means of changing society, and he is averse to open deviations from legality. He may be autocratic in his approach, but he always wants to clothe his actions with ample legal raiment. Moreover, much of his political support comes from genuine conservative forces in India. For these reasons and as a kind of verbal short cut, Desai will often be referred to in this book as a conservative or Right Wing candidate. This description is correct if you always bear in mind that it does not mean the kind of conservatism practiced by the British Tories or the American Republicans.

If he is pragmatic in public life, Desai borders on the fanatic in his quest for personal self-mastery. After his yoga exercises in bed between 5:00 and 5:30 A.M., he says his prayers and has a light breakfast of milk and curds (no eggs, sugar, or tea). By seven o'clock he is ready to receive the day's first callers as he spins khaddar on his special collapsible aluminum charkha, or spinning wheel, in symbolic continuance of Gandhi's campaign against imported British cloth. He takes his only real meal of the day around 10:00 A.M. It consists of bread, butter, milk, and some vegetables and fruit. Then he is driven to his spacious paneled office in New Delhi's North Block, a massive sandstone pile surmounted by a huge cream-colored dome. It is from there that he juggles the finances of the Indian republic. He receives a stream of callers, whose appointments are usually arranged by letter. He can be brutally curt if he disapproves of a visitor or his petition. But at his best he can pacify the unreasonable and chasten the unscrupulous with such winning plausibility that the most disappointed caller goes away without bitterness. He is usually back in his "bungalow" on the grounds of India's presidential palace by 6:30 or 7:00 in the evening. At home he receives another influx of the innumerable favor-seekers who clutter the life of every Indian politician. At 7:30 or 8:00 (often later) he takes some fruit and milk. He is usually in bed by 11:00 P.M.

Weekends are for "touring," as Indians call official speaking and inspection trips. Desai told me proudly that he has never taken a holiday in his life, "except when I've been ill." He considers his fund-raising trips abroad as a welcome break from the files and filibusters of New Delhi. When he is abroad, he relaxes his normal practice of fasting thirty-six hours once a week. He says that even in Delhi he is now not so "rigid" about observing his weekly fast. When he is out of India, he also disregards his private rule against attending any function where alcohol is served. He eats up to three meals a day when he is abroad, and says, "I put on weight."

Whatever poundage Desai acquires outside India is soon lost in Delhi's six-month summers. He refuses to turn on even a ceiling fan in his bedroom; he would have had the fan removed except that such alterations are not permitted in government-furnished quarters. When he was chief minister in Bombay, he slept on a straw mat. He uses a pair of barber's clippers to close-crop his head every week, and shaves himself with Indian razor blades, which he was at pains to popularize when they first came on the market several years ago. He prescribes "nature-cure" treatment for himself whenever he believes it is indicated. He declines all medicines or medical treatment except in surgical cases in which he believes the body cannot heal itself. He boasted to me that the only time he has been hospitalized was in September 1958 when he was successfully operated on for a stone in the urinary tract. He uses homeopathic methods, including fasting, to treat his chronic colitis. In 1935 he fasted for thirteen days to rid himself of malaria contracted in jail. He says it has never recurred.

Desai's dietary rules are incredibly complicated. He takes no tea, coffee, or even soft drinks. At receptions he drinks coconut water as a special concession to his hosts. Invitations to one college convocation where he spoke had a slip attached saying, "The function will be followed by austerity tea." He uses no sugar, relying instead on molasses or honey to sweeten anything he eats. When a Western newsman in Delhi invited him to luncheon, Desai sent advance instructions specifying that he should be served no rice unless it was hand-pounded. Minute directions were also furnished for other food to be served him.

His asceticism permeates everything he does. When he played cricket in September 1954, he declined to use pads or gloves. He played in a silk jacket and a white cap and, not unexpectedly, distinguished himself.

Desai contends that the myriad prescriptions by which he governs his life are aimed at freeing him from "the slavery of habit." He boasts that he has no habits. In fact, he has more self-imposed idiosyncrasies of behavior than any other man in Indian public life. He also insists that he does not believe in tormenting himself. "These are aids to enjoyment," he told me in describing the intricate prohibitions by which he lives. "They should be made cheerfully and naturally. I don't ask anyone else to do them."

I remember sitting for several hours one hot Sunday afternoon with Desai discussing his much-publicized idiosyncrasies. I am sure he is proud of them, but he is careful not to drag them into a conversation unless you ask him. Nor does he simply assume that he has found the true way, as so many re-

ligious fanatics do. He at least makes an effort to explain his
self-denial in rational terms. I never feel the hot breath of
bigotry when I talk to him. That Sunday afternoon he told me
with great earnestness that he hated fanaticism of any sort, because it "distorts the truth." He was fanatic enough, however,
not to offer me even a glass of water as we sat in the sweltering
study of his home. I kept wondering how high the temperature
would have to climb before he might at least think in liquid
terms. I suppose it is some kind of tribute to the strength of his
personality that I, a weak-willed Westerner, never thought of
simply asking if I could have something to drink during that
long talk.

Desai may not demand that others take his hard road to perfection, but he is not averse to making other roads less invit-
ing. When members of Parliament protested in 1962 that his
new budget had caused the price of *bidis* (cheap Indian ciga-
rettes) to rise, the Finance Minister replied severely that it was
nothing to worry about because the common man should not
spend his money on smoking in any case.

Such is the carefully contoured conscience of Morarji Desai,
who began life on February 29, 1896, in the hamlet of Bha-
deli, in the Gujarati-speaking region of western India where
Mahatma Gandhi and Sardar Patel, India's first home minister, also grew up. It is somehow characteristic of Desai that
he should have a birthday only once every four years. The
year he was born, Gandhi returned for the first time from
South Africa to be initiated into Indian politics. Morarji was
the eldest of five children. His family belongs to the Anavil
community of Bulsar, in Gujarat. Anavil means "without
blemish." Anavils are Brahmans by birth but, traditionally,
farmers by occupation. They are famous in Gujarat for their
outspokenness, industry, and physical hardihood.

Morarji's father was a provincial schoolteacher, whom he described as "upright, independent-minded, a man with faith in
God who remained true to himself and never bothered about
getting money in the wrong way." This is clearly Desai's ideal.
His father, who used to call him "More" (meaning peacock),
died just three days before his son, then fifteen, was due to
marry Gajraben, the eleven-year-old daughter of a local rev-

enue official. The wedding took place as scheduled. Morarji suddenly became responsible for his wife, his mother, grandmother, three brothers, and one sister.

"Until I was fifteen," he said later, "I was a coward. I do not know if cowardice has any virtue about it, but looking back I do feel that it was because of my cowardice that I became conscious of the value and importance of courage."

I have always felt that Desai's asceticism is the expression of his lifelong struggle to master his childhood cowardice. He has made a fetish of self-denial in his zeal to overcome the self-indulgent weakness that he blames for making India prey to foreign conquerors through the ages. His intolerance of what he considers weakness is undoubtedly his own greatest weakness.

After passing his matriculation examination, Morarji went to Bombay, where he enrolled at Wilson College under a scholarship from the Maharaja of Bhavnagar, the former princely state from which his father came. He became a free boarder at the Gokuldas Tejpal Boarding School, where the first session of the Indian National Congress had been held in 1885. He invariably sent his ten-rupee (about $2.00) monthly spending allowance back home to support his mother and the rest of the family. "I never felt the pinch," he told me with pride. "I felt no jealousy for the other boys. Even now I don't spend anything on myself. I don't feel the need."

Desai studied science at Wilson College. He could have gone to England for further studies under a scholarship, which would have enabled him to take the Indian Civil Service (ICS) examinations or apply for admission to Sandhurst. He says now that his mother would not have objected to his going to England. But the obligation to support her and his other dependents, including his young wife, overcame the lure of English education. He joined the Bombay government Civil Service as a deputy collector in 1918, at the age of twenty-two, one year after his graduation. For the next twelve years he visited every corner of the old Bombay state, accumulating a wealth of administrative and judicial experience possessed by no other leading member of the Congress party today. A deputy collector under the British was a combination local executive officer and district magistrate. A Briton usually held the collector's post. At this time Desai was a dapper young man in conservative English clothes and a white turban. His reputation for efficiency and incorruptibility was proverbial, although he often clashed with arrogant British superiors. One man who knew him well says that Desai was more powerful as a deputy collector in the districts from 1918 to 1930 than he was as chief minister of Bombay state after independence.

To the extent that Desai can be said to have a personal philosophy of government, it was largely evolved during his service under the British. When he resigned in 1930 to join the Indian National Congress, he accepted a new goal but retained his administrator's approach. The stern-faced young civil servant of the 1920's now presides over India's tangled finances with the same painstaking attention to detail and the same attempt at evenhanded justice that he used to devote to a village dispute over water rights.

Desai had been a Congress volunteer at college in 1915 and had seen Gandhi in Bombay, but his enthusiasm for the national cause did not take concrete shape until he experienced British superciliousness toward Indians in the provincial Civil Service. "The government showed a kind of patronizing and benevolent attitude toward the people," he told me, "but there wasn't the feeling that it was working for the good of the people. I felt it was a wrong thing for an Indian to serve this government in good faith." The day Desai was due to leave the service, the British collector under whom he was serving asked him to turn over the files on all unfinished business.

"I have no papers to hand over," the young Indian replied coldly. "Everything has been disposed of, even today's post."

For the next seven years Desai alternated between spells of what Indians call jail-going and intervals as general secretary of the Gujarat Provincial Congress Committee. He was overshadowed but not entirely overawed by the towering figure of Sardar Patel, the party leader in Gujarat. Desai courted arrest during Gandhi's various civil-disobedience movements. Before India won freedom he had been sentenced to British jails four times, for a total of seven years. His last term was for three years.

Long before he first went to jail, Desai had begun practicing his personal form of austerity. In 1905, at the age of nine, he says he gave up tea-drinking in protest against Lord Curzon's plan to partition Bengal. Curzon was unmoved. When Lokmanya Tilak, the fiery Congress leader, was arrested several years later, the young Desai joined a student hartal, or stoppage of all activity. While he was still in government service, he gave up salt for three years in what he calls "an experiment with myself." Since 1925 he has eaten none of the condiments, chilis, or hot dishes so dear to the Indian palate. Since 1928, he says, he has abstained from sexual intercourse. In prison he continued his self-conscious conquest of self. He insisted on taking "C"-class food instead of the "B"-class fare offered him.

Of his years in prison Desai observes sanctimoniously, "I enjoyed myself and I made myself better physically and mentally by looking within to find out my failings." A former prison official says that Gandhi and Desai were the only political prisoners who never asked for favors. While he was under detention, Desai opposed the common practice of smuggling food and other items into prison. He gave what an Indian biographer calls "perfect cooperation to the gaol authorities in maintaining discipline among the prisoners." In so doing, the same author says, Desai "invariably sided with the gaol authorities." This attitude does not appear to have endeared Desai to all his fellow inmates. The only recorded instance of nonco-operation by Desai in prison was his refusal to be vaccinated against plague. Prison authorities threatened to confine him in solitary. Desai was adamant. Eventually they relented, and the unvaccinated Desai remained with his vaccinated fellow prisoners. Although he avoided plague, he did contract malaria in jail.

When the British conceded provincial autonomy to India and Congress swept the election in 1937, Desai returned to his old role of administrator. He became revenue minister in the Bombay government until it resigned in 1939 because the British had declared India a belligerent without consulting Congress or the country. In his brief tenure Desai demonstrated his capacity for action by sponsoring legislation to improve the status of tenant farmers and to reorganize the police.

His most important disagreement with Gandhi arose over the Quit India movement. Congress was seriously split. Gandhi agreed with the Left Wing that India should offer passive resistance against the invading Japanese. But he insisted that the British should first quit India to satisfy Indian national aspirations and remove any show of provocation against the Japanese. The sanction was mass civil disobedience and nonco-operation in the British war effort. Desai says now that he felt the movement would inevitably lead to violence "but the socialists in Congress deluded Gandhi into thinking that it could be nonviolent." Desai told Gandhi that prolonged strikes were bound to lead to disorder and bloodshed because most Indians were already living on the edge of starvation. After two hours of heated discussion Gandhi finally said, "Well, then let there be anarchy."

"We can't consciously work for anarchy," Desai objected, "when we know that will be the condition."

"Then what do you suggest?" the Mahatma asked.

"It's not for me to suggest a course of action," Desai answered. "You are the leader. I will follow what you propose."

"But some move is necessary, don't you think?" Gandhi persisted.

"Yes, some move is necessary," was the reply, "but I can't suggest that move. I'm willing to follow your lead in whatever move you propose. You alone can give direction."

Desai subsequently courted arrest and was jailed for three years during the war.

In April 1946 Desai was back as home and revenue minister of a new Congress party government in Bombay. He became the acknowledged strong man of the administration. Six years later, with the British no longer on the scene, he became chief minister of Bombay state, an area of 110,000 square miles, with a population of nearly thirty-six million—more than all the Scandinavian countries combined. Desai told the people of the state, "I seek neither popularity nor unpopularity. . . . I am all for discipline."

As the architect of total prohibition, he won more than his share of unpopularity. Despite an elaborate enforcement system, including police check posts around the city and nightly searches of private homes, bootlegging gave birth to a new criminal class. Desai also banned kissing and drinking scenes in the movies. Restaurants were required to close by midnight. He campaigned tirelessly against the use of cosmetics, against female figures in advertisements, against popular music, and against public dancing by unmarried couples. He ordered all students in the state to use old-style pen points and penholders so there would be no inequality between students equipped with fountain pens and their poorer classmates. He admonished students to discard blazers and neckties in favor of "Indian national" dress.

Desai's most conspicuous failure in his quest for public morality came when he tried to clean up Bombay's notorious brothels. He was hamstrung by the fact that the law prohibits pimping, procuring, and owning of brothels but not prostitution itself. When he tried to circumvent the law, the prostitutes formed a procession, marched on his office, and sent a deputation in to see him. Unfortunately, there is no known record of this confrontation between India's premier puritan and its most highly reputed ladies of easy virtue.

Except in the fields of prostitution and prohibition, Desai succeeded in giving Bombay exceptionally efficient administration by Indian standards. He introduced far-reaching land reforms, including legal safeguards for tenants against arbitrary eviction and rent ceilings on their plots. He overhauled the police and separated the judiciary from the provincial executive. Desai the moralist admitted, "One cannot be happy merely spiritually and mentally if the living conditions are awful." But his philosophy of government was and is grievance-oriented. "The test of efficiency," he says, "lies in the removal of grievances."

One grievance eventually overwhelmed Desai in Bombay. It was the explosive agitation for dividing the huge Bombay state into separate Marathi- and Gujarati-speaking states. Even after Nehru accepted the principle of linguistic states in other parts of India, he opposed breaking up Bombay state. Desai stuck doggedly by his chief. The language issue was a façade for the rivalry between the economically backward Marathi-speaking people of the state and the Gujarati merchants who controlled much of the commerce and industry. Since Desai was a member of the Gujarati minority, his position was invidious from the outset. The Communists exploited the language issue to enhance their own prestige and to form a united front with other opposition parties. To quell repeated violent demonstrations, Desai ordered his police to open fire hundreds of times. He told me later that he estimates that almost a hundred people were killed in these clashes. At least 500 shops were looted by agitators.

Desai's one attempt to use Gandhi's weapon of the fast during the language agitation was a fiasco. He announced in August 1956 that he would "fast unto death" in Ahmedabad to halt the violence then sweeping the city. But after only eight days, with stones raining on the heads of his supporters, Desai broke his fast because he "couldn't bear to see the anguish of the people around me." He now says he never hoped to dissuade the Communists, but only "Congress-minded" people, from resorting to violence. He has never tried another public fast.

By November 1956 his position in Bombay had become untenable. The state Congress party was divided on the language issue and in danger of defeat. Desai took the position that he would not continue as party leader and chief minister unless he were chosen unanimously by Congress members of the state assembly. Since this was impossible, it provided a convenient pretext for his escape to New Delhi as minister of commerce and industry in the central cabinet. Yeshwantrao Chavan took over from him in Bombay.

In March 1958 Desai was promoted to finance minister, where he has succeeded in husbanding India's meager receipts with consummate skill. He has withstood pressures and resisted temptations that would have been the downfall of any other Indian politician except Nehru and, possibly, Lal Bahadur Shastri. But unlike Nehru or Shastri, Desai never spares anyone's feelings. He scorns the euphoria of S. K. Patil and the bonhomie of Chavan. Desai is India's Calvin, dourly warning of damnation tomorrow for the sins of today. I remember a speech he gave a few years ago that must have set some kind of record for chastisement of backsliders. He began by reproaching India's textile-mill owners for failing to replace obsolete machinery because they were making fat profits. Then he warned cigarette workers against asking for wage increases beyond the industry's capacity to pay. Next, he admonished manganese-mine owners by telling them that the government would never increase their royalty payments "under pressure." Finally, he issued a blanket warning to businessmen against trying to compel the government to reduce taxes or duties.

On another occasion, when the president of the Bengal National Chamber of Commerce told him that the five-year plan was "overambitious," Desai retorted: "If you think the plan has not been properly conceived and is overambitious, may I know what the plan should be, according to your conception, within the limits of this country, but which would also satisfy our aspirations? Our aspirations are that we must remove poverty from this country and secure satisfactory full employment and a satisfactory living standard for everyone. Do you have any conception of what this task means? Are we anywhere near it at present? If you want to go at a snail's pace in the matter of development, when can we reach that stage? You may not be worried about that stage being reached very late, but 90 per cent of the people will have no patience if they have to wait 200 years or so to be able to live a life worth living. It's from their point of view that we have got to consider and make our plans in such a way that we constantly exert ourselves and raise our output more and more, so that the prosperity of the country increases and the living standard of the common man goes on rising."

Desai says that India can wait for twenty or thirty years "at most." He professes to see a "fair chance" of self-generating economic development by the end of the fourth five-year plan, in 1970, "or two years later at the most." When that happens, he says, India's chronic foreign-exchange famine will disappear. As I said earlier, every available statistic seems to me to belie such predictions. I suspect Desai himself does not really believe in "take-off" by the early 1970's. Nevertheless, he is persuasive when he discusses economics and finance. He exudes a calm lucidity. He rarely indulges in the sweeping ideological generalizations so dear to Nehru. Desai's whole manner is an eloquent appeal for support. His knowledge of fiscal detail is encyclopedic. He is a man of the files, patiently perusing and annotating thousands of sheaves of dog-eared memorandums and correspondence encased in tattered folders and bound with string. Whenever I call on him at his office or home, I have difficulty spotting him behind his mountain of files. If his attention wanders during our conversation, he may pick up one of his folders and begin scanning it with pursed lips and a look of Olympian resignation. Usually, however, I find him a good listener and, what is more important, an articulate exponent of his own ideas.

Desai's obsession with files and the prompt disposal of grievances has not prevented him from taking a broader view, although many would question the depth of his economic understanding. His views have widened considerably since he went abroad for the first time in 1958, after Britain, the United States, and Canada agreed to waive their immunization requirements. He took his charkha abroad and carried on his usual morning spinning unknown to his hosts. He also took with him an unfettered capacity for observation that enabled him to detect sources of Western strength that Fabian socialist blinders have often concealed from Nehru and Menon. He was immediately struck by the absence of class distinctions between employer and employee in American enterprises. "In your country," he told me with genuine enthusiasm, "the manager and the worker sit down together without any embarrassment. Many times the worker's clothes are as good as his boss's and the car he drives to work is also as good."

A State Department official who has accompanied many Indian visitors in the United States remarks that "Indians generally, in my experience, don't always relish the idea of going to other countries and looking and learning. They're proud and sensitive. Desai is too. But he's never overbearing. He gives a definite impression of modesty."

A New York executive who saw Desai in action during his first trip to America says, "He's never embarrassed. He moves with a self-assurance that's almost a physical thing—not necessarily a social, but a spiritual, ease. He has a calm face and a pleasant smile and he talks easily with all kinds of people."

On his first trip abroad Desai was greeted with headlines in London such as "Nehru's heir comes West" and was repeatedly introduced by thoughtless hosts in America as "the next prime minister of India." He concealed his embarrassment at such gaucheries and showed none of the Brahmanical revulsion that Nehru evinces whenever he is subjected to the more bumptious type of American Rotarian. He even managed to sit on Zsa Zsa Gabor's lap without looking too uncomfortable.

When Desai visited Gandhi's former home in London, he asked to be left alone to pray for a few minutes in front of the window from which the Mahatma used to watch English children at play.

Desai arrived in the United States still wearing his immaculate white dhoti and sleeveless Nehru jacket, but he had outfitted himself with a heavy dark-blue overcoat, the first he had ever owned. "On an official tour," he remarked a bit stuffily, "I cannot afford to be an oddity." Nor was he. When an overzealous American host urged him to impress an audience with the virtues of temperance, Desai politely declined. "I am not here," he said, "to tell Americans how to behave," then added with a characteristic twinkle, "But if any of you should give up drinking on his own, I should be only too happy."

With a shrewd awareness of what his audience would want to hear, Desai told a gathering of New York executives on September 12, 1958, "What I want you to understand is that in our concept of socialism the attack is on poverty and not on wealth." When *Time* quoted him as saying that Nehru was "intellectually but not spiritually humble," there was an uproar in the Indian Parliament. Desai also came under fire for appearing to diverge from Nehru's stand that the offshore islands in the Taiwan Strait should go to Communist China. His relations with Nehru were then still close enough that the Prime Minister upheld him against Communist attacks. Today the result might be different.

Although he said a good deal that pleased his hosts, Desai did not abandon his outspokenness when he went abroad. After Per Jacobsson, managing director of the International Monetary Fund, made a speech laden with the usual admonitions about "fiscal stability," Desai made a quick and telling rejoinder: "As we see it, a concern with appropriate fiscal and monetary policies cannot end with the establishment of conditions of stability. The primary and most pressing objective in large parts of the world today is rapid economic development, and in this context the economic content of stability is as important as stability per se. To assume that the Fund is concerned with the preconditions of growth rather than growth itself would be to take too narrow a view of the responsibilities and indeed potentialities of the Fund."

Although Desai has distinguished himself at home and abroad as finance minister, he has found his political growth stunted under the shadow of the Nehru colossus. He is now widely known among Indian businessmen and in educated circles throughout the country, but he still lacks a mass all-India following. In Calcutta and Madras no throngs clamor to hear the austere man from Gujarat.

In 1961 he suffered a damaging political setback when Nehru forestalled his election as deputy leader of the Congress party majority in Parliament. The prime minister is, of course, the party leader in Parliament. The deputy leadership had traditionally been regarded as the second position in the party. Desai's bid for the deputy's post was opposed by Krishna Menon and his allies, who backed the candidacy of the Railways Minister, Jagjivan Ram, the only untouchable in the cabinet. When Nehru returned from the Commonwealth prime ministers' conference in London in late March 1961, he realized that the bitterly contested struggle for the deputy leadership was being interpreted as a qualifying round for the succession to his own position. He postponed the election of a deputy, then reduced the post to meaninglessness by pushing through an amendment to the party Constitution providing for two deputy leaders. The outcome was a stinging reverse for Desai. Relations between Nehru and Desai became noticeably cooler. Desai was obviously unacceptable to his chief as the next prime minister. Indira Gandhi told me later, "No one but Morarji thought he had a chance of winning [election to the deputy leadership] until the very end, when some of his supporters thought they might rally enough support to defeat Jagjivan Ram." This estimate may be biased. Desai himself first said he would stand only if he were assured of unanimous election. Later he allowed his backers to canvass for him.

Menon is reported to have urged Nehru even before the February 1962 elections to drop Desai in favor of T. T. Krishnamachari, who had resigned as finance minister in 1958 in connection with a scandal involving the state-owned Life Insurance Corporation of India. TTK, as he is known in India, is much closer to Nehru in his economic thinking than Desai is. Desai threatened to resign if TTK were given primary responsibility for economic affairs. About this time Desai told me, "If the Prime Minister thinks I shouldn't be here, I'd have no grievance about it. I wouldn't hold it against him. I am willing to leave but I would not take any other position or office in the government. If I'm to be effective in any work, I must have self-respect pure and simple. There can be no compromise on that."

Desai has succeeded in keeping the Finance Ministry and his self-respect. In June 1962 Krishnamachari was named to the new post of minister without portfolio in the Union cabinet, where he will handle planning and economic affairs as a "socialist" counterweight to the conservative Desai. Nehru's habit of balancing contending elements in India by appointing their spokesmen to his cabinet hardly makes for administrative efficiency. However much he may disapprove of Desai, the Prime Minister knows that the Finance Minister's departure from the cabinet would be interpreted by Indian business and perhaps by Western aid-giving countries as a radical swing to the Left. Desai has long been the cabinet's foremost exponent of conservative fiscal and monetary policy. His knowledge in this field is probably more extensive than that of anyone else in India. At a moment of severe foreign-exchange shortage, Nehru cannot drop the man who has proved more adept than anyone else at extracting large amounts of economic aid from the Western powers.

From his political low point at the time of the 1962 elections, Desai has made a striking comeback. He has quietly mended his fences in his native state of Gujarat and elsewhere. He has made discreet overtures to such important state chief ministers as Kamaraj Nadar, in Madras, and even Bijoyananda Patnaik, in Orissa. By midsummer 1962 his position was strong again. Nehru took note of the change by authorizing Desai to preside over the cabinet in his absence. The Finance Minister made a successful trip to the European Common Market countries in July and then accompanied Nehru to the Commonwealth prime ministers' conference in London in September. From London he went to Washington to attend the World Bank and International Monetary Fund meetings. He was warmly received by President John F. Kennedy and other administration leaders. His speech before the National Press Club in Washington was a masterpiece of wit and wisdom tailored to fit American tastes. I have never seen Desai more buoyant and self-confident than during the grim early days of the Chinese offensive in October 1962. He realized he had again emerged as the front-running contender for the succession by reason of his successful negotiations in Washington and his handling of the delicate economic situation. Menon had come under a storm of criticism when the inadequacy of India's defenses was shown up by the initial Chinese successes.

As with every other prominent Indian politician, however, opinions about Desai's future are diametrically opposed. K. M. Panikkar, the Indian historian and former fellow-traveling ambassador to Peking, Cairo, and Paris, whom one would expect to discount Desai, actually rates him as the man most likely to succeed Nehru. Panikkar's order of probability for the succession is Desai, Shastri, Chavan, Patil, and Kamaraj. Panikkar contends that Desai's apparent unpopularity and the noisy agitation against him are inspired by "half a dozen people." "His position is much stronger than you think," he says, obviously not because he is enamored of Desai's economic or political ideas.

On the other hand, a high-ranking American diplomat in India took a totally opposite view of Desai's prospects as late as April 1962. He told me then, "My guess would be that Desai is scheduled to be finance minister for the rest of his life. Desai is ideal for being finance minister and dealing with the Americans, just as Menon is ideal for being defense minister and dealing with the Russians at the U.N." Few observers who know India would put any more faith in the part of this prediction relating to Desai than in the estimate of Menon, who resigned as defense minister barely six months later.

A State Department officer with considerable experience in India expresses a widely held view when he says, "If the big boys decide on a single strong leader to succeed Nehru, Desai is still the front-runner. The deputy leadership contest was essentially a stop-Desai movement. But you can expect another stop-Desai movement after Nehru goes."

Another officer who served in the New Delhi embassy has a contrary viewpoint. "Desai," he insists, "is discredited and deserted by Congressmen. He's proved he doesn't have political finesse. He doesn't get around. He just sits in his office."

One of Desai's predecessors in the Finance Ministry calls him "both tactless and sanctimonious and much less virtuous than he lets on." He says that Desai is much "duller" than the late Pandit Pant, the outstanding former home minister. Desai has acquired the reputation of being a good administrator, this man says, because in both Bombay and Delhi he has had the sense to rely on Indian Civil Service stalwarts. This estimate of Desai's administrative success may be partially justified but it ignores the fact that other ministers have been unable to make effective use of comparable ICS talent. The opinion of one retired ICS officer, who served Desai in a high position in Bombay, is typical. He says: "The Right Wing forces in India would rally behind Desai if Nehru went. Desai is regarded as the conservative leader of the country. He's willing to do things without regard for popularity. This year [1962] he abolished the expenditure tax. Next year he's likely to get rid of the wealth tax, thus returning us to a normal tax situation."

To the extent that the army officer corps is drawn from the same conservative families that produce the top-level civil servants, the armed services are likely to join the Indian Civil Service and the new Indian Administrative Service in supporting Desai's claim to the succession, provided, of course, the Army does not decide to upset the constitutional process and put forth a candidate of its own. The services—both uniformed and civilian—have a vested interest in India's national unity. Their jobs, their promotions, their pensions, their family interests, all depend on the maintenance of the government of India as the effective central authority in the country. The services are undoubtedly supported in their attachment to a strong Center by Indian trade and business, including even small operators, whose position depends on national markets, national access to raw materials, and national leadership capable of checking divisive tendencies. Few army officers have any use for Desai's prohibition mania, and businessmen squirm when he talks of the need for subsidizing cottage industry and khaddar production. These angularities do not, however, vitally affect business and military backing for Desai. The reason is that Desai is rightly considered one of India's most incorruptible politicians. His record has never been stained with graft.

Although no one has ever seriously accused Desai of being corrupt, his asceticism has been questioned more than once. Many insinuations come from the host of political foes he has acquired in more than forty years of public life. Several years ago a Marathi-language newspaper published a series of signed articles accusing Desai of hypocrisy in his show of morality. The paper reported that he had consorted with a Moslem woman. Although the articles were signed, Desai never brought suit for damages, on the ground that such scurrilous charges were beneath his notice. But as one respected former Indian ambassador and ICS officer says, "Desai's action —or inaction—created lots of doubt and suspicion and hurt his following."

Desai's son, Kanti, a Bombay businessman, has been the object of much whispering. He is alleged to have enriched himself by trading on his father's name. This practice is hardly unknown in India. Desai is said to have threatened to commit suicide if his son did not desist from exploiting his relationship to the Finance Minister. Desai told me that when he became minister of commerce and industry he issued orders that no licenses, permits, or other special privileges were to be granted his son without the Minister's personal authorization.

The suicide several years ago of Desai's younger daughter also cast a shadow over her father. The circumstances have never been explained. The story in Bombay is that the girl took her life after Desai refused to let her marry a young man with whom she had fallen in love. Whatever the real reason for his daughter's death, Desai does seem to have softened somewhat since then. On March 19, 1956, a year after her death, Desai told a Bombay radio audience: "For years I believed that truth is bitter and if it hurts it could not be helped. But I have lately come to the realization that truth cannot be truth if it is bitter, and therefore, if in the conveying of truth, truth hurts, the fault lies not with truth but with the person conveying it. For instance, truth conveyed in anger becomes tainted; it no longer remains pure truth. I have always been conscious of my anger, and I have been trying hard to overcome it, and it is only now that I feel I have succeeded to some extent in overcoming it. From weakness, no good ever comes out. Weakness can only destroy us."

These words reflect a certain disenchantment in the man who once prided himself on co-operating with his jailers even to the detriment of his fellow prisoners. "Moralji," as many Indians call him, is still Moralji, but his moralizing is now less astringent, less pontifical, and less obtrusive. As one Indian newspaper remarked, "The years have brought discretion and tolerance; not that they have altered the rigidity of his own views but that they have induced a greater willingness to concede that he might sometimes be wrong. He has also learned that it takes all kinds to make a world."

In April 1962 Desai said in a talk with me, "Even now there may be some intolerance in me." Most people who know him would regard this as a classic understatement. He went on to say that he was striving to eradicate his intolerance, "but someone must have seen it in me." This slightly softened attitude is reflected in his policy on larger questions. As finance minister, he now regularly and unprotestingly allocates funds to propagate the "artificial methods" of birth control that he believes undermine sexual self-control. His attitude toward medicine is now also less fundamentalist. "For me to say all medical systems except nature cure should be dumped in the Ganges is wrong," he concedes. "I can't become Rip van Winkle or Don Quixote, holding up my spear and sword." Yet one feels that the sword has not been permanently sheathed.

Today Desai speaks of plowing "my lonely furrow" and dilates somewhat less on the weaknesses of others. Of course, he would lose much of his following, especially among conservative Congressmen, if he were to abandon the redoubts of traditional morality for anything smacking of foreign modernism. He has no intention of making such an error. But he has tempered his strictures against the stupid, the prolix, and the merely tiresome people who infest his daily life. Indian public life has an abrasive effect on the most equable nature, and Desai has never won prizes in the art of suffering the insufferable.

Regardless of changes in his outlook or political strength, two questions persist with regard to Desai's capacity to lead the world's largest democracy. The first is his understanding of economic problems. The second is his attitude toward India's fifty million Moslems.

Like most Indians, especially old Congressmen, he tends to oversimplify complicated economic issues. For example, in 1955 he explained his approach to labor relations in these broad terms: "The interests of all must precede the interests of a few. The interests of employers and employees also should not conflict and both should live in harmony although there should always be consideration for the weaker party."

Desai is correctly considered a modernizer and a pragmatist. But mixed with his modernism and pragmatism are elements of Hindu orthodoxy and Gandhian revivalism that raise questions about his real standpoint. On July 17, 1959, he told an audience in Ahmedabad, "Voluntary poverty is the key to true happiness." He conceded that it might sound strange for the finance minister of a large country committed to rapid economic development to champion poverty as the road to happiness, but he said he was suggesting "voluntary poverty

and self-abnegation, and not poverty imposed from above."
Desai's Gandhian devotion to khaddar is also hard to reconcile with his commitment to large-scale industrialization.
Seven years after independence, he could still tell a Bombay
radio audience, "If our national economy is to be sound, we
must develop intense patriotism for Indian goods, especially
khaddi and other products of cottage industry."

A note of fatalism creeps into some of Desai's pronouncements although he denies that he is a fatalist. On October 22,
1958, he told a group of Indian and foreign businessmen in
Bombay that Indians were not frightened of poverty, because they had known poverty for so long and it did not really
matter much if it continued a little longer. Of course, he went
on to issue the usual call for raising living standards, but the
idea of living in poverty (provided one has the requisite
strength of will not to succumb to evil at the same time) does
not really appear to repel him. His rejection of misery seems
in the final analysis to stem more from a fear of its demoraliz-
ing effects on weaker spirits than from any belief in the virtues of prosperity. Nehru hates poverty because it offends his
rationalist conception of the universe. Desai, with his at-
tenuated rationalism, often appears to regard poverty as a
divinely ordained tribulation sent to test mankind. Nehru
despises astrology and the thralldom it imposes on so many
Indians. Desai is reputed to have great faith in what the stars
foretell.

As a devout Hindu, Desai is a believer in the Law of Karma
(destiny or fate), which ordains that individuals are born in
the world under certain circumstances and go through certain
preordained experiences as a direct result of their actions in
previous incarnations. The Law of Karma is unchangeable,
although, of course, Desai would hold that it does not exempt
anyone from striving to realize his full potentialities through
his own efforts

Desai's favorite reading is the Bhagavad-Gita, the great
Hindu epic, whose eighteen cantos he memorized in jail, and
the sayings of Ramkrishna Paramahamsa, accounted by
Hindus as one of the saints of modern India. Desai says he
likes to read "anything that has a bearing on a way of life,"

but he is not attracted by what he calls "a mere theoretical dissertation." Most Indian leaders of the present generation cut their intellectual teeth on the Fabian socialists, Harold Laski, and Karl Marx. Those who did not study in England, like the Maharashtra Chief Minister, Y. B. Chavan, were introduced to socialist and communist theory in jail study sessions. Desai, on the other hand, had little acquaintance with Marxism or socialism until he began reading works on economic theory in 1958, when he was named to head the Finance Ministry. He was already past sixty. He discounted Marx's theories on the ground that they arose from personal frustration. There is nothing to show that Desai is inherently any more attracted to conservative economic theory, let alone American-style capitalism. His immunity to doctrinaire economics remains unimpaired. His approach to administration in the economic field remains free of the doctrinal trappings that have slowed India's progress since independence.

If he is pragmatic in larger matters of economics, Desai is irretrievably dogmatic in most of his social attitudes. His attitude toward women is equivocal. He champions complete equality of the sexes but at the same time frowns on women entering professions outside their traditional sphere of social work and child rearing. He also opposes coeducation and the use by women of cosmetics or Western dress. To my knowledge, Desai's wife never appears in public with him. I have visited their home a number of times but have never been introduced to Mrs. Desai or even seen her. Once when we were packing up our equipment after a television interview with Desai, a sari-clad woman appeared momentarily on the rear porch and disappeared immediately. She may have been Desai's wife, although I do not know

After Mrs. John F. Kennedy's visit to India in March 1962, Desai told me bluntly, "We didn't like her spending so much time with the Maharaja of Jaipur, and especially Princess Lee Radziwill's spending that extra night in Jaipur drinking and dancing until morning. This makes a very bad impression. If I had been the Prime Minister, I would have told her 'no.' She should have been advised."

Far more significant than Desai's attitude toward women is

his stand on the vital question of Hindu-Moslem relations. This problem colors everything in Indian life. Desai's public utterances on this score are unexceptionable. He espouses communal harmony and preaches national integration. But his Hindu traditionalism and fervent advocacy of Hindi as the national language have attracted forces behind him that make him suspect in the eyes of many Indian Moslems. Desai himself may be less free of religious bias than he professes to be. In July 1961, when I asked him about a Hindu convention that was then being organized in Delhi as a sequel to a controversial Moslem convention, he said, "The organizers of the Hindu convention are a few extremists. They don't represent the mass of Hindus, who are more detached and less easily aroused than the Moslems."

Many of the more conservative Hindu businessmen and landowners who regard Desai as their best bet politically are unabashed Hindu communalists. This group includes many Congressmen. Michael Edwardes, an English historian who knows India intimately, says that he is deeply perturbed by the "sinister forces" now ranging themselves behind Desai. Whatever course he actually pursues in office, Desai's Hindu orthodoxy naturally attracts reactionary elements both in and outside Congress who realize that the Hindu Mahasabha and the Jan Sangh are not likely to exercise effective political power for many years to come, if ever. The Jan Sangh itself obviously favors Desai over other Congress aspirants for the premiership. What the question boils down to is to what extent Desai has disavowed the support of communalists. In his present ticklish position vis-à-vis other contenders for the succession, he is not likely to reject support from any quarter unless it becomes a positive liability.

In Indian politics the exercise of power is largely a question of alternatives. And the greater one's power, the more inescapable is the need to choose. If Desai inherits the premiership, he will have to make a clear choice between the forces of modernism and reaction. I have little doubt that he would disown reaction, but the choice would not be easy. As prime minister he would probably continue his social faddism, but his main political emphasis would inevitably be on a program of modernization (which means Westernization) that would ultimately destroy many of the traditional values he seeks to uphold. Therefore, from the point of view of the West, Desai's stewardship would probably not impede India's slow advance into the twentieth century. Indeed, because he is more flexible on the larger issues than Nehru, he might well succeed in accelerating the tempo of progress, provided always that India did not disintegrate into regional and linguistic units.

Desai has said, "The present world is witnessing a conflict between the two civilizations—the one in which India believes and the other in which modern Western countries believe. The latter aims at physical happiness while the former aims at humanity, which is the quality of the soul." This bromide conveniently ignores the existence of a form of government that is neither Western nor Indian and cherishes neither happiness nor humanity.

On the other hand, there is no doubt that Desai is conscious of Communism. He abhors its methods and is much clearer and more outspoken than Nehru about the links between the Indian Communists and the Kremlin. He needles the Communists in Parliament mercilessly about their subservience to Moscow. He has also demonstrated an acute perception of the realities of Soviet society. He delights in reminding the Indian Communists how Russia relies on turnover tax and other levies that bear most heavily on the poor. When the Communists in the Lok Sabha blamed rising prices in India on profiteering, which they contended does not exist in a truly "socialist" society like Russia, Desai replied: "They talk of profiteering. Let me tell them something: The Soviet Union purchased shoes from us at twenty-five rupees [about $5.00] a pair and sold them at 100 rupees a pair. Yes, there's no need of a direct tax or even income tax. They simply add the tax to the cost of goods and get all they want."

In a speech to Parliament on May 10, 1962, Desai abandoned his usual restraint and lashed out for the first time at "fellow-wanderers" in the Congress party. He said: "In the Communist party, apart from members, there are fellow travelers and fellow wanderers. Fellow travelers are well known. They are not members of the Communist party, but otherwise they are Communists who have no courage to call themselves Communists. Fellow wanderers . . . are not able to understand the subtleties of the working of the evil ways of the Communists and they get caught. They are the people who are utilized by Communist friends most and they never realize that they are being utilized. We have got such people in many parties, including my own."

This sally was the nearest Desai has come to a public denunciation of Krishna Menon and his coterie of "fellow wanderers" in Congress. In July 1961, in a talk with me, Desai remarked, "Krishna Menon has not been openly active in the deputy leadership question. But people say he took a hand. He feels antagonistic to me. I don't like to say it, but he is openly against me, so why shouldn't I say it?" As he regained his political strength in 1962, Desai became more contemptuous of Menon's prospects. He was fond of calling Menon a rootless anarchist who could just as well be on the extreme right as the extreme left. In private conversation he contemptuously dismisses Menon as a political nonentity with no following of his own and no ability to attract one. He pictures Menon as purely the creature of Nehru, who will evaporate as soon as his protector disappears. A week after the Chinese struck in October 1962, Desai told me smilingly, "Menon is already on the sidelines. He can't throw his weight around any more."

If India had anything approaching cabinet government, the conflict between Menon and Desai and their respective ministerial supporters would long ago have become unmanageable. But important decisions are rarely made by the full cabinet. At best they are made in cabinet committees. And usually they are made by Nehru in consultation with one or two ministers chiefly concerned with a particular problem. Desai is consulted on strictly financial problems. In foreign affairs only Menon's advice is usually sought.

When he visited Washington in October 1961, Desai told President Kennedy that he had advised Nehru against attending the neutral "summit" conference in Belgrade. On this issue he was apparently consulted, or at least felt free to offer his advice. But the upshot is adequate testimony to the weight Nehru attaches to Desai's opinions on foreign policy.

There was no concealment of the divergence between Desai, on the one hand, and Nehru and Menon, on the other, over Goa. In the wake of Nehru's declaration before a "seminar" on Portuguese colonialism in New Delhi in August 1961 that India could not "exclude the use of force" to incorporate Goa, Desai took a diametrically opposed stand. He told the seminar, which included many African nationalists, that it was not India's intention to invade Goa and that even sending a police contingent would be "an act of war." He insisted that India had justified the validity of nonviolent methods in winning her freedom. Referring to Nehru's ambiguous remarks, he said, "If that leads some people to infer that India is going to make an invasion of Goa, I think they are very much mistaken. That is not what he meant." Nehru angrily repeated his own statement a few days later when the seminar reconvened in Bombay. The Indian Communist organ *New Age* demanded that Desai be sacked from the cabinet for his temerity in differing with Nehru.

Four months after Goa was taken over, Desai told me that his view was that India should have given the Portuguese one year's notice before entering Goa. "Then," he said, "no one could have said we didn't give them time to leave. We couldn't wait forever. The people were getting impatient. But I would have done it after the elections rather than before, so no one could have connected Goa with the elections."

If Desai does become prime minister, there will be no drastic change in Indian foreign policy. Nonalignment will continue to be professed, but its practice may be considerably less fraudulent. One irritant to Indo-American relations will disappear with the removal of Krishna Menon from the cabinet. But Desai's Hindu traditionalism is not likely to make him any more sympathetic to Pakistan than Nehru or Menon were. In his public statements he has never openly diverged from the Nehru line on China, but from the beginning of the crisis in October 1962 Desai began acting with increasing independence. While Nehru vacillated and talked about maintaining "pure" nonalignment, Desai was quietly negotiating

terms of payment for American arms shipments to India. He
has always been less inclined than Nehru to parley with the
Chinese and more unwavering in his determination to resist
them by force. He never shared Nehru's conviction that India
should befriend Russia at all costs on the assumption that the
Soviet government would curb its Chinese ally's hostility toward New Delhi. After October Desai became more insistent
that the Indian government should stop its carping and often
gratuitous criticism of the Western powers and concentrate
on the main task of winning Western support in the struggle
against the Chinese.

This background might well lead Moscow to interpret
Desai's accession to power as the final victory of Indian reaction. Such an interpretation would be incorrect, but it could
nonetheless prompt the Russians to reduce or withdraw their
economic aid to India. India would accordingly become more
dependent on Western support. Despite his distrust of all
Communist regimes, I think that Desai would try hard to
maintain at least some of the present ties with Russia. He
would not want India to appear as another client state of the
West.

Foreign policy is secondary, however, to India's explosive
internal problems. In this field Desai's iron-fisted administration would come into play. He could infuse new vitality into a
tired and sluggish administration. Though he is not young,
his physical condition is good, and he is accustomed to a
cyclonic pace. The question remains whether he has the
breadth of vision to guide India through its myriad perils.
For example, would his scruples against contraceptives induce
him to weaken the attack on the population problem? Or
would the scruples themselves give way under the imperious
necessities of survival? More important than his own scruples
and convictions would be the attitude of south Indians,
Bengalis, and Indian Moslems to his premiership. There is
little to show that he commands the allegiance of these groups.
With West Bengal already disgruntled, it would not take too
many of Desai's strictures to drive the state into nonco-
operation, perhaps outright secession. Similarly, his advocacy

of Hindi might turn south Indian regionalism into a serious secessionist movement.

If government in India were like government in Sweden or Switzerland—largely a matter of administrative efficiency— Desai would have pre-eminent claim to the succession as well as an excellent chance of success in office. But in India, per- haps more than in any other country, a leader is expected to possess qualities of compassion that he either lacks or conceals. He fits the Indian image of leadership in his personal austerity, his refusal to indulge in the frank pursuit of power, and his gift for flavoring practical politics with moral precepts, but the indefinable darshana that the Indian masses imbibe from Nehru and the gentleness and humility that characterize Lal Bahadur Shastri are lacking in Desai's stern and uncommuni- cative public demeanor. However effective he may be in office, he lacks the gift of intimacy so valuable in politics. He tends to be slightly aloof, even withdrawn. In public appearances his oratory is flat and his manner uninspiring. His genuine concern for human welfare is expressed in terms of adminis- trative zeal, not in the consoling words so dear to the Indian masses.

Desai has supreme self-confidence. This assurance rein- forces the dictatorial streak in his character as well as the self- centered mentality that dulls his curiosity and restricts his vision. He is one of the few politicians I know who never troubled to see much of his own country before he was sixty. His enemies call him pugnacious, arrogant, and vindictive. He works by the book. For several weeks after I had unavoid- ably missed a scheduled appointment with Desai, his secre- tary kept ignoring my requests for a new appointment. I finally wrote a personal letter to Desai explaining why I had not come to see him as scheduled. An interview was finally arranged, but the atmosphere was glacial for the first twenty minutes.

An American correspondent who spent many years in India says, "Desai sums up what's right and what's wrong with India. He's austere, ascetic, proud, dictatorial, domineering, and egotistical."

Morarji Desai is really the administrator turned politician. He succeeds in extorting respect from all but the inveterately biased. Whether he could ever seduce the affection that Indian leadership ultimately depends on is one of the many questions about India that remain unanswered.

V. K. Krishna Menon

"I CHARGE HIM with wasting the money of a poor and starving nation. I charge him with having created cliques in the Army. I charge him with having lowered the morale of our armed forces. I charge him with the neglect of the defense of the country against the aggression of Communist China. I charge him with having lent his support to totalitarian and dictatorial regimes against the will of the people to freedom."

The peroration was over. Acharya J. B. Kripalani, a gaunt wraithlike Indian Cicero in flowing white robes, sank back exhausted on the Opposition front bench in the high-domed chamber of New Delhi's Lok Sabha. The object of his defiance rested his chin on his desk on the opposite side of the house; his eyes darted venomously from side to side. Vengalil Krishnan Krishna Menon was at bay.

It was not the first time I had watched him under fire. I knew he derived a perverse kind of enjoyment from being hated. Conflict has always been the thread of his life, as rigidly prescribed as the sacred thread a Brahman wears on his chest to denote his high caste. In the beginning there was the matriarchal Malabar society of India's extreme south, which disowned Menon before he disowned it. Then there were the long years in London, the fight to stay alive in cold, dirty little boardinghouse rooms and the even harder fight to help persuade an imperial race to part with its brightest imperial jewel. Even in love there was conflict and the aching anguish that made Menon vow he would fast until he died. He lived to find himself beset by new contention, his dreams of sitting in the House of Commons shattered, his record as free India's first envoy to Britain sullied, his influence in the United Nations reduced. Now the thread of conflict threatened to snap, to plunge Krishna Menon into oblivion. His past, his present, and his future were under attack.

Earlier that afternoon I had watched Menon defending himself, like an Epstein Lucifer come to life. And he would speak again in reply to the Opposition. But he knew, as we in the press gallery did, that his scornful sallies would win no friends and change no votes in the Lok Sabha. All but a handful of the legislators seated around the big semicircular hall feared and hated India's acerbic Defense Minister. His political survival depended on one man, whose seat, in front of Menon, happened to be empty at the moment. Jawaharlal Nehru was occupied with a foreign visitor at the moment, but he would return to speak in Menon's defense and ensure that the huge Congress party majority voted down all Opposition efforts to discredit the Defense Minister.

Nehru has always been Menon's redeemer. He delivered him from anonymous squalor in England and has upheld him against all enemies, foreign and domestic. Over and over Nehru has said much as he did in 1957: "There are some in India and abroad whose job in life appears to be to try to run down Mr. Menon because he is far cleverer than they are, because his record of service for Indian freedom is far longer than theirs and because he has worn himself out in the service of India."

The impassioned indictment delivered in the Indian Parliament by Kripalani on April 11, 1961, was the opening salvo in a struggle that was eventually to raise Menon to new heights of power and influence in India and abroad. I followed the course of the battle in Delhi, Bombay, and other parts of India. I watched Menon win one of the most sweeping electoral triumphs in Indian history and emerge as a contender for supreme leadership. I watched him consolidate his position as India's defense minister and seek to build a personal following in the Indian armed forces. I could feel his grip tightening on New Delhi's External Affairs Ministry to the point where he often seemed to be running Indian foreign relations.

To me he has always been the most fascinating man in India. He has long been Nehru's closest adviser on foreign affairs and one of the Prime Minister's few trusted confidants. He has sat on more cabinet committees, made more speeches, and covered more ground inside and outside India than any other man in the government. He also draws larger crowds in more places than anyone but Nehru. He is by turns brilliant, irascible, charming, cantankerous, malign, and benevolent. His smile seems to conceal a whole armory of daggers. I shudder when he fondles babies although his affection for children is well known. I have conversed happily for an hour with him one day, only to find him abusive and almost hysterically anti-American the next day. He is a teetotaling, vegetarian bachelor who spurns food and sleep. His health is as unpredictable as monsoon weather. His fainting spells are famous. I have seen him practically carried to his seat on a speakers' platform, where he slumps corpselike until it is his turn to speak. Then he comes alive with a start. His harangues rarely last less than half an hour; often they go on for as long as three hours. He speaks without notes and always in English, the only language he really knows. He admits that he could no longer make a speech in his mother tongue, Malayalam.

Menon is the main topic of conversation for diplomats, journalists, and politically minded Indians in New Delhi. He is India's gray eminence, the brooding figure whose shadow falls across the entire country. Everything about him is controversial except his brilliance, although even that is sometimes called in question. The widow of Menon's English idol, the late economist and Labour party leader Harold J. Laski, told me that her husband thought Menon was "something of a windbag." She also recalled that Menon "didn't know much about India and never expressed an economic philosophy as such." K. M. Panikkar, who shares Menon's far Left outlook, dismisses him as a "good technician who could possibly be used by a new leader." He says that Menon is one of the most overrated Indians alive today. I am more inclined to agree with Nehru, who told a former cabinet minister, "Menon has a colossal intellect," and then added rather plaintively, "I wish I were more clever."

Whatever others may think, there is no doubt of Menon's opinion of himself. "What I have to say is not meant for today or for next year," he once boasted, "but for a generation or more hence, when people are ready to accept what today they criticize." Answering charges of crypto-Communism after his 1962 election victory, he said of himself, "Krishna Menon could have shaken the whole country in a single day had he been a crypto-Communist." He is convinced that his oratory holds audiences spellbound. When the gallery booed him at the United Nations in 1956, he first denounced delegates who pander to popular sentiment, then warned that he too could "arouse passions." The first time I saw him after the North Bombay election, he told me, "You couldn't get better people than at those election meetings I held. They came out for me." I have never seen him more exhilarated. When a *Time* correspondent asked if he could interview him for a cover story, Menon confided, "I know what the Americans want to know. They want to know why Krishna Menon is so popular." Every time someone approaches him in a New York department store, he professes to see new proof of his popularity in the United States.

There is a harsher side to Menon's conceit. Such epithets as "fool" and "idiot" fall easily from his curled lips. He browbeats and even kicks subordinates. Never one to practice racial discrimination, he treats Africans, Asians, Europeans, and Americans with equal contempt. Another's will to agree with him never stops Menon from getting in the first insult. I have never seen anyone so apoplectic with rage against him as were the Yugoslav Communists who endured his whiplash tongue in the drafting committee at the neutral "summit" conference in Belgrade in 1961. At the U.N. he has come to be known as "the arrogant apostle of tolerance" and "the great I am." Discussing another U.N. delegate, Menon snapped a sugar cube in his fingers as he sneered, "The man has no courage. I broke him like that." When General Pran Nath Thapar took over as chief of the army staff in 1961, Menon told him that the service chiefs could not expect to understand everything that he as defense minister was doing, but they need not worry, because it was "for the best."

Menon's egoism is equaled only by his persecution complex. As an American correspondent observed, he assumes intellectual dishonesty in almost everyone else but explodes when his own integrity is questioned even by indirection. Criticism is criminal. He really thinks everyone is both for and against him. "I have no enemies," he will boast, and lament in the next breath, "It's no use, they're all against me." The most innocuous questions in Parliament acquire a sinister significance in Menon's eyes. At home and abroad he conducts a kind of running warfare with the press, which he accuses of deliberately misrepresenting him in an effort to malign India and destroy his popular appeal. My own relations with him have been comparatively good. Everything depends on his mercurial mood. His news conferences at the airport in New York after the long flight from India are classic demonstrations of ill-humor. He shakes his cane at cameramen, demands that reporters apologize, and abuses everyone in sight.

A yawn or a sidewise look by a member of any audience he is addressing may draw an instant reproach from Menon. He is incapable of enjoying a joke on himself. As Frank Moraes, an Indian author and newspaper editor, has remarked, he suffers neither fools nor wise men gladly. He rebels at the thought of being indebted to anyone. The offer of an American Embassy car (which, for example, was made when he arrived unexpectedly at the Manila airport several years ago) provokes the withering retort that he will not be humiliated by American charity. He even hints that American surgeons deliberately failed to remove part of a blood clot in the brain that incapacitated him briefly in the fall of 1961.

Menon heatedly denies that he is anti-American, but there

is no doubt that much of his persecution mania is focused on the United States. His cabinet colleagues all agree on this. The London *Observer* has noted his "almost malevolent hostility" to America. Menon has told friends in Delhi that he will be anti-American as long as the United States is allied to Pakistan, which he regarded as India's number-one enemy until the Chinese attack in October 1962. A more convincing explanation seems to be that he has inherited Marxist and Fabian socialist suspicions of America as the citadel of capitalism and reaction. However, many Americans are surprised when I say that Nehru is almost equally anti-American, the only difference being that he dissembles more artfully than Menon.

Such are the externals of this "wicked fairy complete with wand," as one Western newsman called him. It may be, as Indira Gandhi says, that even Menon could not explain himself, but an attempt must be made because he is already important and may one day be supreme in India.

Krishna Menon (who uses two names, like Lloyd George, to distinguish himself from other Indian Menons) was born on May 3, 1897, in Tellicherry, now in the state of Kerala, in the extreme southwest corner of India, the area where Vasco da Gama made the first European landing in India. Some accounts say that Menon's family were "rebellious," but my information indicates that they were not politically inclined. His father was a middle-class lawyer with enough land to provide for the family comfortably. His mother died when Menon was still in his teens. His brother is also dead, but he has three living sisters as well as a favorite niece, with whom he likes to stay in Madras.

Menon's verbal belligerence may arise from the fact that the large Menon subtribe historically supplied scribes and bookkeepers for the even larger Nair caste, which furnished the warrior rulers of south India for many generations and still dominates Kerala. But the most important members of the ultraorthodox Malabar society in which Menon grew up were women. It was a strictly matriarchal system, based on matriarchal laws of inheritance, until the second quarter of this century. Such a background makes Menon's confirmed bachelorhood more understandable.

Unlike most other contemporary Indian leaders, Menon did not join student boycotts for nationalist objectives in his youth, although he does profess to remember writing "India for the Indians" on his school slate in 1905 during the agitation against Lord Curzon's plan to partition the province of Bengal. At fifteen he defied his matriarchal family to enter Mrs. Annie Besant's Theosophical Institute near Madras, where he again found himself under female tutelage. Mrs. Besant was an opinionated, eccentric Englishwoman who propagated home rule for India and metaphysical salvation for mankind. She recognized unusual qualities of intellect in the shy, studious, introverted boy who arrived in 1912 at the institute. Menon, however, found little in theosophy that attracted him. His mind was already groping toward the radical rationalism he now espouses.

After being graduated with an A.B. degree in arts and letters from the Madras Presidency College, Menon ignored his father's pleas that he enter the law college there. He lectured on history for a time and served for four years as an unpaid commissioner in the Indian Boy Scouts. The Scout code seems to have interested him less than the fact that the movement was being opened to non-Europeans. He also worked on Mrs. Besant's newspaper, but without developing a lasting affection for journalists.

An Indian biographical sketch says that Menon went to England in 1924 as a "young propagandist" for the Home Rule movement. In fact, he was interested in continuing his education, not in making propaganda for any cause. Mrs. Besant bought his passage and he traveled as an unpaid secretary to one of her assistants. He went to England for six months. He stayed twenty-eight years.

They were the formative years. Menon was scholar, politician, and propagandist rolled in one. He excelled as a scholar and propagandist but failed as a politician, because he insisted on going his own way. His three roles in London were related. He accumulated degrees because socialist theory intrigued him and because London University was the best place to recruit British intellectuals and Indian students for the India League, which he used as a propaganda platform for preaching the gospel of Indian independence. He joined the British Labour party in 1930 and served on the St. Pancras Borough Council in London to prove that he, an Asian, could win elective office in England. Membership in the party also enabled him to influence Labour's stand on India more effectively.

In the course of his long self-imposed exile, Menon became deeply attached to London. Today he finds it politic to discount this phase of his life. "I survived England somehow or other," he sneers. The fact is, he prefers it to any place else on earth. "It's a country where you can easily be at home," he has conceded in a rare moment of self-revelation. "London is such a friendly place. Nobody is ever lost in London or unhappy there, except the loud, vulgar type of American."

At the London School of Economics Menon was electrified by the socialism of Professor Harold J. Laski and other Left Wing English intellectuals. He eagerly applied their Marxian analysis of imperialism to India and found it fit. He was a good student. Mrs. Laski told me that her husband liked Menon, who used to spend hours at the Laski home expounding his ideas about socialism and Indian independence. He received a Bachelor of Science degree with first honors and a Master of Science degree from the London School of Economics, a Master of Arts with honors from University College, London, and a Doctor of Laws from Glasgow University. His thesis was entitled "An Experimental Study of the Mental Process Involved in Reasoning." He has more degrees and far more education than any other Indian cabinet minister.

When Dean William H. Beveridge barred Menon from taking further courses at the London School of Economics because he was not a bona fide student, Laski objected. He won his point, and Menon continued buttonholing people in the common room.

Menon was called to the Bar from the Middle Temple, but chose to remain a briefless barrister most of his life. When he handled tenants' cases, he worked without fee. His real passion was Indian independence. In 1929 he took over the moribund Commonwealth of India League, renamed it the India League, and turned it into one of the most effective lobbies in English history. From the League's cold, grubby little offices in the Strand, Menon turned out a flood of pamphlets, organized thousands of meetings, and lectured everyone in sight. The League was never, as is often said, the London branch of the Indian National Congress party. Menon preferred to operate as a lone wolf. He still does. He did not even join Congress until after independence. As he says now, "I had no link with the Congress party. I didn't want to be tied to anyone at home." The India League aimed at influencing Englishmen, especially the Bloomsbury intellectuals and members of the Labour party. An Englishman was always chairman of the League. Bertrand Russell headed it for a time, and Laski and Stafford Cripps served as officers. But in fact the League was its secretary-general, Krishna Menon. He served without pay and often contributed whatever he earned as a lawyer or free-lance writer to pay the League's bills. He almost never left the office. One of the Indian students who volunteered to help Menon at the League was Indira Gandhi, then an undergraduate at Somerville College, Cambridge. Despite his habitual rudeness, he persuaded more than a hundred members of the Labour party to join the League. He concentrated on Labour, although it was out of power, because he believed the Conservatives would never free India.

Menon had little to sustain himself except work. He subsisted on tea, buns, and rancor. His life in London, as Philip Deane has aptly remarked, was marked by "penury, perpetual colds, large cheap scarves and a kettle that bubbled endlessly on a gas ring to replenish the teapot from which he seemed to get his only nourishment." He moved from one cheap boardinghouse to another in the grimy Camden Town district of London. As one English member of the League recalls, "No one knew precisely which little room in Camden Town he was living in at any particular moment." A member of the St. Pancras Borough Council told me, "Krishna never went to anybody's home. He wasn't social at all." His health was already poor. He suffered from tuberculosis of the kidneys, stomach trouble, and fits of coughing. He managed to keep going only with heavy doses of drugs. One day in 1934 he disappeared. Reginald Sorensen, a Labour member of Parliament and of the India League, learned after some time that Menon had been taken to a workhouse ward for indigent patients. "When I went there," Sorensen says, "the ward attendant told me, 'Yes, we have him. It's that bloke down there under the big pile of blankets. He'll be dead in the morning.' " He did not die, but he spent three months in the crowded ward.

Menon had never been religious. London and Laski made him an agnostic. But when his father died, Menon made one of his rare trips to India to conduct what he called a "proper funeral" for the parent whose wishes he had flouted.

To supplement his meager income, Menon edited paperback books. He says that British publishers scoffed when he first suggested paperback editions on economics, history, and science. The first printing of twelve titles sold out overnight. This new Pelican series was more of a literary than a financial success for its editor. Menon accuses the publisher, Sir Alan Lane, of denying him his agreed share of the proceeds. He remarks bitterly, "They later knighted him for it. He never has read the books himself."

Menon was not knighted, but his knowledge of the book business enabled him to arrange for publication of Nehru's works, thereby earning the lasting gratitude of India's future prime minister.

Books were not Menon's only love. His extended romance with an English girl ended unhappily in the thirties. She was not a member of the India League and appears to have had no special interest in politics. She is said to have decided, after much soul-searching, against attempting marriage with the unpredictable Menon. He reacted melodramatically. He announced that he had no further interest in life and took to his bed. He ate nothing. Harold Laski and his wife held his hand as he lay on a cot in his shabby rented room. Mrs. Laski was unimpressed. "I think he was dramatizing himself," she says.

It is widely believed that Menon thought color prejudice was to blame for the girl's decision and that this feeling accounts for much of his present hostility to Westerners. Vincent Sheehan sees a look of "ancient and remembered wrongs" in Menon's smoldering eyes and concludes that he must have been dreadfully insulted or maltreated at some time. My own feeling is that it would be wrong to ascribe too much to his unrequited love, although, of course, if he had married and had children, he would probably be a different person today.

One unforeseen result of Menon's blighted romance was that he and Nehru were brought together for the first time. After giving up his fast, Menon announced that he would stake everything on a giant rally in London for Indian freedom. He wrote to Nehru, who was in Switzerland at the time, and asked him to address the meeting. "Who is this Menon?" Nehru asked when he got the letter. Minoo R. Masani, then a friend of Menon and now one of his bitterest foes, happened to be with Nehru and described the young Keralan in glowing terms. Nehru reluctantly agreed to go. He and Menon found immediate rapport.

In 1938 Nehru and Menon met in Barcelona and toured the trenches of the Spanish Republican Army for five days. They underwent nightly bombing attacks. The experience moved Nehru deeply. "There, in the midst of want and destruction and ever-impending disaster," he wrote later, "I felt more at peace with myself than anywhere else in Europe. There was light there, the light of courage and determination and of doing something worth while."

Afterward, when he returned to London with Menon, he says that he "met people of all degrees and all shades of opinion." Purshottam Trikumdas, a leading Indian socialist who also visited London in 1938, told me, "Menon threw no one but Communists at me during my one-month stay. He did the same thing with Nehru." Menon and Nehru spent long hours discussing politics in a London vegetarian restaurant. Nehru was delighted to find someone who did not repeat the cautious platitudes of the conservative Congress party majority. He envied Menon's incisive mind and revolutionary daring. Menon, for his part, recognized in Nehru the future leader of independent India and lavished attention on him.

Menon already had more ward-level political experience than Nehru would ever acquire. St. Pancras, Menon's borough, is traditionally radical. He was one of the few lawyers on the Labour side in the Borough Council. "He often raised legal points," one Council member recalls, "and you knew you could always support him, because he was always right." He was named chairman of the committee on libraries and amenities, normally the least important and most despised borough office. But he brought culture to St. Pancras with the same energy that Tammany Hall used to expend on a wavering borough before an election. He founded and developed the highly successful St. Pancras Arts Council, which became a model for the rest of Britain. He made arrangements with the Royal Academy of Dramatic Art and leading orchestras and opera companies to put on performances in St. Pancras. He even started a ballet circle. He is remembered in the borough as being hypersensitive about his color, but the only time that it is known to have been used against him politically was during one election campaign when some Tory extremists put up posters saying, "Don't vote for Menon or you'll get a black man." Menon was quick to repay any slight, real or fancied. He once threatened to stop speaking at a Labour meeting until a party member apologized for yawning.

Menon twice missed being nominated as a Labour candidate for the House of Commons. He lost the first time by one vote after shocking the sober working folk on the party selection committee with a display of political iconoclasm. On the second occasion he was forced to withdraw his candidacy because he attended a Communist meeting, which was against Labour party rules. The London *Daily Worker,* to which Menon occasionally contributed, came to his defense with several page-one articles. Until Russia was attacked by Germany in June 1941, Menon followed the Communist line in denouncing the war as an imperialist struggle. He could see no difference between British and German imperialism as far as India was concerned. "You might as well ask a fish if it prefers to be fried in butter or margarine," he scoffed.

Russia's involvement in the war caused a startling about-face by all Communist parties and by Menon. Overnight the war became a righteous struggle against fascist tyranny in which all freedom-loving peoples must join. In articles published in the British Communist party's *Labor Monthly* in August 1941 and January and June 1942, Menon argued that the character of the war had been transformed for colonial peoples by the attack on Russia. He wrote: "To them the victory of the Soviet Union is not merely the hope of freedom, but the guarantee of its achievement. They realize that the Soviet people have unfailingly recognized the common interests of the peoples of the world. . . . The Soviet Union has consistently championed the struggles for national independence and the autonomy of nationalities. . . . [It] has given great inspiration to the colonial peoples. . . . It has also inspired and enabled national movements of liberation to recognize their role and to seek to play their part in a freer world and in the world struggle for freedom."

German aggression against the USSR, Menon said, "calls for the fullest mobilization of all the forces of freedom everywhere." For him, participation in the "world anti-fascist front" was now an "integral" part of Indian policy. The demand for Indian freedom, he added almost as an afterthought, was "equally" part of that policy.

In fact, Indian policy as expressed by Gandhi and the majority of the Indian National Congress leadership was the exact opposite of what Menon advocated. In its famous Quit India resolution of August 8, 1942, the Congress demanded unconditional freedom as the condition for India's participation in the war effort. Menon refused to be bound by the resolution. He argued that it would hinder the prosecution of the war. He demanded the release of Communist prisoners in Indian jails who, "despite the obscurantism of the British government, would rally the people in resistance and prevent a repetition of the experience in Burma." He ignored the Congress and insisted that India should be led by its "most

vital elements," which he defined as the Communists, Socialists, and other working-class leaders.

Was Menon a member of the Communist party at this time?
Like everything about him, the question produces more heat
than light. The *New Statesman* says that the Labour party
leadership "believed or at least alleged Menon was a Communist." Trikumdas says that Menon was a Communist card-
carrier from 1937. Masani, a Socialist turned conservative,
who has known Menon since 1926, says that Menon has been
a "consistent fellow traveler" since 1936 or 1937. The people
I have talked to in London who were closest to Menon in the
thirties and forties insist that he was not a member of the
party, if for no other reason than his anarchic individualism
and abhorrence of discipline. He could as well be a perfect
Communist as he could be a member of the Ku Klux Klan. In
any event, he is infinitely more valuable to the Communists
out of the party than in it.

Menon resigned from the Labour party in 1941, but was re-
admitted a year later. It is now said that he left because the
party refused to press for Indian independence until after
the war. It seems more probable that he left before he was
kicked out. He was allowed to return to the party with other
extreme Left Wingers when Labour's relations with the Communists improved during the height of the "grand alliance"
between Russia and the Western powers.

By 1946 Labour was in power in Britain and independence
was in sight for India. Menon still hesitated over whether to
enter Indian politics or stay in British politics. His course was
decided by a message he received in London from Nehru, then
head of the provisional Indian government and premier-
designate of the new Indian state. Long years of separation
had not caused Nehru to forget his companion in the Spanish
trenches. He asked Menon to make a quick tour of European
capitals as his personal representative. Menon accepted the
mission. When India achieved full independence the following year, Nehru named Menon the country's first high commissioner (ambassador) to the Court of St. James's. Menon
was so little known at that time that his name did not even
appear in the Indian *Who's Who*. Except for Nehru, the few

Indian leaders who had met Menon in London were not impressed. Sardar Patel, the man who unified India after independence, and Maulana Azad, one of Nehru's closest advisers, opposed Menon's appointment as high commissioner. Azad says in his autobiography: "Krishna Menon professed great admiration for Jawaharlal and I knew Jawaharlal often listened to his advice. I did not feel very happy about this because I felt Krishna Menon often gave him the wrong advice. Sardar Patel and I did not always see eye to eye but we were agreed in our judgment about him."

Menon visited Delhi briefly, then returned in triumph to London. He shed his shabby flannel bags and grubby overcoat in favor of tight, rather unfashionable but faultlessly tailored Savile Row suits. He never appears in anything else outside India. In India he affects Keralan national dress. For the high commission, Menon selected expensive crockery, cutlery, carpets, and curtains with obvious relish. Although he preferred to live in a single room behind his office in India House, he purchased a comfortable residence in Kensington Palace Gardens for official entertaining. He also bought a fleet of limousines, despite his own preference for traveling by bus.

The financial scandals connected with Menon's term as high commissioner in London are as notorious in India as the Billie Sol Estes case is now in America. He began by losing £17,000 ($47,600) of government funds on the purchase of additional office space for the high commission. He was publicly censured for allowing the government to be grossly overcharged for 4,275 cases of whisky ordered by the Indian Army. But the most serious allegations against him arose from the now famous "jeep case." In July 1948 he signed a contract for the supply of 2,000 jeeps for the Indian Army with an unknown and nondescript English firm named Anti-Mistant Ltd. He advanced £143,162 ($400,853.60) in Indian government funds to the company, which went into liquidation after delivering only 155 jeeps. The vehicles were found to be useless and unserviceable. No spare parts were included.

The Indian Parliament's Estimates Committee demanded an urgent inquiry. Two years later no steps had been taken

to open the investigation. In March 1951 Menon signed a new
contract with an equally unknown firm named S.C.K. (Agencies) Ltd. for the supply of 1,007 jeeps at almost twice the unit
price quoted in the previous contract. The new firm promised to absorb the losses on the first contract. Only forty-nine
jeeps were delivered. Then S.C.K. stopped further shipments
on the ground that the Indian government had reneged on an
oral promise to give the spare-parts contract to the company.
The Indian Parliament's Public Accounts Committee censured the authorities concerned and declared, "It is not possible to hold that the lapses were merely procedural or due
to defects in the rules." The auditing committee that finally
visited India House to investigate the jeep scandal was headed
by R. P. Sarathy, who has since become a Menon protégé and
a key official of the Defense Ministry. General K. S. Thimayya,
the former army chief of staff, who opposed Menon, told me
that Sarathy "tore from his report the pages with incriminat-
ing evidence against Menon." India brought suit against
S.C.K. in London for the recovery of £254,498 ($712,594.40).
Menon would have been the principal witness called by the
firm. In April 1961, with the case due to come up on May 2
in the Queens Bench Division of the High Court, Law Minister Ashoke K. Sen was dispatched to London to arrange an out-
of-court settlement. India waived its entire claim.

It has never been determined whether Menon was corrupt
or merely careless in the jeep case and on other questionable
contracts he negotiated in London. Trikumdas says, "Menon
is completely dishonest in his deals. The money he got from
these deals went to the Communist party." Reginald Sorenson,
who generally dislikes Menon, says, "He is a man of tremendous self-sacrifice and supreme integrity. But his judgment can be very faulty." An American-trained Indian businessman with close connections in Delhi agrees. He says,
"Menon is honest in all financial transactions. He has no
personal fortune. But he's completely unscrupulous in choosing his friends." My own feeling is that Menon is irresponsible
financially, as well as in every other way, but that he is not
crooked.

The jeep scandal overshadowed Menon's successful efforts

to work out a formula to enable the new Republic of India to remain in the British Commonwealth of Nations. By 1952 he was under attack from all sides. Even Nehru is reputed to have decided to drop him. Trikumdas visited London at the time and says: "Menon thought he was finished in Indian politics. He would come to my hotel in London at eight o'clock every morning and telephone me in my room asking me to help him. He went into great detail to exonerate himself. This went on for ten days."

It was Nehru who, as usual, came to Menon's rescue. About this time the Prime Minister visited Paris to attend a conference of Indian ambassadors in Europe. Menon presented a pitiable spectacle. He seemed about to die. He walked with difficulty, leaning heavily on his cane and the arm of an aide. Nehru was suitably impressed. He told an Indian diplomat that he thought it would kill Menon if he were dropped from government service just then. So Nehru appointed his old friend deputy chief of the Indian delegation to the United Nations. The change appeared to have had a miraculous effect on Menon, who reportedly began walking normally soon after Nehru left Paris.

At the U.N. Menon was supposed to serve under Mrs. Vijaya Lakshmi Pandit, the Prime Minister's sister, and later the first woman president of the U.N. General Assembly. Madame Pandit had already served as India's ambassador in Moscow and Washington, and there was no doubt where her sympathies lay. Nehru had once rebuked her for being "the only one among us who defends the American empire." From the beginning she and Menon came into violent collision. Menon even refused to show her the cables he sent to Delhi. She complained bitterly against him, but Nehru dismissed her objections as "too personal." Menon won the day. Thereafter he took orders from no one but Nehru.

India's voice in the U.N. suddenly took on a rasping, caustic quality unknown in the days of previous Indian spokesmen. As A. M. Rosenthal, of the New York *Times,* says, Menon made a reputation for himself and lost it for his country. Menon had no difficulty putting the blame on South Korea for the refusal of Communist prisoners of war to return home. And when Communist China accused America of waging germ warfare in Korea, Menon said that it was not for him to deny the charges. He produced a Korean peace plan which Henry Cabot Lodge, the only American official for whom Menon has publicly demonstrated his regard, called "a splendid and sincere effort for peace." Russia rejected Menon's plan, but he blamed its failure on American bombing beyond the Yalu River.

Menon reached the summit of his international prestige at the 1954 Geneva conference that brought the war in Indochina to an end. Although India was not a full-fledged participant, Menon was the most indefatigable toiler in the diplomatic pastures. He produced formula after formula to induce the Western powers to accept the partition of Indochina. For him, the only issue was the liquidation of French imperialism. He ignored the extension of Communist influence in southeast Asia. Seven years later he told me, "The United States tried to sabotage the conference. Dulles kept coming in and out like Talleyrand." He blames all of southeast Asia's subsequent woes on American interference in Laos and on South Vietnam's refusal to co-operate with the Indian-led International Control Commission.

In October 1954 Menon anticipated Soviet proposals on Germany when he told the U.N. General Assembly that a solution of the German problem lay in "direct talks . . . for the unification of Germany." He declared, "German peace is necessary for world peace and German peace means the unification of Germany in whatever way it is brought about." He could see no difference in the sovereign status of East and West Germany. Such views led Andrei Vyshinsky, the former Soviet delegate in the U.N., to applaud Menon as "an honest man," while making clear that he thought differently about other Indian delegates.

Hungary provided the most striking example of Menon's depths of tolerance for the Communist bloc. He dismissed Soviet repression of the 1956 uprising as an internal affair of Hungary and compared it to a linguistic riot in Ahmedabad. With new-found reverence for legal niceties, Menon told the U.N. General Assembly on November 8, 1956: "Even with all

the emotional environment that surrounds the present situation, we may not forget the sovereign rights of a sovereign
state in the Assembly. We may not refer to a member state
as though it were struggling for its independence. . . . It is
our view that in dealing with a member state, the General Assembly cannot deal with the problem in the same way as in
the case of a colonial country where the people have no representation. We anticipate with hope and with confidence that
the Soviet Union, having announced its intention to withdraw
its troops from Hungary, will implement that decision soon."

Menon's hope and confidence turned out to be as well based
as his respect for Hungary's sovereign rights.

The following day his scruples found new expression. "Any
approach we make," he cautioned, "as though this [Hungary]
is a colonial country which is not represented at the U.N. is
not in accordance with either law or the facts of the position."
India, he said, was informed that Soviet troops would be withdrawn from Budapest "as soon as order is restored." The information was authentic. It came from Marshal Nikolai Bul-
ganin. Later that day Menon voted with the Soviet bloc and
Yugoslavia against a five-power resolution denouncing Soviet
repression in Hungary, again calling on Russia to withdraw
its forces, and asking for free elections in Hungary under U.N.
supervision. The vote was 48 to 11, with 16 abstentions. India
was the only non-Communist country to oppose the resolution.

Menon's action unleashed a flood of criticism in India and
the West. His political enemies rashly assumed he was
through. Nehru backtracked with a weak explanation that,
"Mr. Menon does not always speak for India." Stories were
circulated, presumably for the benefit of the Western press,
that the Prime Minister had sent a stern rebuke to his U.N.
representative. It is true that Menon had not received specific
instructions from New Delhi on how to vote on the five-power
resolution. But he had studied Nehru's speech of the day
before to the All-India Congress Committee in Calcutta in
which the Prime Minister paralleled the Soviet line on Hungary. Nehru called the explosion in Hungary a "civil war"
and, except for one indirect criticism, ignored the Russian
attack. In these circumstances he appeared to condone the

intervention of Soviet forces at the request of the "legitimate government." Menon simply applied Nehru's reasoning to the five-power resolution on Hungary. He complained that parts of the resolution were unacceptable because they "prejudged" the results of the on-the-spot inquiry that Secretary-General Dag Hammarskjöld had been asked to make in Hungary. He said that India preferred to await Hammarskjöld's findings, although he knew as well as everyone else that the Russians had no intention of allowing the Secretary-General into Hungary. He could see no point in passing a resolution unless it could be carried out in practice, a subtlety he has never applied to Indian-sponsored resolutions on such subjects as racial discrimination in South Africa or an uncontrolled nuclear-test ban.

Both Nehru and Menon repeatedly lamented the lack of "reliable information" from Hungary, although they were receiving regular and detailed reports from their Chargé d'Affaires in Budapest, M. A. Rehman, and from K. P. S. Menon, then Indian ambassador in Moscow, who went to Hungary in November to investigate the situation. Both these diplomats were reporting fully and objectively on the course of events. Their dispatches were ignored.

As late as November 21, 1956, when the Hungarian revolt was already history, Menon told the U.N. General Assembly: "We have kept ourselves under restraint, without pronouncing judgment on events which we have not been able to observe ourselves, and in spite of whatever newspaper criticism there may be, whatever epithets may be used, my government and people will not shift to a position where we are called upon to condemn without evidence. Even though we may believe something, even though all the facts point toward that, even if there is what a magistrate calls a prima facie case, we have as a sovereign government in relation to another government the responsibility of permitting a judgment or inference to be made on the basis of facts. . . ."

Such punctilious regard for facts has never deterred India from issuing blanket condemnations of regimes in Angola, Algeria, Western Samoa, South Africa, or any of the many other places where there is no official Indian representative

Finance Minister Morarji Desai at his desk, 1960
Press Information Bureau, Government of India

W. B. Iliff, Vice-President of the World Bank, with Morarji Desai
at a reception, October 1960
Press Information Bureau, Government of India

At right, former Defense Minister V. K. Krishna Menon with
Minister of Food and Agriculture S. K. Patil
Central Newsphoto Service, New Delhi

Minister of Home Affairs Lal Bahadur Shastri in his office
Press Information Bureau, Government of India

At left, Krishna Menon addressing *jawans* at Ferozepore in
January 1960
Armed Forces Information Office, New Delhi

Lal Bahadur Shastri
Central Newsphoto Service, New Delhi

Y. B. Chavan, Defense Minister
Press Information Bureau, Government of India

Y. B. Chavan in his office in Bombay when he was Chief Minister
of Maharashtra

on the spot. Nor is it correct to say that India simply adopted the position of other Afro-Asian neutrals on Hungary. Burma, a much smaller and weaker country, which also receives Soviet economic aid, repeatedly denounced Soviet aggression in Hungary in categorical terms. Menon, on the other hand, sought to equate Soviet armed intervention with what he hinted was interference by Western intelligence and propaganda agencies. He spoke feelingly of "the populations of Hungary which are trying to unite and, I hope, stand against the elements of dismemberment, from whichever quarter they may come, either from within or from without." During the entire Assembly debate on Hungary, he never used the terms "Soviet aggression" or "Soviet intervention."

Again Menon had taken his cue from Nehru. The Prime Minister had told the Rajya Sabha on November 19 that "fascist elements" and "outsiders" had joined the Hungarian uprising, although he conceded, "That is not the major fact." According to Nehru, "There was no immediate aggression there [in Hungary] in the sense of something militarily happening as there was in the case of Egypt. It was really a continuing intervention of the Soviet armies in these countries based on the Warsaw Pact."

On December 4, 1956, a full month after Russian tanks smothered the Hungarian revolt, Menon could finally discern the true outlines of the situation. "We have no doubt," he said, "that the beginnings of the movement in Hungary were the national uprising against a tyranny, whatever happened to it afterwards. We have equally no doubt from the experience of our own country and others that all kinds of irresponsible elements get into a tumult of that sort." The solution was simple. The world should "allow Hungary to settle down a little by itself, without foreign intervention of any kind."

The record indicates that there was never any real divergence between Nehru and Menon on Hungary. They were always in step, although, as usual, Nehru trod a bit less heavily on Western sensibilities. Menon was made the scapegoat for India's unpopular vote against the five-power resolution because Nehru had misjudged Indian reaction to the slaughter of the Hungarian rebels. Frank Moraes has pointed out that Hungary was the first major international issue on which Indian public opinion challenged Nehru's wisdom. The ground had been laid for the outcry three years later over China's repression in Tibet and occupation of Indian territory.

Before passing on to the question of India's relations with Peking, it is worth inquiring why Nehru and Menon refused to condemn Soviet imperialism in Hungary. One reason, I believe, is that they regard imperialism as the domination of white capitalist powers over nonwhite colonial peoples. Hungary did not fit the definition. Nehru and Menon said, and may possibly have believed, that Russia's reoccupation of Hungary on November 4 was a defensive reaction prompted by the Western attack on Suez. Menon is reported to have exclaimed at the time, "Hungary! The Russians should have bombed London after the Anglo-French attack on Egypt." Privately he told African and Asian delegates that the West was making much of Hungary to divert attention from Suez. He accused John Foster Dulles of feigning illness so that he would not have to lead the condemnation of Britain, France, and Israel in the General Assembly. The Indian leaders' suspicions of the West were equaled only by their reluctance to offend Moscow. Nehru had just succeeded in establishing friendly relations with the post-Stalin Russian regime. For Menon, such ideological and tactical considerations were reinforced by the working of his "rebound mind." He habitually takes positions as a reaction to opposing positions. As an old Laski socialist, he is chagrined to be found on the side of major capitalist powers. Politically, I have always felt that he derives more satisfaction from embarrassing the United States than from overtly supporting the Communist bloc. For Menon, facts can be made to suit the circumstances. I remember him telling an American television interviewer, "There is no objective truth. Truth is dynamic."

So also is Chinese expansion. Menon's equivocations on Tibet and the border problem with China had already cost him dearly in Indian eyes before the Chinese launched their massive attacks along the Himalayan border before dawn on

October 20, 1962. The call to arms on that black day in Indian history may well have sounded his political death knell. As the full magnitude of Indian military unpreparedness became apparent, Nehru was deluged with demands for Menon's removal as defense minister. Congress party stalwarts who had not dared challenge Nehru for years quietly told him that unless he made a sacrificial offering of Menon, the country's wrath would be directed against the Prime Minister himself. India would then have a discredited leader at the head of a discredited government in the country's worst crisis since independence. Nehru's sure instinct of political self-preservation was aroused. He accurately sensed the nation's angry mood. Eighteen days after the Chinese offensive began, Menon was dropped from the cabinet.

In restrospect there is no doubt that Menon shares responsibility with Nehru for the disastrous policy of *Panch Sheel,* or the "five principles of coexistence," originally enshrined in the now defunct Sino-Indian treaty of 1954 on Tibet. The five principles, relating mainly to noninterference in each other's affairs, lulled the Indian leaders into complacency while the Chinese Communists fastened their grip on Tibet and encroached on Indian territory. Menon helped Nehru introduce Premier Chou En-lai to African and Asian government chiefs at the Bandung conference in April 1955. At Chou's invitation, Menon visited Peking on May 11 to continue discussions of the Formosa question begun at Bandung. He came back to announce that at India's request the Communists would release four United States airmen imprisoned in China. In further efforts to improve Chinese-American relations, Menon visited London, Ottawa, and Washington, where he conferred with President Eisenhower. Menon is said to have left Washington resentful of the credit being given Hammarskjöld for the airmen's release.

When the Tibetan revolt broke out in March 1959, Menon told an interviewer that he had no reason to doubt Peking's version of events. Later he told Charles Mohr, then *Time* correspondent in Delhi, "We have done a lot more for Tibet than you have. You used Tibet as a pawn in the game of cold war.

We provide asylum for Tibetan refugees." In the U.N., Menon has upheld the position that since Peking is not a member of the organization, it cannot be held to account for the suppression of human rights in Tibet. He also wonders how U.N. resolutions on Tibet can "help the cause of peace." Menon, like Nehru, regards Tibet as a domestic Chinese problem and says, "We have no desire to interfere in the internal affairs of China or Tibet. The issue has become clouded in cold war."

Menon's replies to criticism of defense measures on India's northern border are masterpieces of obfuscation. On October 21, 1959, nine members of India's Tibet Border Force were killed and ten taken prisoner by Chinese Communist forces fifty miles inside Indian territory in the Chang Chenmo Valley of Ladakh. A few weeks later Menon told a Bombay crowd that India had not been invaded. On November 26, 1959, he told Parliament that it was impossible to speak of Chinese aggression against India because the U.N. had not yet defined aggression. He said that India's policy had been to have "no military deployment anywhere on our international frontiers," ignoring the fact that more than half the Indian Army was then concentrated near the Kashmir cease-fire line and elsewhere on the Indo-Pakistani border. As for the frontier with China, Menon proclaimed: "That frontier has been left not to police protection, as some people make out, but has been very much like the frontier between Canada and the United States, in the hope that neighborly relations will prevail and no cause for military action would arise."

This statement was made more than five years after Peking had registered its first official claim on Indian territory; more than two years after Chinese troops had completed a military highway through Indian territory on the Aksai Chin plateau; nine months after Chou En-lai had formally laid claim to 14,000 square miles in Ladakh and 36,000 square miles in India's Northeast Frontier Agency (NEFA); two months after Chinese troops had fired on an Indian frontier post in the east, and one month after the bloody Chang Chenmo clash had electrified India. By Peking's own admission Chinese troops had started patrolling the Ladakh province of Kashmir in July 1951. At that time, when Communist China was still weak and distracted by the Korean war, it might have accepted a compromise with India on the border. But Nehru failed even to mention the subject with Peking. He later admitted in Parliament, "I saw no reason to discuss the frontier with the Chinese government because, foolishly if you like, I thought there was nothing to discuss."

From 1954 to 1955, while Nehru was extolling 2,000 years of Sino-Indian friendship, Chinese frontier units conducted what Peking later called "military investigations" and surveyed more than ten routes for the proposed Aksai Chin highway to connect Chinese Sinkiang and Tibet. Several of the alternate routes were even deeper in Indian territory than the one finally chosen. Of all this activity on their own territory the Indian authorities remained inexplicably ignorant. India did not even know the Aksai Chin road existed until Peking obligingly announced in September 1957 that it would open to traffic the following month. Nehru and Menon, who became Minister of Defense the same year over bitter objections from Congress conservatives, did nothing until the following summer. Then two small reconnaissance parties were sent to the area. One party returned after a long time. The other did not. Its fifteen members had been seized by the Chinese. But not until October 18, 1958, did Nehru bring himself to send a note to Peking protesting the construction of the road and inquiring helplessly about the missing Indian reconnaissance party. In a pathetic gesture of appeasement that must have provoked smiles in Peking, the note said, "As the Chinese government are aware, the Government of India are anxious to settle these petty frontier disputes so that the friendly relations between the two countries may not suffer."

The Chinese replied tartly on November 1 that the Indian party had been "arrested" and later released after intruding on "Chinese territory." Peking also insisted that the Aksai Chin highway passed through Chinese territory. Nehru later admitted that he was "worried" when he learned that the road ran through what India regarded as its own domain, but he neglected to inform Parliament or the public until another year had passed. He offered the feeble excuse that, "No particular occasion arose to bring the matter to the House, because we thought we might make progress by correspondence and when the time was ripe for it we would inform Parliament." He conceded, "It was possibly an error or a mistake on my part not to have brought the facts before the House." But Nehru still sought as late as the fall of 1959 to minimize the whole border question. He dismissed the 17,000-foot Aksai Chin plateau as a wasteland "where not even a blade of grass grows." He was later to acknowledge that the collision of India and China in the heart of central Asia is one of the most fateful developments of the second half of the twentieth century.

To me, the secrecy and appeasement that marked Nehru's handling of the border issue throughout the 1950's will always carry the trademark of Krishna Menon, although K. M. Panikkar undoubtedly had much to do with it. The policy itself was undoubtedly conceived by Nehru in hopes of keeping the Chinese dragon at bay. But the execution and the rationale reflect Menon's influence. Even after the Chinese were attacking all along the border in October 1962, Menon continued to admonish Nehru against divulging routine military information or taking any step, such as the use of Indian combat aircraft or retaliatory raids into Tibet, that might displease Peking. Earlier, when he was asked in Parliament why the Indian Air Force failed to bomb the Aksai Chin road, Menon replied, "I can answer it. But it is not wise to answer. Therefore, that is the position in regard to the frontier, and there is no question of our running away from any resistance that is required." In the same speech on November 26, 1959, he declared grandly, "The frontiers of other countries, by and large, are violated; our frontiers are violated and, therefore, we must take action against it." Menon repeatedly assured Parliament that no further Chinese incursions into Indian territory were possible. But the incursions continued until the full-scale Chinese attack of October 1962, when all Menon's assurances were shown to be worthless. A second Chinese military highway was built through Aksai Chin, and Chinese check posts have been pushed deeper into Indian territory. Asked about the situation after meeting

President Kennedy in November 1961, Menon replied sooth-ingly, "There is no active hostility." The following spring, when still more Chinese posts were spotted, he stoutly refused to take any step "which will expose our troops to unnecessary jeopardy."

He was as sanguine as ever about the border when I talked with him in his large corner office in New Delhi's South Block office building in April 1962. When I asked him about sug-gestions to arbitrate the Sino-Indian dispute, he countered, "Who's to arbitrate?" Then, after stifling a yawn, he con-tinued in a schoolmasterish voice, "Arbitration is a procedure that only operates when the main principles are common ground." He expressed deep concern about the behavior of the then Royal Laotian government, but dismissed the danger of armed conflict on India's northern frontier with the remark, "The Chinese know they can't wage war against us any more than we can wage war against them. The Chinese fear losing prestige in a border settlement." They evidently did not fear losing India's good will by barefaced aggression only six months later.

In the summer of 1962 Menon was responsible for drafting Indian notes in an increasingly acrimonious exchange with Peking. The Indian note of July 26 provoked an outcry in Parliament and the country because it merely asked the Chinese to "restrain" their forces from going beyond Indian territory that they had claimed in 1956. The note made no reference to the Chinese returning to the old boundary and offered to resume talks "as soon as the current tensions have eased and the appropriate climate is created." Although Nehru later sought to make a distinction between "preliminary talks" and actual negotiations on the border issue, it was clear that Menon favored keeping up the dialogue with the Chinese under any circumstances. Even after full-scale Chinese attack, Menon told an audience that India was fighting "to negotiate."

The U.N. debate on a nuclear-test ban in the fall of 1961 brought Menon into conflict with American spokesmen and many articulate Indians. In private he justified the powerful Soviet tests in the atmosphere on the ground that Russia had to catch up with American nuclear capability. But when the

United States announced that it would resume underground testing, Menon protested that such explosions were actually more dangerous than atmospheric testing, because they would pollute underground rivers and contaminate the earth. When I questioned him on this, he proceeded to paint a fearsome picture of vast subterranean caverns costing millions of dollars and poisoning the whole globe. For a politician whose stock in trade is anti-Americanism, Menon, I sometimes feel, shows more concern for the burdens of the American taxpayer than the Republican National Committee.

Before he returned to Delhi, Menon left orders with the Indian delegation at the U.N. Assembly to vote against an eight-power resolution appealing to the Soviet Union not to explode its fifty-megaton bomb. The delegation leader had doubts and queried Delhi. Nehru promptly ordered him to support the resolution. What one New Delhi editor called Menon's "pervert distortions" of Indian policy on the eve of Nehru's visit to the United States in November 1961 provoked bitter condemnation from all major Indian newspapers. At Nehru's suggestion, Menon called on President Kennedy at the White House later that month, but, as one American official said, "Nothing happened. There was no meeting of minds."

Menon's stand on disarmament has been less flagrantly partisan but equally irksome to Western diplomats. He has followed the Russian line in consistently disparaging the controls demanded by the United States and urging an advance commitment to the "principle of complete disarmament" by the major powers. Each side, Menon insists, is guilty of "gamesmanship" on disarmament, but he throws the burden of responsibility for the deadlock on the capitalist West. "There is a general fear," he told Parliament, "particularly in the circles economically and militarily affected by these things, of what is called the 'outbreak of peace'; that is to say, that people may be out of work, business may go down and so forth." He likes to identify the Russian line on disarmament with the stand taken by the nonaligned countries.

Menon may twist Nehru's foreign policy, but he rarely tries to nullify it on a particular issue. He tried and failed during the dispute over Russia's "troika" plan for a three-man U.N.

directorate to succeed Dag Hammarskjöld. Nehru rejected the troika soon after it was first proposed, and insisted that the U.N. Secretariat have one executive head. While he was in New York, Menon quietly promoted his own plan for alternating secretaries-general. When he returned to Delhi, the Indian delegation at the U.N. co-operated with the United States in supporting U Thant's nomination as acting secretary-general.

Diplomats who endured prolonged spells of Menon during the Geneva conference on Laos in 1961 and 1962 tell me that he was disagreeeable to all sides, although his sharpest thrusts were reserved for the United States, Britain, and Canada. He refused to acknowledge that India had agreed to the withdrawal of the International Control Commission from Laos in 1958. His prickly personality irritated even the Russians and Chinese Communists. His deputy, Arthur Lall, scrupulously avoided offending the Communist delegates, even if it meant reneging on a previous Indian position.

I have never seen Menon more incoherently abusive than when I talked to him about Laos and other subjects at his New Delhi home early on the morning of November 2, 1961. I found him sipping black tea—he drinks up to sixty cups a day—as he slumped on a couch in his book-lined sitting room. He had undergone a minor brain operation in New York a few weeks before, and his Indian physician kept coming in and out of the room to caution him against becoming overexcited. The conversation began calmly enough with some discussion of the nuclear-test-ban issue. Disarmament proved more thorny. By the time I raised the subject of Laos (then torn by a fresh outbreak of warfare), Menon was indignant. "American arms started flowing into Laos," he said sourly, "long before the Russian airlift last December. The Russians only sent transport planes, while you sent fighters." When I persisted with questions about Communist interference in Laos, Menon blurted, "I feel sorry for countries subjected to American and Russian interference." Then, quivering with rage, he exploded, "Ugly Americans giving dollars and arms in a cantankerous way!" The interview was interrupted at this point by the physician, who took his patient into the next room, saying he had been under "great strain."

Only later did I realize how great the strain was. Menon was already hatching plans to seize the 1,394-square-mile Portuguese enclave of Goa, on the west coast of India. I have authentic information that Menon and Lieutenant General B. M. Kaul, the chief of the general staff, planned to send a party of Indian border police into Goa, some of whom would allow themselves to be captured by the Portuguese. The rest were to fall back and give the alarm. Under the pretext of rescuing the captured border guards, a small Indian force would move in and engage the Portuguese. The main body of Indian troops would then quickly overrun Goa, which is about the size of Rhode Island. In late November 1961 Nehru got wind of the scheme and summoned Menon and the senior military chiefs. He rebuked them for plotting direct action against Goa without his permission. Menon persisted. With the help of hand-picked lieutenants like G. K. Handoo, a top security officer, he stepped up subversion against the Portuguese in Goa. The Indian border police under Handoo's direction recruited, trained, and equipped saboteurs, who were slipped across the border into Goa. Fabricated stories about Portuguese "border provocations" were fed to the Indian press.

On December 7, 1961, Menon lent the weight of his official position to the concoctions. He told the Lok Sabha: "Reports have been pouring in for the last two weeks of intensified firing activity, oppression and terrorism in Goa and of heavy reinforcements of Portuguese armed forces. . . . There was a report of 2,500 troops having been deployed along the Goa border . . . also a report of a fleet of two Portuguese frigates standing guard . . . 2,000 more troops from African and other places have also arrived. . . . It was also reported that dawn-to-dusk curfew had been imposed and that anyone coming after the curfew hours would be shot at sight. . . . Another report said that in Daman [another Portuguese coastal enclave in India] over 1,000 Portuguese soldiers had landed. . . . The Portuguese armed forces are thus poised near the border at various points to overawe and intimidate both the residents of Goa and those living in the border villages on the Indian side. Hit-and-run raids across the border already seem to have started. A raid in a village near Savantvadi was reported two days ago."

There was indeed a military build-up under way, but it was on the Indian, not the Portuguese, side. Rail traffic throughout northern and western India had been disrupted to move the elite 50th Paratroop Brigade and the 17th Infantry Division to jumping-off positions near the Goa border. Elements of the First Armored Division were also deployed. In full view of the Goan coast, India had assembled a task force composed of the newly acquired aircraft carrier *Vikrant*, two cruisers, a destroyer flotilla, at least two antisubmarine frigates, two antiaircraft frigates, and supporting craft. Canberra jet bombers and Gnat and Vampire fighters had been concentrated at Belgaum to support the ground and naval units.

Contrary to what Menon had said, no Portuguese reinforcements ever reached the 3,500-man garrison in Goa and the two smaller enclaves in India. Against India's heavy Centurion tanks, the Portuguese could muster only a handful of 1942-vintage armored reconnaissance cars. They had no air force whatever. Their only warship was the seventeen-year-old sloop *Affonso d'Albuquerque,* which went into action against the entire Indian armada. I know these facts firsthand because I spent ten days covering every part of Goa before the Indians invaded, and I was there during the take-over. My own observation leads me to credit the estimate by foreign military attachés that India enjoyed at least a ten-to-one numerical superiority over the hopelessly ill-equipped and outmanned Portuguese defenders.

The invasion of Goa actually began more than twenty-four hours before India announced early on December 18, 1961, that its troops had been ordered to move in. On Sunday morning, December 17, several other Western correspondents and I ran into bearded Indian troops dug in at least a quarter of a mile inside Goan territory. They had taken over the Sinquervale frontier post, abandoned three days before by the Portuguese, who feared that its exposed position would give the Indians an opportunity to provoke a shooting incident. The Indians needed no pretext.

The other correspondents and I alighted from our taxi to walk several hundred yards to what we expected would be a Portuguese frontier post. There was an ominous silence until we heard a voice shouting to us in Hindi to stop. A turbaned Sikh trained his machine gun on us. We explained that we were British and American newsmen and asked to see the officer in charge. We were then taken into custody and held at the post for an hour, until an Indian Army captain in paratroop uniform arrived on the scene. He questioned us about the condition of the roads in Goa, then told us to return to Pangim, Goa's capital, in the taxi we had brought. As we left, he said matter-of-factly: "It's all right—your coming here in daylight. But tonight—or, rather, at night—we couldn't guarantee your safety." That night the push was on.

Soon after the invasion began, Menon called a news conference in New Delhi. He was in a jaunty mood. India, he explained, had been "forced" to send troops into Goa to protect the civil population against the breakdown of law and order and the collapse of the "colonial regime." I know from my own observation that there was no breakdown of law and order and no collapse of the regime in Pangim or any of the many other places I saw in Goa. I had twice visited the central prison in Pangim, and found it occupied by only eleven bored inmates, seven of them political prisoners. There had not been a single case of arson, looting, or terrorism in Pangim in the ten days before the Indians invaded. There was no curfew there or anywhere else in Goa. Where isolated acts of terrorism or sabotage had taken place, it was established that most of them were committed by infiltrators trained and equipped by Handoo's Indian border police.

Menon had talked about the people of Goa being "shot down, repressed, and massacred." He had said that the Goans must achieve their own liberation. But the striking thing about Goa on the eve of the Indian take-over was its tranquillity. There was no popular resistance movement worthy of the name. Portugal was not particularly popular, but neither was India except among a section of Goan Hindus (mostly lawyers, teachers, and other middle-class professionals), who hoped their status would improve under Indian rule. They are already showing signs of disappointment. Many of Goa's 228,000 Christians (out of a total population of 640,000) might have preferred to maintain some link with Portugal as insurance against being swamped by the fast-growing Hindu majority. My own feeling is that a majority of politically conscious Goans would have elected for autonomy or actual independence if they had been given the choice.

Ten days before Indian troops had moved onto Goan soil, Menon told the lower house of Parliament, "The position of the government is that there is no question of our going and liberating Goa. The question is that we shall not leave our places undefended. . . ." He termed Indian troop movements "precautionary," and said flatly, "There is no question of suddenly hitting or attacking; Government . . . is not thinking of any operations."

A few years before, Menon had publicly affirmed, "I say categorically that India will not take one step that involves the use of force to alter a situation, even if the legal right is on her side." Nehru had been even more specific. Speaking of Goa in Parliament on September 17, 1955, he said, "We rule out nonpeaceful methods completely." Even a police action, he said, would lay Indians open to the charge of being "deceitful hypocrites." He insisted that reliance on peaceful methods to bring Goa into India "is not only a sound policy, but the only possible policy."

Such is India's record on Goa. It has earned Menon the epithet of the "Goa constrictor." I have never been able to understand why the resort to force to seize Goa surprised so many people in America and Britain. Nehru champions many Gandhian ideals, but pure nonviolence is not one of them. He has used violence before—in Kashmir and against the princely state of Hyderabad in 1948. He is still using it against the Naga rebels fighting for their independence in extreme eastern India. During the first fifteen years of independence, Indian police have fired on Indian crowds at least as frequently as the British used force during the last fifteen years of their rule. For his part, Menon has never even paid lip service to Gandhism. He calls it "good merchandise" but boasts that he does not need it.

For me, the most significant thing about the Goa operation is the light it sheds on Menon's power at that time to manipulate Nehru and the rest of the Indian government for his own ends. To what extent Nehru believed Menon's fraudulent version of events leading up to the take-over is difficult to say at this stage. The Prime Minister was under heavy pressure from the Army and public opinion on the eve of the 1962 elections to demonstrate that he could deal firmly with foreign intruders. No action being possible (in Nehru's judgment) against the Chinese, he may have felt compelled to move on Goa. I have never accepted the notion that Goa was primarily designed to enhance Menon's electoral prospects in North Bombay. Menon was convinced he could win without Goa because he had Nehru and the Congress machine working for him.

The North Bombay campaign in the fall and winter of 1961-1962 was the most bitterly contested and lavishly financed election in Indian history. It aroused strong passions in India and abroad. Its outcome, although never really in doubt, was thought likely to affect the future of India and Asia for many years to come.

North Bombay is what is known in India as a "prestige constituency." Its 762,775 eligible voters, living in an area of 254 square miles, include many Bombay cinema artists, writers, and professional people. But the majority is composed of illiterate slum dwellers, poor artisans, petty traders, and manual laborers. Tiny stall shops and thatch huts sprawl over the tidal marsh land of North Bombay. The constituency has been solidly Congress for many years. In 1957 Menon was elected from there without difficulty, although the local tide was running against the Congress party at the time.

When Menon sought renomination from North Bombay in 1961, he met surprising opposition. The district Congress party committee voted by a narrow margin to choose an old-school party stalwart over Menon. Nehru was furious and demanded that Menon run from North Bombay. Local party leaders finally bowed to the Prime Minister, but twenty-six members of the Congress party youth organization resigned and declared in a statement, "We are convinced Menon is procommunist and the future of the country is not safe in his hands as India's defense minister and spokesman of our foreign policy. . . . We feel it is our bounden duty to see that he is defeated." Nehru later told 200,000 people in Bombay that the defectors could "go to hell." At the end of his speech, he turned to Menon, sitting behind him, to ask, "Is that all you wanted me to say?"

Menon was opposed by the perennial maverick of Indian politics, seventy-four-year-old Jiwatram Bhagwandas Kripalani, who carries the honorific title of Acharya (teacher) and once served as president of the Congress party. He resigned from Congress in 1951 in a dispute with Nehru, formed his own party, and finally became an independent. In North Bombay he was backed by an unlikely coalition of the Praja Socialist party, the traditionalist Hindu Jan Sangh, and the Right Wing conservative Swatantra party. As a long-time associate of Gandhi and friend of Nehru, Kripalani was loath to attack Congress or Nehru. He concentrated his fire on Menon, whom he called "the spearhead of the creeping march of Communism in the country and in the Congress." He insisted that it was dangerous to entrust the defense of the country against Communist China to such a man.

This issue, however well chosen, evoked little response among the largely illiterate masses of North Bombay. Kripalani's own supporters were often at odds. His campaign was badly organized.

Menon, on the other hand, rode to victory on the well-oiled machines of Congress and the Communists, with a powerful assist from Nehru. Congress and Communist party workers carried on door-to-door campaigning for him in every ward of the constituency. The movie colony, attracted by Menon's radicalism and flattered by his attentions, was mobilized. A. M. Tariq, a Moslem member of Parliament and former tonga-driver from Kashmir, was imported to rally North Bombay's 80,000 Moslems. Mrs. Violet Alva, a south Indian Christian, who was then deputy home minister, appealed to the 50,000 Christians (mostly Goans). Even Bombay's powerful bootleggers were told to muster their supporters. But by far the most effective support for Menon came from Nehru. Driving himself at an inhuman pace, Nehru toured India from Kashmir to Kerala defending Menon at every turn. He campaigned in North Bombay a month before the elections and offered to return in the last days, but the Congress party bosses assured him that Menon's victory was already safe. Nehru's theme was: "A vote against Menon is a vote against me." He even threatened to resign if the Defense Minister were defeated. While Menon remained silent in the face of charges that he was a crypto-Communist, Nehru heatedly denied them, insisting, "Mr. Menon is a socialist like me. But he is a real socialist and not an armchair socialist." Overexertion during the campaign contributed to the illness that incapacitated Nehru for several weeks in April.

In Bombay, the Communists concentrated on ensuring Menon's re-election to the exclusion of all else. They took over the Citizens Committee for Menon. They broke up Kripalani meetings and burned anti-Menon newspapers. They were so engrossed in Menon's cause that they made little effort to save their veteran organizer and Lok Sabha leader, Shripad Amrit Dange, from defeat in another Bombay constituency. "One Menon is worth a hundred Danges" was the word that went out to party activists. The Communists eagerly exploited charges by Menon and Nehru that "outside interests"—clearly meaning the United States—were conspiring to defeat the Defense Minister. When I asked Nehru at a news conference after the election which "interests" he was alluding to, he said he would rather not identify them.

Menon's campaign manager and constant companion in Bombay was Dr. A. V. Baliga, fellow-traveling Indian surgeon and former president of the Indo-Soviet Cultural Society. He treated Menon's physical complaints as well as his political infirmities.

The Defense Minister had been "nursing" his constituency with patronage and such favors as new suburban railway stations for several years. He visited every corner of North Bombay, including six tiny offshore fishing islands included in the constituency. He spoke in churches, on street corners, in public parks, and anywhere else a crowd could be found. Since he is unable to speak any vernacular Indian language, much of Menon's English rhetoric was lost on his auditors, but they were flattered by his presence. He never referred by name to Kripalani and never specifically denied the charge that he was partial to the Communist bloc. Instead, he harped on the theme that he was a loyal lieutenant of Nehru and faithful exponent of the socialist policy espoused in resolutions of the Congress party. He attacked vested interests and spoke vaguely about the need for disarmament and coexistence. It is an irony of politics that his themes and the way he approached them would have been far more understandable to American voters than would the Gandhian metaphysics of Kripalani.

Kashmir was the only foreign-policy issue Menon stressed. It had paid off in 1957, when Menon was hailed as the "hero of Kashmir" for his twenty-hour defense of India's position in the U.N. Security Council. When he collapsed at the end of one eight-hour stretch of oratory, he revived long enough to ask, "Where is the A.P. [Associated Press] man?" The Indian government's Films Division thoughtfully released propaganda films on Menon and Kashmir before both the 1957 and the 1962 elections.

The outcome of the North Bombay contest was apparent to any unbiased observer long before the votes were cast. But Menon and Kripalani campaigned intensively until the end. I will never forget watching Menon, on the last night of the campaign, being hoisted to his feet by two burly helpers. Clutching the microphone, the tottering figure in long Keralan robes addressed the crowds in a hoarse whisper. Kripalani was equally exhausted. His last speech was a fervent warning against Menon. As police sirens wailed to signify the official close of campaigning, Kripalani uttered his last exhortation to the voters, "Beware of Communism!"

When the votes were counted, Menon was the victor, with 298,427 votes to Kripalani's 157,069. It was the second biggest landslide in the 1962 elections. The next day Menon made a well-publicized courtesy call on his defeated rival. Under the headline "Menon Routs Reaction," the pro-Communist Bombay weekly *Blitz* cried, "The electorate of North Bombay has saved the Nehru ideology from a fascist coup. The will of God and history has been asserted." Kripalani went into temporary retirement. Menon told me that his election was a "fresh mandate for socialism." Delhi buzzed with rumors that Nehru would now make a drastic shift to the Left. The Bombay Stock Exchange sank giddily, and Right Wing members of the cabinet trembled for their political lives.

The exultant and the fearful were equally deluded. The real victor of North Bombay was not Menon, but Nehru and the Congress machine. The stop-Menon movement had failed, but the Defense Minister still lacked the support of any important faction of the Congress party. The massive Menon vote did not reflect mass popularity. In caste-conscious, symbol-ridden, tradition-governed India, the verdict of one constituency is a poor clue to a politician's national following. Since the election, Menon has plunged into an endless round of speechmaking before garden clubs, student groups, dramatic societies, and anyone else who will listen. He attends flower shows, inaugurates sports events, gives away prizes, opens schools, and sits on any platform in sight. This frenzied activity reflects Menon's realization that he still lacks a political base outside Nehru. His native state is no source of strength. The reason, of course, is that Menon is as much a stranger in Kerala as anywhere else in India.

You feel the intellectual chasm between Menon and any Indian audience the moment he starts speaking. I especially remember a little talk he gave at the opening of a dramatic festival for clerks and other lower-ranking civilian employees of the Defense Ministry in New Delhi. Menon stared at his audience a moment and then began speaking as if he were carrying on a monologue. "There is a curious social mathematics in this country," he mused. "When we speak of people in India, one and one don't make two. They cancel each other out because fellowship is lacking." His audience gazed at him in bewilderment. "You can't abolish slums simply with brick and mortar," he continued. "You have to create an anti-slum mentality. You have to develop a mind that is against dirt." He spoke the last word as if he could taste it in his mouth. I could sense the old undercurrent of bitterness in his voice as he went on. "Unless the mind is against dirt, people get used to it. Even microbes get immune to medicines. That's what makes medicines less effective. This immunity to evil is what education must prevent." Then he stopped speaking as abruptly as he had begun. His definition of the role of education struck me as the quintessence of his brilliant negativism. I doubt if he could formulate a thought that did not include at least one negative.

When Menon is not speaking to baffled mass audiences, he is lecturing his small coterie of admirers in Parliament. They include the ambitious Leftist Oil Minister, K. D. Malaviya; A. M. Tariq, a political hack; and a handful of others. T. T. Krishnamachari, the former finance minister who resigned under fire, was brought back into the cabinet as a minister without portfolio, reportedly at Menon's behest. Krishnamachari's socialism is supposed to coincide with Menon's, but the two men are more likely to be rivals than partners after Nehru goes. In the fall of 1962 they were reported to have quarreled bitterly over economic policy. Two other cabinet ministers, Law Minister Ashoke Sen and Minister of Scientific Research and Cultural Affairs Humayun Kabir are often said to be close to Menon, but have not been notably active in his behalf. Jagjivan Ram, who was then railways minister and who now holds the transport and communications portfolio, got Menon's backing for the deputy leadership of the Congress parliamentary party in 1961 and might some day return the favor if Menon's political fortunes improve.

The real power in the Congress party after Nehru will not be with members of Parliament and ministers in the central cabinet. It will be in the hands of chief ministers in the states and party bosses in the countryside. Menon's support among this group is practically nil at the present. Maharashtra's powerful Chief Minister, Y. B. Chavan, supported Menon's campaign in North Bombay on orders from Nehru, not out of fondness for the Defense Minister. Kamaraj Nadar, chief minister of Madras and Congress party powerhouse in south India, has little use for Menon. Bakshi Ghulam Mohammed, the strong-arm prime minister of Kashmir state, has sometimes been regarded as a Menon supporter, but may have fallen out with him recently. Menon has poured defense funds into the Punjab, possibly in hopes of winning the state's hardhanded Chief Minister, Sardar Pratap Singh Kairon, a former

Ford assembly-line worker and graduate of the University of Michigan. But Kairon, like Menon, depends on Nehru. Once Nehru goes, Kairon's bitter foes among the Punjab's Sikhs are likely to strike him down.

The only chief minister who might be willing and able to give Menon effective support in a bid for power is Bijoyananda Patnaik, the ruthless and unprincipled young multimillionaire who runs the state of Orissa, in eastern India. Patnaik is a kind of Indian Huey Long. He is addicted to authoritarian methods and will stop at nothing in his pursuit of power. He won repute in Congress by retrieving the party's fortunes in the 1961 mid-term elections in Orissa. The state, long one of the poorest and most backward in India, has become in effect another department of Patnaik's giant Kalinga Enterprises. Patnaik's business deals became so notorious a few years ago that the then Union Finance Minister notified all government departments, "The Finance Minister will not support any project with which Mr. Patnaik is associated." Patnaik, Malaviya, and Menon have each rented a floor in the New Delhi office building recently erected by the Communist-line weekly *Link*, and Patnaik is a major stockholder in the publication, which unfailingly backs Menon.

India's Communists would undoubtedly support Menon for the premiership unless they saw a chance of winning power themselves. In that event they would have no difficulty forgetting the cantankerous Keralan. The Indian Communist party is divided and nowhere in power today. If it adheres to constitutional methods, the party could help Menon little in the next five or six years. In the unlikely event that the Communists reverted to the agitational tactics they practiced in the early independence period, they would have to subvert or overpower the Indian Army. They are incapable of doing either today.

Whatever other support Menon may have, his political strength is still the shadow of Jawaharlal Nehru. Many Right Wing Congressmen long believed that Nehru's refusal to designate a successor—even by implication—was a stall aimed at giving Menon time to build a political base. Nehru's decision to take over the Defense Ministry himself after the military debacle of October 1962 was made only under intense pressure from an aroused party and public. Although Menon had been dropped from the cabinet, it was not clear in the closing months of the year whether he retained Nehru's confidence in such measure that he might eventually hope to make a political comeback. It is clear, however, that Menon's position, once Nehru goes, will probably be more vulnerable than ever. Frank Moraes predicts that once Nehru is gone, "the Congress pack will descend on Krishna Menon like hungry wolves and tear him apart politically."

One tactic Menon may adopt to escape such a painful denouement is to support Indira Gandhi for the premiership. Her ideas are to the left of the Congress majority, but all factions in the party might be persuaded to accept her because she is an all-India figure whose name and successful tenure as Congress president have brought her considerable prestige. Mrs. Gandhi is probably closer to Menon than to anyone else in the cabinet except her father and Home Minister Lal Bahadur Shastri. She disagreed with Menon on Tibet and on Congress participation in an anti-Communist coalition in Kerala, but on most questions their views coincide. Menon has recently gone out of his way to flatter Mrs. Gandhi, but he probably deludes himself if he thinks he can rule through her. Indira Gandhi is no one's mouthpiece.

If all constitutional roads to power are blocked, Menon can hardly have failed to think of the alternative. He is authoritarian by nature. The use of force has no terrors for him. The question is whether he could muster the force to fulfill what he undoubtedly regards as his historic destiny. Menon's removal from the Defense Ministry in October 1962 followed the bitter reaction among army officers to disclosures of Indian weakness in the Himalayas. Whatever following he had in the officer corps appeared to have vanished in the nationwide wave of resentment at his handling of frontier defenses.

During his five-year tenure as defense minister, Menon succeeded in forcing out a number of senior officers, including General Thimayya, who resisted his dictation. He was less successful in breaking up the Army's long-established units based on caste or province. He twice raised officers' pay scales and improved billets and other amenities. He was also more successful in extracting appropriations from Parliament than any previous defense minister. Under his supervision, the volume of India's military production has more than doubled, and now includes jet fighters, recoilless rifles, antitank guns, trucks, jeeps, and other items previously imported. But few of these weapons had reached front-line troops by the time the Chinese attacked in October 1962. The real cost of Indian-produced military equipment is impossible to determine, because Menon refuses to permit even Indian government auditors to inspect the books of the ordnance factories and other defense establishments. The quality is still below Western standards.

In July 1961 Menon organized an elaborate demonstration of the Indian-made HF-24 fighter, which he hailed as the first supersonic jet war plane produced in Asia. The HF-24 was a fraud. It is incapable of reaching supersonic speeds in level flight. After a British manufacturer declined to underwrite development costs for a new engine for the HF-24, Menon persuaded Nehru to take up a Soviet offer to sell India supersonic MiG-21 fighters for rupees. The United States and Britain made vain eleventh-hour efforts to block the MiG deal by offering Western fighters on attractive terms. Many Western observers concluded that India was moving toward the Soviet bloc. In fact, the MiG purchase had little to do with politics except that the Indian leaders interpreted it as a tacit guarantee of Russian support against Chinese Communist expansionism. India's hopes were disappointed when the Soviet Union made clear its ultimate sympathies were with China after full-scale fighting began on the Indian-Chinese border in October 1962. American discomfiture at the talk of MiGs was all the more surprising in view of the fact that everyone in Delhi had known since July 1961, when the first American supersonic fighters were promised to Pakistan, that India would shop for equivalent planes. As in so many other situations, American Ambassador John Kenneth Galbraith appears to have failed to alert Washington to Indian intentions until it was too late.

Under the guise of stimulating domestic production of critical military equipment, Menon has partially broken the West's monopoly on the supply of arms to India. He rejected a lightweight American plastic rifle in favor of an Indian model although qualified Indian officers strongly endorsed the American weapon. He ignored an American offer to demonstrate the C-130 turboprop transport for him. Instead, he contracted for the purchase of eight Soviet AN-12 transports, which have proved unsuitable for airlift operations at Ladakh's high altitudes. Russian MI-4 helicopters, ordered by Menon in preference to American and French models, have also failed to fulfill expectations. India has now arranged to produce helicopters under license from a French firm.

Menon was out as defense minister the day after it was announced that India had asked for emergency shipments of American military equipment in the face of the Chinese onslaught in October 1962.

Despite such blunders, Menon gave India's armed forces a new feeling of importance. He helped remove the "anti-patriotic" stigma that clung to the services for their generally pro-British stand during the independence movement. He ruthlessly brushed aside government regulations and administrative procedures to get things done. "We have all kinds of civilian help doing army jobs," General Thimayya told a foreign military attaché in Delhi, "and other government agencies have to pay for it. I don't know how in hell Menon gets away with it, because he tells the government nothing." Menon carried the cult of secrecy to the point of requiring senior officers to swear in writing to disclose nothing.

The cult of his own omniscience made the Defense Minister anathema to many Indian officers. In the fall of 1961 a Bombay weekly published an anonymous letter from a group of army officers who said, "We are fast coming to the belief that the defense minister is the evil genius of independent India. He seems to wield some black magic over the mind of the prime minister." A British Labour M.P. who knows India well says that he has never met an Indian officer who really liked Menon. Michael Edwardes, an English historian who has served in India, reports that even younger officers are anti-Menon. There is evidence that a group of high-ranking Indian officers actually approached a Western attaché in New Delhi for help in arranging to have Menon assassinated. Money was offered but the attaché in question declined the honor.

My own feeling is that much will depend on the stand taken
by Lieutenant General B. M. Kaul, the brilliant spark plug of
India's military services. He rose to his present eminence with
Menon's help and against bitter opposition from General
Thimayya and the old guard at army headquarters. Kaul is
now consolidating his grip on the Army. He has succeeded
in scotching the notion that he is Menon's man. I doubt that
there is any ideological or emotional affinity between the two
men.

So much for the prospects and problems of Krishna Menon.
Such a balance sheet of strengths and weaknesses can be drawn
up for other Indian politicians, and though it might come out
wrong, you would still feel you were dealing with natural
political phenomena. Menon is different. Like Stalin, he uses
language not to convey, but to conceal, his meaning. He
harbors a kind of political death wish that goads him into
alienating those whom he most needs to befriend. I have seen
him exude charm for two hours and then fly into an un-
controllable rage over some imagined slight. Some Indian and
American friends recall spending a delightful evening with him
at a New York night club (where he drinks nothing but tea)
until, for no apparent reason, he suddenly picked up a pin
and plunged it with fiendish glee into the arm of the lady
sitting beside him. Such aberrations deepen the mystery that
surrounds this slightly satanic figure. Exploring the dark
universe of his mind is like celestial navigation when all stars
are extinguished. He is the undeciphered apocrypha of India,
the sum of all negation; like Goethe's Mephistopheles, "a part
of that part that always denies." A former American ambassador to India believes that Menon expresses the evil in Nehru
just as the portrait of Dorian Gray did for its subject. The
idea might sound fanciful, but there is much that is somberly
complementary in the characters of the two pre-eminent figures
of contemporary India. Nehru is the reluctant despot, and
Menon the unwilling democrat. Nehru, the disappointed
idealist groping for a rational road to salvation, seems to have
enlisted the malignant powers of Menon's intellect, much as
Faust made his evil compact with Mephistopheles to escape
despair. Nehru, like Napoleon, "went forth to seek virtue,
but since she was not to be found, he got power." The loneli-

ness of supreme power has been intensified by Nehru's supreme frustration at his inability to project his power through a world-conquering ideology of his own making. His dreams of entering a pantheon of seers as a nonviolent Lenin or Mao have crumbled in the unchanging Indian dust. What remains is Menon's intellect and Nehru's instinct. On November 7, 1962, Nehru yielded to intense pressure from Congress party leaders, including, ironically, T. T. Krishnamachari, and accepted Menon's resignation from the cabinet. But there are no signs that he has dispensed with Menon's advice on a wide variety of subjects. The Prime Minister's long-time confidant and trusted lieutenant continues to wield immense backstage influence. Nor has Menon's following in the country evaporated since he resigned his portfolio. On the contrary, there were signs of an upsurge of sympathy and support for him late in 1962 by those who felt that Menon had been made the scapegoat for military setbacks for which Nehru shared responsibility. Menon seemed more relaxed and confident after his removal from the cabinet than during his years of ministerial office. He clearly has no intention of relinquishing the pursuit of power or his special place in Nehru's confidence. The two men approach a mentally foreign country with the rusting doctrinal apparatus they heard described in the lecture halls of a bygone Europe. They are the rootless reformers of Asia, filled with hatred of the past, revulsion at the present, and dread of the future. History will be generous to Nehru, for it will account as achievement what he regarded as prologue. Menon has no prologue and no achievement. Now sixty-five and increasingly dependent on drugs to sustain his energy, Menon may not even live to see Nehru in his grave. Or the two men may vanish together into the mists of history. But my own feeling is that Menon will outlive his protector. When Nehru is gone, when the mighty banyan tree is removed and Menon is exposed to the pitiless elements, he will make a brave pretense of competing in the open political market by fair means or foul. But when the game is up, as it must soon be, I venture to predict (as Philip Deane has) that he will go home to that drab boardinghouse in Camden Town. There you will find him wrapped in cheap scarves, brewing endless cups of tea, and writing mordant articles on the folly of mankind.

Lal Bahadur Shastri

LAL BAHADUR SHASTRI occupies a position in Indian life today that gives him broader powers in more fields than any man except Nehru. As minister of home affairs of the government of India, he controls half a million police, a nationwide intelligence network, and one of the largest armies of civil servants in the world. He is ultimately responsible for protecting the lives and welfare of 443 million people in various stages of evolution from the Stone Age to the twentieth century. India without a Union home minister would be a geographical expression.

Lal Bahadur (Shastri is an honorific surname referring to the course he pursued at college) is India's premier compromiser, conciliator, and co-ordinator. More than Nehru or any other member of the cabinet, he labors to harmonize the often contradictory workings of the central government and fifteen state administrations (with a sixteenth in formation). He umpires their disputes and referees seemingly irreconcilable claims. He directly administers eight Union territories (centrally administered areas akin to territories of the United

States) with a combined population of almost seven million souls. As father-confessor to the onetime rulers of India's 555 former princely states, Lal Bahadur has more retired royalty on his pension-roll than any other man in history. At the other end of the social spectrum, he is specially charged with the uplift of India's sixty-five million untouchables and almost thirty million members of backward tribes, the largest socially benighted community on earth.

When Nehru and Morarji Desai were both out of India in September 1962, Shastri functioned as acting prime minister although he was never formally given that title. At other times he is in fact, if not in name, deputy prime minister. Without appearing to seek self-aggrandizement, he wields immense authority in all domestic matters. He enjoys Nehru's complete confidence and is the one person (other than Indira Gandhi) with whom the Prime Minister discusses internal politics frankly and in detail. He is the most popular man in the Congress party and the main channel of communication between Nehru and the party organizations. He had more to do with selecting Congress candidates for the 1962 elections than anyone except Nehru and Indira Gandhi. S. K. Patil and a very considerable body of Indian opinion openly regard Shastri today as India's next prime minister and first among equals in a post-Nehru collective leadership.

The repository of this vast power and popularity is a small (just over five feet), shy, self-effacing man who speaks in an almost inaudible whisper. The first time I met him I kept staring hard to make sure he was not an office messenger. Anyone who had not seen pictures of the Home Minister would certainly mistake Shastri for a minor clerk in the office. He is the most unpretentious government official I have ever met in India. Looking at him across the glass-topped expanse of his office desk in Parliament House, I remember thinking how out of place he looked. All I could see was a miniature face set on a scrawny neck and surmounted by the inevitable white Gandhi cap. He began by apologizing profusely for being late—something Indian ministers do not usually bother doing. He is the only Indian official I have ever heard say "please" to a telephone operator or "thank you" to a messenger. His diffidence can be excruciating. Just before we began a television interview one day, I mentioned to him that I would open by asking him what the home minister does in India. "I don't really know. I can't say," he blurted in a paroxysm of embarrassment made worse by the snickers of his assembled aides. But by the time the interview began, he had collected his thoughts and answered the question lucidly.

Shastri is the only Indian minister I know who prefers not to sit on the speakers' platform at public meetings. When he travels outside Delhi, he usually avoids the VIP government guesthouses in favor of more modest lodgings. In Allahabad, his adopted home in the state of Uttar Pradesh, he always went back to his family's small rented bungalow in a working-class district of the city, instead of staying at the well-appointed government quarters available to him. In the spring of 1962, when his family had to vacate the bungalow and return it to the owner, the Home Minister publicly appealed to the citizens of Allahabad to help him find new accommodations. He said he did not think it proper to use his "official influence" in the matter. Shastri's plea led to his being dubbed "the homeless Home Minister."

Shastri is the unusual Indian minister who will share his lunch with his office staff and leave his home to converse on a street corner with a disappointed petitioner. When he returned to his home constituency to vote in the 1962 election, he found that his aged mother had been barred from the polls because her name did not appear on the voters' register, owing to an oversight by local election officials. Any other cabinet minister would have excoriated the erring bureaucrats and ordered their instant removal. He took the matter philosophically and refrained even from calling it to the attention of the election officials. As far as I know, his mother's name still does not appear on the voters' roll.

Shastri is a truly humble man who, in the Churchillian phrase, may have much to be humble about. But his rare humility and genuine compassion set him apart. He has never succumbed to the disease of feeling superior, which afflicts so many educated Indians, especially those mistakenly called government servants. Without flaunting his convictions, he is probably more profoundly Gandhian in his attitude toward the world than are any of his cabinet colleagues, including Nehru. His reputation is untainted by faction or fraud. He is the target of few political attacks, not because he lacks enemies, but because, like Duncan in *Macbeth*, he

> Hath borne his faculties so meek, hath been
> So clear in his great office, that his virtues
> Will plead like angels trumpet-tongu'd. . . .

Again like Duncan, Lal Bahadur is not a great man; he is not even outstanding, except by comparison with the depressingly low run of Indian politicians. He describes himself as a "mediocre" and "not an important person." A well-informed New Delhi editor calls him "a loyal, colorless party wheelhorse who does what Nehru tells him." An Indian Civil Service officer who held high posts under Shastri and India's first home minister, Sardar Patel, says that comparing them "is like comparing a mule with a thoroughbred." Another senior civil servant who worked with Shastri for many years says that he was never able to tell where he stood on the larger issues facing India. Such uncertainty is justified. S. K. Patil, for example, insists that the Home Minister really sympathizes with the Congress Right Wing, "but he doesn't dare do anything against Nehru's wishes." He predicts that Shastri will rally to the conservatives in Congress once Nehru is gone. I am sure that Shastri is a social conservative, but he identifies himself too closely with the underdog ever to feel really at home with Indian big business. He calls himself a Gandhian socialist (a practically meaningless term) and says simply, "I like socialism because it will reduce the wide gulf that exists between the rich and poor." G. D. Birla, an Indian industrialist, is probably right when he says, "Shastri is not Leftist, but not Rightist either. He's a good, clean man who has no great ideas about economics." Nor, it might seem at first glance, has he about anything else. No one with whom I have talked about him could recall one idea that he had originated except his solution of the Cachar language dispute in Assam. In both governmental and Congress party councils, the little man has been a faithful echo of his master, Jawaharlal Nehru. A former

American political officer in Delhi says flatly, "Shastri can't make decisions for himself. He always refers to Nehru."

What will he do when Nehru goes? Will he be bereft of ideas and lost in indecision? I believe not. Lal Bahadur Shastri regards himself today purely and simply as a lieutenant of the Prime Minister. He applies to this role the same strict construction that he places on his constitutional powers as home minister. He may lack imagination, but no one can accuse him of disloyalty. He is an example of constancy in a country where allegiance is too often negotiable. I do not expect the constancy to disappear with Nehru. Shastri has a will of his own and, what is more unusual, a conscience. Neither is transient. Under the right circumstances they could assert themselves with possibly telling effect. Moreover, he is not deluded by visions of grandeur. He knows his own limitations, which is more than most Indian politicians can say for themselves. Like so many other compromise candidates throughout history, he might well surprise those who chose him for his apparent pliancy. The mouse might well roar.

It is unlikely, however, that he would ever try to imitate the Nehru roar. His voice is better suited for calling a cabinet, not a nation, to order. He appears to be a likely choice to lead the collective government that is likely to follow Nehru's long one-man rule. No one in the upper reaches of the Indian government today can produce a consensus more deftly than the Home Minister. No one is more universally trusted by Congressmen, from chief ministers down to ward secretaries.

Shastri's early career, like the man himself, conforms rather colorlessly to the approved pattern for Congressmen of the preindependence generation. The most important fact of his life even today is that he was born in the old United Provinces, now Uttar Pradesh, where Indian politics is brewed and Congress leaders are bred. U.P., as it is called in India, is the largest state in the Union and the home of one Indian out of six. Its population, of more than seventy million, is larger than that of Britain and the Benelux countries combined. The state is the center of the enormous Hindi-speaking heartland of India that stretches from the Great Indian Desert, in the west, to the Bay of Bengal, in the east, dominating the

country politically and economically. U.P. was the birthplace
of Motilal and Jawaharlal Nehru, of Pandit Pant, and of a host
of other Congress leaders. The era of its hegemony may be
passing, but U.P., usually seconded by neighboring Bihar, still
considers itself mistress of Indian politics and the Congress
party.

Lal Bahadur was born in the Hindu holy city of Banaras,
by the Ganges, on October 2, 1904, about eighty miles and ten
incarnations removed from the big mansion in Allahabad
where Jawaharlal Nehru, then thirteen, was discovering the
world with the help of his private tutor. Nehru's family were
aristocratic Brahmans of ample means. Lal Bahadur, whose
family name is Srivastava, is a member of the Kayastha caste,
who served as clerks, scribes, and petty government officials
under the Moguls when Indian Brahmans still boycotted the
Moslem conquerors. His father was a schoolteacher who became a minor government official. He died when Lal Bahadur
was only a year and a half old. It is a curious fact that most
of the main persons in this book lost one or both of their
parents at an early age. "I led a very poor life," Lal Bahadur
told me without rancor. He is still one of the poorest men in
Congress, a fact that may help account for his sympathy for
the underdog. His maternal grandfather helped him get his
early education at the local Harischandra school and supported
the boy's mother and two sisters, the younger of whom is now
a member of the Bihar Legislature. The turning point in the
young man's life came in 1920, when he was only sixteen. It
was then that he heard Gandhi appeal to students in Banaras
to boycott government schools. "I immediately decided to give
up my studies and join the nonco-operation movement," he
says. The following year, after being arrested but not jailed,
he enrolled at the Gandhi-sponsored Kashi Vidyapeeth, or
National College, in Banaras. Gandhi opened the school and
visited it several times while Shastri was there. But the man
who had the deepest impact on his thinking was the scholarly
Dr. Bhagwan Das, principal of the college and authority on
humanistic philosophy. Shastri studied philosophy under him
and absorbed his compassionate outlook. The young man
lived in the same building with Acharya Kripalani, then a

faculty member. The faculty also included Sri Prakasa, later governor of Maharashtra, and Dr. Sampurnanand, the Hindu traditionalist who served as chief minister of U.P. and is now governor of Rajasthan. The Kashi Vidyapeeth devised the so-called Shastri course and its own degree, roughly equivalent to the Bachelor of Arts. Some graduates were called "Shastri" (one versed in a particular branch of learning). "I keep telling my friends," Lal Bahadur said to me in a voice that reminded me of Eddie Cantor's, "not to call me Shastri. But they persist, and hundreds of thousands of voters in my constituency know me as Shastriji [the diminutive form]." It is like calling the graduate of an American arts college "Mr. A. B."

Equipped with a college education, a degree, and a new name, the young man from Banaras went forth to do battle with the British. He joined Congress and donned khaddar with thousands of other Indians his age. When he was twenty-three, he married Lalita Devi, then eighteen years old. They have four sons and two daughters, which he ruefully admits is "not a good example of family planning." His wife rarely appears in public and never attends official functions. I have never seen her when I have visited the Shastri home.

At midnight on December 31, 1929, Shastri stood among thousands of excited Congress enthusiasts as they roared approval for a resolution demanding unconditional independence proposed by a handsome, intense young man with a Cambridge accent. Lal Bahadur was twenty-five on that fateful night, which is still one of his most vivid memories. He little dreamed at the time that he would one day be considered by some the logical successor to the mover of the independence resolution.

Before a year had passed, Shastri was in jail for the first time. He was sentenced to two and a half years for participating in Gandhi's famous march to the sea to make salt in symbolic defiance of the law. He was jailed again in 1932, 1934, 1941, and during the Quit India movement in 1942. Altogether, he spent six terms in prison totaling seven years. At Allahabad he was in the same prison with Nehru, but they were confined in separate barracks. "We couldn't meet," Shastri recalls, "but Nehru was very kind about sending books to us."

For three years beginning in 1935, Shastri was general secretary of the U.P. Congress Committee, already dominated by the redoubtable figure of Pandit Govind Ballabh Pant. When Congress entered the provincial elections in 1937, Lal Bahadur won a seat in the U.P. Legislative Assembly. He was re-elected to the legislature and named secretary to the U.P. Parliament Board (a Congress organ) after World War II. At the same time, he and C. B. Gupta, now chief minister of U.P., were appointed parliamentary secretaries to Pant, then chief minister of the province. It is largely to Pant that Shastri owes his entry into the upper echelons of Congress.

Pant was one of the supreme figures of the independence movement. He was a massive, hulking man with bushy eyebrows and drooping walrus mustaches. His hands shook uncontrollably from palsy caused by injuries received when police lathi-charged a procession he and Nehru were leading in 1928 to protest the presence of Sir John Simon's commission to investigate India's political grievances. Pant was a lawyer of formidable skill, a masterful parliamentarian, and India's last mogul. He transacted most business while reclining on a couch at home. Visitors would kiss his feet as a mark of deference. Such customs might offend the younger generation, but no one questioned Pant's Olympian vision and sagacity. After Sardar Patel and other old-line Congress stalwarts had disappeared, Pant exercised a more effective restraining influence on Nehru in internal policy than anyone else in the cabinet. Pant was a conservative and a traditionalist. He could impose agreement on squabbling Congress factions, especially in U.P., by the sheer weight of his prestige. His position was assured to the point that he did not hesitate to speak his mind to Nehru or anyone else on any issue. When Premier Chou En-lai visited Delhi in April 1960 to discuss the Sino-Indian border dispute, the aged Home Minister was more outspoken and caustic in his comments to the visitor than any other Indian leader, including Nehru. But with most people Pant was considerate and gravely courteous. He was one of the most adept Indian politicians of his generation. He never went abroad and rarely ventured outside Delhi and U.P., yet his mind easily transcended provincial and national frontiers.

He built a first-class machine as Union home minister from January 1955 until his death on March 7, 1961, at the age of seventy-three. Some observers assert that Pant was building a following in other government departments, but he probably knew he would not live to succeed Nehru.

Lal Bahadur served his political apprenticeship under Pant. Pant picked him because he was likable, hard-working, devoted, and trustworthy. He was also noncontroversial. Pant relied on him to assess the political impact of measures the state government proposed to take. In 1947 Pant named him to take charge of public security throughout U.P., a traditionally turbulent area twice the size of England and Wales combined. Shastri became minister for home and transport in the state government.

In 1951 Nehru, who had just been elected to the Congress presidency, called Shastri to New Delhi to organize the Congress campaign in the 1951-1952 general elections. He became the party's secretary-general. As one veteran party member remarked, "The whole show was in Lal Bahadur's hands." He worked around the clock, rarely leaving his desk at the All-India Congress Committee headquarters on New Delhi's tree-shaded Jantar Mantar Road. His labors contributed significantly to the landslide victory that made Congress undisputed master of the country. His reward was election to the Rajya Sabha and appointment as Union minister for transport and railways in May 1952. He resigned from the cabinet in 1956 because he felt responsible for the disastrous Ariyalur rail accident in which 144 persons were killed and 115 injured. The following year all was forgotten. He was elected to the Lok Sabha from Allahabad and served as minister of transport and communications until March 1958. In that month he took over the important commerce and industry portfolio in a cabinet reshuffle following the resignation of Finance Minister T. T. Krishnamachari in the wake of a scandal involving the state-owned Life Insurance Corporation. Opinions are divided on Shastri's performance as commerce and industry minister. His record was not outstanding, but most businessmen seem to think he was hard-working and reasonably efficient. There has never been any question about his honesty. In February 1961, when Pant began to fail, Shastri was named acting home minister. On March 7 the old lion breathed his last, and his onetime disciple inherited the awesome powers and prerogatives of the Union home minister.

Watching Shastri enter the high-domed chamber of the Lok Sabha for the first time after Pant's death, I was struck by the contrast. Shastri seemed almost furtive as he slipped unnoticed onto the Government front bench. Pant's entrances always sent a stir through the huge hall. The emperor Akbar could not have commanded more deference. The contrast was even more marked when Shastri rose to speak in a small monotone. His words were lost in the hubbub of heedless legislators. Pant, on the other hand, always held Parliament spellbound. Out of consideration for his infirmities, Pant was allowed to keep his seat while he spoke, with hands trembling and with a quavering voice of doom. To me it seemed as if Oliver Wendell Holmes had been replaced by the clerk of the court. But the clerk made sense. I soon realized that he was neither overwhelmed nor overawed by the immense responsibilities that had been thrust upon him.

The Home Ministry is an octopus whose tentacles hold India together. One tentacle helps the state government quell language riots in Assam while another probes a corrupt stationmaster in Kerala. If a maharaja packs his bags for Europe, if a deputation of tribesmen petitions for rice, or if a highcourt judge misbehaves, the Home Ministry's tentacles react almost immediately. The Ministry deports subversive Chinese aliens, combats tree blight, recruits clerks, and advises the president of India on whom he should appoint to the superior courts and whom he should spare from the gallows. The home minister has at his disposal fourteen armed battalions of the Central Reserve Police (CRP), the most effective force in India outside the military services. He is also assisted by the Intelligence Bureau (IB) and the powerful Special Police Establishment (SPE), which have, respectively, broad powers to investigate organized crime and corruption. The Ministry's Political Department reports on every facet of Indian political life, with special attention to Communist activities.

India has a federal system. But contrary to American practice, the Indian Constitution provides that all power not specifically vested in the states belongs to the Union government. It is the Home Ministry that exercises many such "residuary" functions on behalf of the Center. Even if there were no such provision in the Constitution, government in India would become increasingly centralized because the states depend on money from the Center to carry out their development plans. The Union government's budget is expanding much more rapidly than the finances of the states. Shastri believes that the Center will continue concentrating power in its hands at the expense of the states for another twenty-five years. Then, he says, the states will have developed economically and politically to the point where they can effectively reassert a larger measure of autonomy.

The all-India services, including the far-flung Indian Administrative Service (IAS), successor to the old Indian Civil Service, the Indian Police Service (IPS), and the newly revived all-India engineering, medical, and forestry services, are recruited, trained, and supervised by the Home Ministry. A member of the all-India services assigned to serve in one of the states gets his pay from the state government and is generally regarded as a state official. But the Home Ministry decides where he is to be posted, how much pay he should receive, and when he should be retired. The collector, highest-ranking official in each district, is from the IAS. Under him in each district there is an IAS officer in charge of local police. Members of the all-India services, especially the 200 ICS officers still on active duty, are better paid and have higher *esprit de corps* than the provincial bureaucracy. They owe primary allegiance to the central government. They are the backbone of the administration and one of the most important unifying elements in India today.

No man in the country wields more effective power in more fields than V. Viswanathan, the capable and little-known home secretary. This veteran ICS officer is the top-ranking civil servant in the Home Ministry, in charge of security, intelligence, and relations with the former princely rulers. His authority is so broad as to seem limitless. Viswanathan is the *de facto* home minister except on the rare occasions when Shastri intervenes personally to overrule his lieutenant. Viswanathan is assisted by two other home secretaries, L. P. Singh and Hari Sharma, also ICS stalwarts, charged respectively with administrative services and government of the Union territories. This triumvirate runs the Home Ministry and with it a great deal of India. Home ministers come and go, but the triumvirate endures.

I shall never forget the elation I felt the first time I was ushered into Viswanathan's office in one corner of the enormous South Block office building in New Delhi. There is nothing unusual about the room itself. In fact, it is smaller than what an official of comparable rank would occupy in other ministries. But in Viswanathan's office I had the feeling that I was at the nerve center of the Indian state. A moment after I entered, he was on the telephone to Bombay giving orders for a particular police inspector to be assigned to "special duty" at the Center. A few minutes later he curtly told an External Affairs Ministry official not to concern himself with the European travel plans of an Indian maharaja. The next moment he had put through a call to the maharaja and was suavely probing to find out what the royal traveler had in mind. Before a quarter of an hour had passed, Viswanathan had issued orders on several clemency cases and disposed of a mass of other business that would take most senior Indian civil servants months to handle. The Home Secretary is the uncrowned king of India.

Shastri's own daily routine reflects his reliance on Viswanathan and Company. He rarely visits his Ministry until 5:00 or 5:30 P.M., by which time official papers requiring his signature and particularly important files are ready for him. Everything else is handled by the triumvirate. Shastri may work at his desk in the South Block labyrinth until 10:00 or 10:30 in the evening, but he usually prefers to return home or to his office in the circular Parliament House. Callers invariably await him at both places. He receives them until 11:00 P.M. or even later.

Shastri devotes mornings to party affairs. He is up by 5:30 or 5:45 A.M. He likes to spin, and says he can make "fine yarn" but rarely finds time nowadays. He used to do yoga exercises, but gave them up after a serious heart attack in October 1959. "I was careful the first year after my heart attack," he says, "but now I follow a normal routine," "Normal" in his case means surrendering to his compulsive tendency to overwork. Many political observers discount his chances for the succession for no other reason than his frail health. L. P. Singh says, "If you judge his health by the way he functions, you'd think he was one of the immortals. His working hours and the way he allows visitors to eat up his time are compatible only with a determination to end his life quickly."

Long before Shastri awakes, his house, at 1 Motilal Nehru Place, resembles a metropolitan railway station at rush hour. Waiting there, you feel as if you were at the crossroads of India. Turbaned Sikhs, dhoti-wearing Congressmen, and half-naked sadhus are among the flood of audience-seekers who fill his sitting rooms and spill out into the garden. When Shastri is ready, he receives each caller individually, rather than having them come in delegations as Pant used to do. He rises to greet each visitor; he would not dream of lying on his couch, let alone allowing petitioners to kiss his feet. Despite the milling throng outside and the other pressures on him, I have always found him calm, courteous, and seemingly unhurried. As one of his aides remarks: "Shastri is always anxious to be fair and very human. He always puts himself in the position of the supplicant in cases involving the administration. This makes difficulties for me. He treats every individual as an individual rather than part of the mass."

The practice of treating every person as an individual, regardless of what Indians call "recommendation," has made Shastri the most popular Congressman and a well-liked figure among the townspeople and villagers of northern India. Over and over I have heard the expressions "a man of the people" and "a pure man" used about him. A member of the Rajya Sabha from Bihar told me, "He represents the common people. He's popular everywhere because you feel quite at home with him when you talk to him."

Shastri is characteristically modest about his popularity. "I think the essential thing," he says earnestly, "is devotion to work with some detachment. This is essential if feuds and conflicts are to be avoided." Then, lest he sound too pontifical, he adds with a wry smile, "This is easy to say but difficult to practice."

His most notable personal triumph to date was working out the so-called "Shastri formula" to resolve the menacing language dispute in the Cachar district of Assam. The formula has already been applied in one district of West Bengal and may be applied in other parts of India to reconcile the conflicting claims of majority and minority language groups.

A word of background may be useful. Language in India is much more than a medium of communication. It is an insigne, a badge, that proves an Indian belongs to something more than the dust and the air, that he is part of a community and that his community survives. More than anything else, language defines an Indian's native region; it is often the most emotionally charged expression of his culture and religion. A devout Sikh will never desecrate anything bearing even one word in the sacred Gurmukhi script. The Urdu-speaking Moslem regards the Arabic characters of his language as a divinely bequeathed link with the holy Koran. The Devanagari script has profound religious significance for many Hindus. Language assumes even more importance in India when it corresponds to caste or economic interests. These interests can be advanced under the politically acceptable cloak of linguistic rights to the disfavor of rival groups.

Language was the spark that ignited long-smoldering economic jealousies in the Brahmaputra Valley of Assam in late June and early July of 1960. The backward Assamese-speaking majority had long resented the fact that the Bengali-speaking minority held the best jobs in the bureaucracy and dominated trade and commerce. It would be difficult to find two languages more similar than Assamese and Bengali, but the Bengalis' reluctance to accept Assamese as the state's sole official language was used as a pretext for a wholesale assault on their communities. At least 40,000 people were driven from their homes, of whom almost 32,000 took refuge in neighboring West Bengal. At least three villages were burned to the ground and 600 other Bengali homes were set on fire. The Army was

ordered in after the police opened fire on a crowd in Gauhati
on July 4, killing one student and and injuring six others. But
before the troops could reach remote areas, anti-Bengali frenzy
had become a hurricane of violence. The Assam government,
twenty-five of whose officers were charged with gross derelic-
tion of duty in connection with the outbreaks, now says that
twenty persons were killed and "about 100" injured in the
bloody July days. But Indian correspondents (foreigners were
barred) who visited the affected areas at the time insist that the
toll of killed and injured was much higher. As is so often the
case in India, the actual numbers will never be known. The
extent of the devastation can be judged from relief expendi-
tures by the state government equivalent to $2,250,000 in the
first nine months after the carnage. I will never forget the
picture published in the Indian press of an ashen-faced Nehru
walking among the hordes of homeless during a tour of the
stricken villages. It was the kind of catastrophe that seems
endemic to the Indo-Pakistani subcontinent.

Pant was still Union home minister at that time. He was
already too old and feeble to visit the scene. It needed all his
still-formidable forensic talents and his unassailable prestige
to meet attacks on the government in Parliament. Eight
months later, Pant's voice was stilled, but the communal
volcano still rumbled ominously in Assam. On May 19, 1961,
it erupted again. This time it was the Bengalis, agitating for
the recognition of Bengali as an additional state language of
Assam, who clashed bloodily with the police. At least eleven
persons were killed and seventy-seven injured (fifty-five with
bullet wounds) when the police opened fire on a crowd of
2,000 Bengalis in Cachar district. Hundreds were arrested.
The nervous state authorities flooded Cachar district (where
the Bengalis are in a majority) with troops, police, and detec-
tives. On May 20 the Bengalis of Cachar and other parts of
Assam observed a hartal during which not a single bus, car, or
train was allowed to move. All shops and offices in the Bengali
areas shut down. This was followed by similar stoppages of
activity on May 24 in Calcutta and other West Bengal towns.
The ghastly events of the previous summer seemed about to be
repeated. Pant had failed not long before his death in an

effort to work out a compromise on Assam's explosive language problems. Nehru had vainly offered his advice. Now Shastri staked everything on finding a solution. He flew to Cachar and surveyed the situation. At first it looked hopeless. Passions on both sides were at fever pitch. Blood had been shed only a few days before, and memories of the wholesale carnage of 1960 were still fresh. Shastri decided the only way was to listen to each side until it had exhausted its invective against the other. Then there might be a chance of compromise.

As one high Home Ministry official says: "Shastri went on probing and pursuing this thing until people started thinking in terms of human tolerance and their obligations to the country. It required tremendous patience. He had to convince all groups of his own deep sincerity and firmness. He would go as far as he could with each group. Then when he thought they were being unreasonable he would tell them so."

Shastri himself says simply, "I listened to different viewpoints. I have the capacity of understanding different viewpoints. I keep an open mind. I talked to different sets of people."

The best that Nehru expected was a year's truce in Cachar. Shastri returned with a permanent solution acceptable to all parties. It was based on the use of English, Assamese, and Bengali. Correspondence between Cachar district and Assam government headquarters is conducted in English. Both Assamese and Bengali are used in Cachar government offices and schools, but Bengali has the preference because it is the language of the local majority. The result of his labors has been communal harmony in Assam. There is now even a Cachar representative in the state cabinet. Congress improved its majority in the Assam Legislature in the 1962 elections as a direct consequence of Shastri's work of reconciliation.

The announced "fast unto death" by Master Tara Singh to obtain a Sikh-controlled Punjabi-speaking state in the Punjab proved to be a more intractable problem for the Home Minister in the late summer and fall of 1961. In this instance, the demand for a Punjabi-speaking state was used to disguise dreams of a Sikh state. The motive was religious but the justification was linguistic. Shastri's efforts to mediate were abortive, principally because Nehru refused to mollify the extremist Sikhs by according full official status to the Punjabi tongue in the Gurmukhi script. Master Tara Singh, the leader of the Sikh opposition party, Akali Dal, in the Punjab, eventually broke his fast when it was clear that the government would not grant his demand for a Punjabi-speaking state.

Shastri might have succeeded in compromising with the Akali Dal if he had not had to conduct most of his negotiations in New Delhi in the shadow of the Prime Minister. But even in the capital, the Home Minister has shown that he can take independent action. In the spring of 1962 he moved quietly to initiate what he regards as long-overdue reforms in the administration.

On April 29, 1962, talking to Delhi newspapermen, Shastri depicted the evils of Indian bureaucracy in graphic terms: "I have been connected with the administration for some time past and I know that the administration has yet to gear up to the needs of the situation. . . . There is delay in the disposal of papers or disposal of cases, sometimes our procedures cause delay; then there is corruption at different levels. . . . Recommendation plays an important part when matters big or small are decided at different levels. Well, everyone talks of these things but it must be admitted that these problems still stare squarely in our face."

His words were homespun and his manner as diffident as ever as he stood there before the assembled Delhi press. With painful sincerity he went on to say that the senior civil servants "can quote things admirably well but the point is whether they can bring about a change in the existing situation." He answered his own question in the negative. "It seems to me that they are not able to think in advance and they only think when the situation is almost out of control. . . . Although I am a mediocre, yet I find that a mediocre like me is able to produce something new and original, not in a very high sense, but whatever new things are suggested in the Ministry, well, they generally come from me, and the officers who are far, far abler than myself go on with their routine way of thinking and perhaps routine way of working."

To overcome the problem of bureaucratic inertia, which underlies so many of India's other problems, Shastri has launched a radical experiment (by Indian standards) to curtail time-consuming procedures and speed up the whole administrative process. Most innovators in Indian officialdom like to suggest improvements in departments other than their own. Shastri has started his experiment in the Home Ministry. He told me that he wants "important matters" taken up at higher levels from the beginning. The normal procedure is for a district superintendent of police to send a file, no matter how urgent, to the state inspector-general of police, who passes it to the Home Ministry, where it must go through a deputy secretary, a joint secretary, and the home secretary before it finally reaches the minister's desk. By that time the communal tension reported by the district superintendent has probably erupted twice over in bloody rioting.

Another source of appalling delays is the central government's habit of referring important questions to the fifteen state governments for their comments and recommendations. This unwieldy procedure literally consumes years. Shastri is trying to short-circuit the process. For example, in connection with a long-awaited report on the status of Scheduled Castes (untouchables) and Scheduled Tribes, he called a conference in Delhi in July 1962. There the subject was thrashed out in two days by key Center officials and state chief ministers and their principal assistants. In the previous two months not one state had replied to Delhi's questionnaire about the report.

On the question of corruption, Shastri is less hopeful. "We can certainly reduce corruption," he says, "but we can't eliminate it completely. Certainly we can and should eliminate extortion and harassment." The crux of the problem is salaries. They are abysmally low. But there are two million civil servants on the payroll of the government of India. There is no possibility of significantly increasing their emoluments without wrecking the five-year plans and further widening the disparity between the pay of central and state government workers. And reducing the number of public servants is anathema to a vote-conscious government.

Shastri's concern with corruption stems from more than a

desire for administrative efficiency. He knows at firsthand how dishonest officials torment Indian villagers. And he is not blind to the dangers posed by the continuing gulf between the masses and their government. "It is the poor and the weak who will shape the coming India," he says with conviction. "Any party that appeals to the poor and attacks those with wealth has a certain appeal. The Communists do that. But we have avoided class war so far, and I think we should avoid it in future." This credo leads Shastri to discount Swatantra and other economically conservative parties. But he thinks that the Right Wing communalism represented by the Jan Sangh and other parties like it is a real menace which threatens to disintegrate India. His only answer to divisive forces is the patient redress of minority grievances, which means the grievances of all, because every Indian is a member of at least one minority.

The dismay Shastri feels at the emergence of Right Wing obscurantism does not prevent him, as it often does Nehru, from seeing the Communist shadow across India. Nor does he copy the Prime Minister in minimizing the international character of the Communist movement. "Indian Communist leaders go to Moscow," he told me in May 1962, "and get the line there which they then try to carry out here." When I asked him if he agreed with Nehru that Right Wing parties are more dangerous than the Communists, he replied obliquely, but nonetheless clearly: "Well, there's no doubt that if the Communists ever won here, India would change completely. Democracy would be no more. Parliament and our other institutions would be finished. Everything that distinguishes India today would be changed." Shastri's understanding of international Communism as it actually functions today is more remarkable in view of the fact that he has never been out of India, not even to Ceylon or Burma. "So you see," he says disarmingly, "I am a very conservative person. But I try to read foreign books." He is also able to perceive what goes on in the Indian Communist party because his vision is not distorted by the refractive lenses of outworn doctrine.

Neither the Left nor the Right opposition can do anything like the damage to Congress today that Congress is doing to itself. Shastri is acutely aware of the problem. He says: "The

Congress party organization has to be a more compact and well-knit body. We need to know if the membership is properly enrolled. Admission standards for active members [those who can hold office] should be higher. We must be stricter about officeholders in the party."

The selection of Congress candidates in the 1962 election was made by Nehru, Indira Gandhi, and Lal Bahadur Shastri. The other nine members of the party's Central Election Committee, including Sanjiva Reddy, then Congress president, S. K. Patil, and Jagjivan Ram, were so completely ignored that they soon stopped attending committee meetings. Shastri was consulted because he is known to be free of factional bias. As home minister he maintains closer day-by-day liaison with provincial and local party leaders than anyone else in the government. He is far more important than the Congress president or any other purely party officeholder because he has the power to dispense government patronage and resolve disputes between state administrations. He is accessible to all and has Nehru's ear. As one New Delhi editor has written, "The kingpin of the whole central machinery is, of course, the Home Minister, Mr. Lal Bahadur Shastri, who can predict Mr. Nehru's views with rare certainty."

Thanks in part to Shastri's influence, at least one third of the Congress incumbents in the central Parliament and in the state legislatures were dropped in favor of new candidates before the 1962 elections. The aim was to bring in new blood and break up entrenched and quarreling groups in the party. "Groups within Congress," Shastri concedes, "are reflected outside the party among the people at large. If the chief minister heads one group, you may feel you have a better chance to get into the university or to get a job if you're with his group. So our feuds spread out and affect people outside the party."

Shastri's views on party affairs are illuminating. The same can hardly be said for his pronouncements on socialism and the state's proper role in the economy. These tend to be masterpieces of oversimplification. "We should try as far as possible," he says, "to have equitable distribution of wealth. We should decentralize wealth, although this doesn't mean the same salary and the same house for everyone. Every person should have enough to live on, to clothe himself, and to educate his children." Shastri is not so biased by ideology against private enterprise as Nehru is, but he is less sympathetic to big business than Patil or Desai.

"The difficulty arises," he insists, "more from the private sector's suspicions of the public sector than the public sector's encroachments on the private sector. Government is keen to increase production and improve techniques in different directions. I feel India is an example to the world that the public and private sectors can work together for the growth and expansion of the country."

The example is admittedly less edifying when the state of Indian agriculture and cutbacks in the third five-year plan are taken into account. Shastri says he now agrees that there should have been more emphasis from the outset on developing power and transport. He is less impressed than Nehru is by the Soviet-style crash approach to heavy industry. "I don't forget myself," he says smilingly, "when I see dazzling things like brand-new plants." The fact is that Shastri has had little voice in formulating India's economic policy. He usually confines himself to echoing the Nehru line. What he would do in this field if he became prime minister is impossible to predict. My own hunch is that he would try to muddle along with the hodgepodge of economic expedients now being applied.

What would Shastri do in other fields as prime minister? Again the answers are obscure. I doubt if he himself knows. He would certainly adhere to some form of nonalignment in foreign policy, although he (like most of the other major figures in this book except Krishna Menon) would probably be disinclined to temporize with the Chinese Communists on the border issue. When I asked him point-blank in the spring of 1962 if he thought adequate steps were being taken to protect the northern border, he hesitated for a long moment and then answered simply, "No." When the Chinese intruded into India's Northeast Frontier Province in September of the same year, while he was acting as prime minister in Nehru's absence, Shastri said flatly, "They must be driven out. There's no other way." Shastri's outspokenness on this occasion belies the general notion that he always simply parrots Nehru.

Shastri is a democrat by temperament if not by conviction. He is no Hindu communalist despite his parochial background and his long association with the late Purshottamdas Tandon, a traditionalist who was ousted by Nehru as president of Congress. My feeling is that Shastri would never knowingly jeopardize India's secular parliamentary institutions. Autocracy is repugnant to his nature. So is violence. "I, for one," he says, "can never support any kind of encouragement towards violence or violent activities." He is disinclined to utilize the Preventive Detention Act or the other legal weapons by which India could be transformed into a virtual police state. Moreover, he is humane. I remember the anguish that filled his voice when he told me of the "unspeakable way" Brahmans used to treat untouchables in south India. Being of the people, and not simply from them, he feels their woes more intensely than other cabinet ministers. He wants to lift the weight of corrupt and inefficient bureaucracy from their backs. So far, it must be admitted, there is little to show for his efforts to reform the administration. The Home Ministry continues more or less as before. But the impulse for change still animates the Home Minister.

At a time when other Congress leaders were loath even to whisper the words "deputy leader" for fear of antagonizing Nehru, Shastri told me calmly, "There should be a deputy leader of the Congress parliamentary party but I don't think the Prime Minister is thinking in those terms." Shastri never sought the honor for himself. "I may be better as a conciliator," he told me, "if I don't have such an office."

This reluctance to thrust himself into the limelight has prompted many observers, including knowledgeable Indian politicians, to dismiss Shastri as a straw man. But a high civil servant who knows him intimately gave what I consider an accurate appraisal of the man. "Shastri," he said, "doesn't have firm ideas on every subject, but he has strong moorings. I know few people so free from brutality and with so strong an aversion to anything smacking of violence. He's intelligent but not an intellectual. He has the capacity to feel and think like the decent common people of India. Instinctively, Shastri can share the feelings of the common man in the village."

Another long-time co-worker says, "Only a crisis will bring out his true qualities." The question is whether this extremely dedicated, industrious, and high-principled little man could master the convulsive forces unleashed in a crisis. Would his popularity in Congress outlive Nehru? A leading party official remarks doubtfully, "Shastri is liked and respected in the party but his standing depends on the favor Nehru shows him." On the other hand, a qualified American student of Indian politics says that the Home Minister has turned out to be "the real power" in the party organization because the state chief ministers look to him to solve factional disputes in their party organizations and to help them with patronage and in other ways. By reason of his official position, one New Delhi editor feels that Shastri is already the front-runner in the succession race.

Shastri's popularity among many Hindi speakers in the north is specially notable in view of his comparatively recent emergence on the national scene. He is not an impressive speaker, either on the hustings or in Parliament. There is nothing magnetic in his appearance. Nevertheless, a poll conducted in 1961 by the Indian Institute of Public Opinion showed that Shastri ranked fourth among those favored to succeed Nehru as prime minister. The percentage supporting Shastri was far smaller than for the three front-runners, Jayaprakash Narayan, Morarji Desai, and Krishna Menon, but greater than that for Y. B. Chavan, S. K. Patil, and other leaders.

Shastri says privately that he will not contest the premiership with Desai. If he plays his cards right, he may not have to. Desai's own thrust may evoke a counterthrust that would deadlock the Congress party and open the way for Shastri. There is considerably more guile in the little man than his manner indicates, and the appearance of mediocrity is often an advantage for a politician. Shastri absorbs praise and abuse from Nehru with equal grace. His equanimity has even won him the Prime Minister's affection, and he is also very close to Indira Gandhi, whom he used to visit when she was a lonely child in the Nehru family mansion at Allahabad. If she came to power, he would be assured an important place in the government. I have even heard it said that Shastri is planning to use Mrs. Gandhi as his front, but this seems a little farfetched. It seems more likely to me that Mrs. Gandhi would back Shastri as a compromise minister, thinking she could use him for her own ends. In any event, the two are not likely to be at odds when the showdown comes.

Shastri's most serious handicap, besides his unassertive personality, is probably his health. A former colleague in the Union cabinet says that his first heart attack caused no lesion but that a second or third attack could be crippling. By driving himself eighteen hours a day without letup and moving around the country by jeep and on foot, Shastri takes risks that Pandit Pant avoided. He never suffered the kind of injuries that incapacitated Pant, but he is still far from robust.

Shastri is the most authentically Indian of the personalities described in this book. He is nearest the mind and soil of India. He reflects the strengths and weaknesses of the Indian villager. If he is to enter history as the second prime minister of independent India, he must do so with the mandate of the party bosses, including Nehru. If he is to be more than a footnote to history, the mandate must be upheld against all challengers by the overwhelming will of the Indian people. Armed with the party mandate and sustained by the popular will, Lal Bahadur Shastri could take his place with vastly magnified stature on the world stage.

Y. B. Chavan

ONE NIGHT IN NOVEMBER 1943 a young Indian underground leader slipped into the village of Phaltan, in Bombay state. He groped his way through the darkness until he reached the modest cottage where his even more youthful wife lay seriously ill. It was a time of stress for India. The burdens of war had ignited violent resistance to British rule. A kind of guerrilla warfare had broken out in parts of the country. The young underground leader was one of the guerrilla fighters. He had taken exceptional care to conceal his movements from the British, and knew he should spend only a few hours with the girl whom he had married six months earlier. But when he saw how ill she was, he forgot his usual prudence and spent all day and the following night at her bedside.

He felt guilty because his wife had fallen ill in prison after being arrested for no other reason than her relationship to him. The British had released her when her condition became critical. He wanted to send her to Poona, where better treatment was available. But the next morning, before she could be moved, there was a knock at the door. Someone had informed the police. They had come to arrest Yeshwantrao Balwantrao Chavan, saboteur, poet, criminal lawyer, journalist, ex-convict, student agitator, and leader of the resistance in the most turbulent district of western India. He was twenty-nine years old at the time.

This wartime episode reflects the courage and compassion of the man who is now regarded as India's most promising younger leader and a leading candidate for the office of prime minister. Chavan (pronounced with the accent on the first syllable) had risen, before his appointment in November 1962 as defense minister, to be chief minister and undisputed political boss of the state of Maharashtra, which includes the city of Bombay. He is now enshrined as the latter-day hero of India's martial Marathas, who make up almost half Maharashtra's population. The impulsive young resistance fighter has proved dynamic, intelligent, earthy, and massively self-assured in his role of popular leader.

A Westerner's first meeting with an Indian politician is often icily formal. Many are ill at ease and hesitate to speak openly. It usually takes several talks to establish any rapport. Not so with Chavan. The first time I met him I felt as if I were conversing with an Indiana politician. Although he had been up until five o'clock that morning selecting candidates for district elections, he showed no sign of fatigue. He was genial, hearty, and affable. He laughed more easily and more often than any other Indian leader I have met. His English is by no means exceptional, but he sensed the purport of every question before I finished speaking.

Chavan is of medium height, with heavy eyebrows, thick features, and dark, expressive eyes. His burly, almost shapeless Maratha figure makes him look short. His complexion is so dark that an Indian photographer once told me, "When I am developing his pictures, I always lose him in the darkroom." Indians are intensely color-conscious in their social relations, especially when making marital arrangements for their offspring, but color is not a political handicap. Chavan's face is constantly mobile. He reacts to everything. When he smiles—which he does often—his heavy face is illuminated by a set of apparently perfect teeth. His crumpled dhoti hardly matches the sartorial elegance of Menon and Desai, but it seems to go with his forthright character.

The Chief Minister looks the part of a provincial Indian politician. But he combines rustic charm with a taste for books and ideas notably lacking in most of his party colleagues. He has outward simplicity and inward sophistication. His bulky frame seems to vibrate with energy.

Chavan has a more balanced combination of political attributes than any Indian leader I have met except Nehru. All things being equal—which they rarely are in politics—I think Chavan has a better chance than any other politician now in the running to become a durable and distinguished prime minister of India. It was felt until recently that he was not likely to succeed Nehru directly if the Prime Minister died or retired before 1967, because the Congress party chieftains would want someone familiar with the central government, and Chavan would have to serve at least a brief apprenticeship in New Delhi before he would be eligible to take the reins. His appointment as defense minister should go far toward removing this difficulty, and by virtue of his comparative youth, he can afford to wait.

There is a new generation about to inherit power in India today. Chavan is its political expression. He is the only Congress leader I have met who did not call himself a Gandhian. He feels no need to conceal his sharper political contours in the loose cloak of Gandhism. He makes no ritual obeisance to *ahimsa* or to *sarvodaya*. He was brought up politically in the harsh school of the underground movement in his native Satara district of western Maharashtra. For four years he maintained Bombay by force as a bilingual state against violent opposition from Maharashtrians and Gujaratis who demanded the creation of separate linguistic states. Nor has Chavan ever regulated his private life according to Gandhian precepts. He strikes no ascetic poses. He enjoys rich food, sleeps late, and relishes such modern conveniences as air conditioning. As chief minister of a prohibitionist state, he finds it politic to be a teetotaler, but he has no squeamishness about seeing others drink. He eats meat and much else that the strict Gandhians deny themselves.

Chavan is no rebel against Gandhism. My impression is that he simply feels that most of the Mahatma's injunctions are irrelevant to Indian society today. He has no interest in antagonizing the Gandhians; neither will he bow to them if he thinks they are obstructing something essential.

For Chavan, the most essential thing is close contact with the masses and with the Congress party. He has achieved this by becoming a mass leader and a party leader at the same time. His second objective is effective administration. He served his apprenticeship under Morarji Desai, probably the ablest administrator in the upper reaches of the Indian government. Like his mentor, Chavan can dispose of 200 to 300 official files every night. But he never plays the Hindu despot. He never takes himself more seriously than he does his work. And he extracts far more work from his subordinates than Desai ever did. Above all, Chavan makes himself liked, rather than feared, by his colleagues and constituents. Gandhi was revered as a saint, Nehru is loved as a father, and Desai is respected as an administrator. Chavan is no saint, but, at least in Maratha eyes, he combines the attributes of father and administrator. This could become a new pattern in relations between ruler and ruled in India.

When I first started asking people in Bombay about the Chief Minister, the chorus of approval was so unanimous that I began to suspect I was the victim of a conspiracy. But I soon realized that Chavan is genuinely popular—and for good reason. He has given Maharashtra, and, before it, the old Bombay state, clean and relatively efficient government. By Indian standards his performance has been outstanding. He may not be as personally efficient and painstaking as Desai, whom he succeeded as chief minister, but he more than makes up for such shortcomings by his abounding humanism and gift for ingratiating himself even with political opponents. Unlike Nehru, he never talks down to his audiences, never lets himself be provoked into public outbursts of temper, and rarely betrays impatience.

I think the thing that strikes me most about Chavan is his uncanny knack for making all parties in a controversy think he is on their side. Until the last days of the bitterly fought North Bombay election, both the Menon and Kripalani camps were telling me that the Chief Minister was really with them.

Some of this talk may have been wishful thinking, but much of it stemmed from Chavan's friendly overtures to both sides. When he finally did make his position unmistakably clear in speeches for Menon, he couched his appeals in language that would cause the least possible offense to the Kripalani camp. He made it clear that he was campaigning as a loyal Congressman and lieutenant of Nehru for a candidate officially designated by the party high command.

People on both sides still believe that Chavan was with them on the hotly debated question of applying land ceilings to Maharashtra's large sugar estates. The sugar-mill owners, who control the big estates, argued that breaking them up would cut production and raise costs. "Progressives" in Congress insisted that the big operators should not evade the land-ceiling law. Dr. Rafik Zakaria, a socialist Congressman and minister in the state government, told me that Chavan opposed the Planning Commission's effort to exempt the sugar plantations. The same day, A. D. Shroff, a prominent Bombay financier and member of the conservative Swatantra party, told me, "If Chavan was compelled to apply the land ceiling to the sugar estates, it was not by his choice."

The upshot was typically Indian: the ceiling has been duly applied to the sugar estates but the big operators have formed co-operatives, thereby evading the acreage restrictions. Chavan's popularity, Maharashtra's sugar output, and socialist predilections for land reform have all been safeguarded.

It would be wrong to conclude that Chavan tries to be on all sides of every issue. He takes firm positions on many questions. But he does so in a way calculated to minimize resentment on the opposing side. He shuns political vendettas and never gives the impression that he is acting out of spite or vengeance. He actively strives to befriend all factions and compromise all viewpoints. I sometimes feel that he may overreach himself in the pursuit of popularity. His distaste for making enemies tends to blur his political outlines and leaves many Indians, especially outside Maharashtra, wondering where he really stands on the larger issues facing the country. Like the governor of an American state, he is able to avoid committing himself on many controversial issues.

Chavan is a product of the rugged Satara hills south of Bombay, an area whose people have been historically addicted to freedom. He was born there in the squalid village of Deorashtre on March 12, 1914. His father, who was a small farmer and part-time bailiff of the local court, died of plague when Yeshwantrao was barely four years old. Chavan calls himself "a typical product of village life." In his boyhood, he says, "when we compared life with village urban life, we found it rather oppressive. That paved the road to the demand for equality on our part in the sense that we yearned for equal opportunities." After his father died, his mother, an illiterate peasant woman, devoted her energy to educating her four children—Yeshwantrao, his two older brothers, and one older sister. Young Chavan was enrolled in high school in the nearby town of Karad, and there he won prizes in essay writing and elocution contests on "patriotic" subjects. He was a thin, intense young man in those days, overshadowed by his brother Ganpatrao in both studies and athletics. But Yeshwantrao already possessed unusual self-confidence. When his teacher once asked students whom they most wanted to be like, the first reply was "Sivaji," the seventeenth-century Maratha chieftain; another was "Tilak," the first Congress party extremist; and a third answer was "Gandhiji." But when Yeshwantrao's turn came, he announced firmly, "I just want to be Yeshwantrao Chavan."

Even today Chavan differs from his Congress colleagues in refusing to call himself a Nehruite or to identify himself with any single personality of the independence movement. He says, "I was never the worshiper of any personality." He first went to jail when he was sixteen years old, for agitating among students in his school. He was released after a few weeks. His mother and his eldest brother, Dnyanoba, who had succeeded his father as the local bailiff, were shocked. But Yeshwantrao told his mother that he was doing nothing that Sivaji and Tilak would not have done. The old peasant woman was eventually pacified.

At eighteen Chavan was again arrested by the British. He had joined Gandhi's nonco-operation movement in a new outburst of patriotic fervor. He recalls, "They found a bulletin on my person and they prosecuted me. I pleaded guilty and I was sentenced to eighteen months' rigorous imprisonment."

Jail was his campus. There the young agitator from Satara met leaders of the independence movement. He attended political lectures, joined a prison study circle, and devoured books secretly circulated among inmates. India might yet be British if so many Congressmen had not gone to universities behind bars.

In prison Chavan read everything he could. Despite the heat and the "C"-class food, he mastered some abstruse works on political theory. He read everything available on Marxism, imbibed Lenin, and went through several works of the English Fabian socialists. The program of the British Labour party drafted by Sir Stafford Cripps caught his imagination. He liked the books of Bertrand Russell and Lord Morley's essay "On Compromise." But he was most deeply influenced by the Marxism of M. N. Roy, a pioneer Indian Communist who was later expelled from the party for defying the Comintern line on India. Chavan was attracted by Roy's historical perspective and his revolutionary approach. He calls this second jail term "the year of revolution for me."

From his studies in prison, he went on to further studies. He passed the matriculation examination in 1934 and entered Rajaram College, in Kolhapur, from which he was graduated with a degree in history and economics four years later. After India had been taken into World War II, he was awarded a Bachelor of Laws degree from Poona Law College and started practice as a criminal lawyer in Karad. "In our taluka [district]," Chavan told me with a wry smile, "every pleader is a criminal pleader." Such is the combative temper of the Satara hills. But politics remained his first concern. The year he was graduated from law school, he became a member of the Congress party's Maharashtra provincial committee. He visited every village in his district. "I knew the whole district as I know the palm of my hand," he boasts. And he still knows it.

World War II was a turning point for Chavan, as for so many other Indians. He parted ideological company with M.

N. Roy when the Bengali Communist called the war an accidental conflict.

"It took a long time for me to make a rational analysis of the whole thing," Chavan told me. "It was said that Hitler's Nazism was the greatest danger to human rights in their democratic form. But at the same time we couldn't make much of a distinction between British and German imperialism. I felt it was intellectual romanticism to say we should support British imperialism against German imperialism. This struggle within myself went on for a long time."

The moment of decision came on the night of August 9, 1942, when word spread that Gandhi had been arrested for espousing the Quit India movement. Chavan was attending a meeting of 300 Congressmen in Bombay that night. He remembers the angry crowds that gathered in the streets of the city when news of Gandhi's arrest became known.

"Finally," he recalls, "I said I must be with the freedom forces in India. For me, British rule was an equal evil."

He thereupon joined the resistance movement in Satara and soon carried a price of 1,000 rupees (about $200), set by the British for his capture dead or alive. He described his role to me in these words: "Our idea was not to court jail. We had to prepare the people for some sort of mass action." The action took the form of violent protest marches on district government offices. "We tried to plant the national flag on the *kucheris* [local government headquarters] in symbolic capture of power," Chavan said as his eyes lighted up. "The police reacted sharply. They opened fire on several processions, killing nine marchers at one place and injuring dozens of others." Chavan was deeply affected when a man who had been with him the night before was shot dead as he held the national flag aloft. "After the firings," he said, "we decided this was wasting manpower. We decided we should start a no-tax campaign and nonco-operation movement, a game of hide-and-seek with the authorities."

The underground distributed anti-British pamphlets, trained recruits in sabotage, and organized clandestine study groups. But Chavan admits that it was difficult to keep up popular enthusiasm for the cause. After eight or ten months there was a lull. The police went on the offensive. Chavan says that they were assisted by landowners and "other vested interests" in the villages. The underground leaders decided the time had come to deal severely with this "reactionary element." Their decision was the origin of the famous Patri Sarkar, or parallel government, movement in Satara during the war. On a small scale it resembled Chinese Communist guerrilla warfare. Most of the Patri Sarkar leaders later joined the Indian Communist party.

Chavan's role in the movement is now minimized in his official biography. It is said that he never took a direct part in sabotage operations except to observe the attempted derailment of one freight train. The attempt failed. Chavan now says that he went on that particular expedition "for the thrill of it." In July 1960 he told an interviewer, "I did not like the violent turn of the Patri Sarkar. Once violence is started it is difficult to fix the limit." But he admits that the leadership of the movement had decided to carry out some "effective sabotage work" and that he belonged to one of the terrorist squads set up for this purpose. I have reason to believe that he took a more active and sanguinary part in Patri Sarkar than he now cares to admit. In any event, his terrorist career was short. Late in 1942 his young wife, Venutai, and his brother Ganpatrao were arrested as a means of bringing pressure on him. "My wife naturally had a severe shock," he said, "because she did not know any politics." She fell seriously ill in prison. When the British released her, she went to stay with her father at Phaltan. It was then that Chavan made his ill-fated night journey to be at her bedside. "I found her in so bad a condition," he told me, "that I thought I should stay one day more. By that time my identity had been secretly betrayed to the police by someone." The last word came out with a hissing sound. His eyes hardened in remembrance and his massive Maratha frame became taut. Watching him, I had the feeling that his account with the "someone" who betrayed him had not remained unsettled.

Chavan was arrested, convicted, and sent to jail. There he returned to intellectual pursuits. He took more large doses of

Marxism and wrote patriotic poetry. "At that age," he remarks, "everybody is a poet." The subject matter of his verse was, he says, "naturally, political revolution." In 1944 he was released from prison by mistake and spent a week at liberty before he was rearrested. The next year he was freed and was forthwith selected as the Congress candidate from Karad for the old Bombay Legislative Assembly. He won the election by a towering margin. He was thirty-one.

Chavan was not content to become a potbellied parliamentarian. Satara continued to seethe in the early postwar years. Economic conditions were unbelievably bad. A bloody struggle continued against Brahman landlords and British overlords. British control had never been effectively reimposed since Patri Sarkar days. Law and order were nonexistent. One Western political observer with considerable experience in Bombay and Delhi says that he has authentic information that Chavan had a hand in two political murders in the factional infighting in Satara after the war. The truth may never be fully established, but I doubt that any political leader in the district came out of that period with clean hands.

When the Congress party ministry was formed in Bombay in 1946, the young man from Satara was appointed parliamentary secretary to the minister for home and revenue, the imperious Morarji Desai. The two men, completely different in outlook, temperament, and background, had never met before. Surprisingly, their association quickly ripened into friendship. Chavan was shrewd enough to realize he could learn much from the master administrator who was his chief. As he says now, "I was certainly observing Morarji at close quarters." Desai, for his part, found his energetic young lieutenant a refreshing change from the file-bound senior ICS officers.

Chavan soon discovered that what he now calls his "romantic" ideas of socialism had little relevance to the scarcity-ridden postwar Bombay economy. Distress was universal. Food was short. So was housing, transportation, power, and almost everything else except misery. Prices skyrocketed. Chavan found that the controls so glibly propounded by socialist theorists were easily evaded. Corruption had eaten deep into the fabric of Indian society.

When Desai became chief minister of Bombay in 1952, he named Chavan to head the Ministry of Civil Supplies, with responsibility for food and other scarce items like fuel. Chavan was also put in charge of local self-government and community development. He soon won general esteem for his skill in introducing decontrol of food in Bombay state.

He is remarkably clear today in his understanding of economic realities. As he puts it, "The problem [of prices] is there and the solution lies in more production of essential commodities, i.e., food and cloth." Unlike the Chinese Communist leaders, he has never ignored the importance of monetary incentives in stimulating agricultural production. China's agrarian problems are, of course, much vaster and more complex than anything Chavan has faced in Bombay, but the way he has accommodated himself to the realities of the situation is impressive.

In July 1960 he told the editor of the Communist-line weekly *Blitz:* "If you go to a man who has five acres of land and tell him the country is in need of more food, he goes by his own economics. If he thinks that he does not get more money by food crops and he can get more money by growing sugarcane or other commercial crops, he will say, 'Let your country go to hell. I want money for my children.' So the approach should be to the problem."

Although voluntary "co-operative farming" is an official goal of Congress party policy, Chavan has been equally pragmatic in his approach to this explosive subject. He told *Blitz:* "So far as the question of agriculture is concerned, this is a sector of economic activity where the incentive to produce is very vitally linked up with the idea of ownership. . . . That is why to take this idea of ownership from the peasants without giving them the proper idea about it would naturally take away that incentive of production."

He pointed out that in Yugoslavia and even in some Soviet-bloc countries collectivization has been stopped or slowed down because "it is not serving the purposes for which it was meant." He contends that Congress must "prepare" the Indian peasant for co-operative farming by successfully launching service co-operatives to provide him credit, seed, improved tools, and marketing facilities. But he admitted in a talk with me in 1962, "If the cultivator is never convinced, it's possible there will never be co-operative farming in India." The prospect does not alarm him.

In Bombay state after 1952, one problem fast came to overshadow all others: language. The agitation for carving separate linguistic states—Maharashtra and Gujarat—out of Bombay state reached hurricane fury. As mentioned in the chapter on Desai, the Communists took up the cry and plunged the movement into bloody conflict with the police and the Army. The iron-willed Desai became intensely disliked for the repressive measures he instituted and for his refusal to make concessions on the language question. By 1956 linguistic fever was running high all over India. Under the States Reorganization Act passed that year, Bombay was enlarged and made a bilingual state, with Marathi and Gujarati sanctioned for official use. Desai escaped to New Delhi. On the eve of the reorganization of Bombay state, Chavan was elected to lead the Congress party in the state assembly by a vote of 333 to 111. On November 1, 1956, he became chief minister of the enlarged Bombay state. He faced what seemed a hopeless political situation. Congress was committed to maintaining Bombay as a bilingual state. Chavan was young and unknown. Even Nehru wondered if he could hold fast against opposition that had shaken the redoubtable Desai. Chavan hung on grimly. Later he admitted that the pressure "took its toll of any vitality."

Nehru paid public homage on three occasions to Chavan's performance as chief minister. By the end of 1958, Chavan was persuaded that Congress could not maintain its stand against the linguistic agitation and hope to recapture Bombay state in the 1962 general elections. He is widely credited in Maharashtra with bringing this truth home to Nehru and the Congress high command. His role may be exaggerated in retrospect, but it is tribute to his Rooseveltian sense of timing that he escaped from the collapsing edifice of old Bombay state in time to avoid serious political injury and not before he had made his name with Nehru as a fearless lieutenant of the central government.

Following the advice of Chavan and others, Nehru retreated,

and the new linguistic states of Maharashtra and Gujarat were born on May 1, 1960, to the relief of almost everyone except the Communists. They had lost their last effective issue in Bombay. The united front they had forged against Congress quickly disintegrated.

Chavan now says that the reorganization of India on linguistic lines was inevitable. "The basic idea of having linguistic states is a correct thing," he says. "It's an expression of the diversity of Indian life. This diversity is a fact and should be a source of strength." He contends that a linguistic state also brings the machinery of government closer to the people and provides an opportunity for the development of indigenous literature, theater, and films.

On this issue Chavan differs from Desai, who believes that linguistic states are a bad thing. The divergence reflects the different approach of the two men: Desai, the administrator, thinking first of administrative efficiency; Chavan, the politician and humanist, with his eye on what the electorate wants.

Chavan could never have weathered the years after Desai's departure and before the decision to divide Bombay state had it not been for his extraordinary tact in dealing with the opposition. Whereas Desai can alienate even his most fervent admirers, Chavan can disarm the most partisan critic. His courtesy and good humor are now proverbial in the Bombay Legislature. He is regularly in his seat during the question hour in the legislature and handles the most embarrassing queries with candor and an easy manner. When he first succeeded Desai, Bombay expected him to retain the regulations and restrictions imposed by his puritanical predecessor. What happened was, as one young Indian businessman recalls, "a refreshing contrast." House searches by the police for suspected bootleggers or illegal distilleries were largely abandoned. The cosmopolitan city of Bombay heaved a sigh of relief. Many residents felt as if they had been released from a reformatory. They were pleased to see their young Chief Minister relaxing at evening receptions and were delighted to hear him give speeches that did not end in homilies on the evils of self-indulgence.

I was impressed by the easy way Chavan mixed with some of Bombay's leading industrialists and financiers at a reception I attended. He has no particular fondness for big business, but he bantered with the tycoons as naturally as with a gathering of Maharashtra Congress party workers. He listened gravely to their complaints about Bombay's chronic power shortage and promised to do something about it. When he rose to speak, he began by praising the business community's contribution to Maharashtra, then gently chided them for concentrating their plants around Bombay instead of pioneering in the backward areas of the state. He ended with a happily turned phrase about providing electric power for any industrialist who went into the back country.

Unlike Desai and Nehru, Chavan never lectures his audience. He is succinct. Even more unusual for an Indian politician, he can talk about what he is supposed to talk about when he gets up to speak. If he opens a girls' school, he will discuss women's education. In the same situation Desai might sermonize on the virtues of self-denial. Nehru, who often forgets what he is supposed to be inaugurating, is likely to soliloquize on nuclear testing or the future of Asia.

The formation of the first Maratha state in 142 years (albeit under New Delhi's control) has prompted the inevitable and absurd comparison of Chavan with Sivaji, the great Maratha empire-builder. Maratha patriotism has swelled. Typical of the prattling hero worship now lavished on Chavan is the discovery by one newspaper that "Chavan has materialized Sivaji's dream of a strong and unified empire on India's west coast." A more thoughtful observer says that Chavan has given Maharashtrians self-respect and a feeling of individual identity for the first time since 1818, when they were subdued by the British. The tough, warlike Marathas provided some of the finest soldiers in the old British Indian Army, and they fulfill the same function in the present Indian Army. They are a sturdy, self-reliant race with a 300-year-old imperial tradition. They are accustomed to helping shape the political destinies of the rest of India. Maharashtra has an active, intellectual middle class based on Bombay, Poona, and other cities. The peasantry, vigorous and progressive by Indian standards, has never suffered the burden of feudalism that crushed the Bihar country folk. Historically, Marathas have advocated education. Every sizable town in the state has a secondary school. Most of them are privately run although they receive state aid. Marathas have traditionally been farmers, teachers, clerks, soldiers, or policemen. Business has been in the hands of Parsis and Gujaratis. The state's natural resources are largely untapped. Consequently, Maharashtra has always had a slight have-not complex, resulting in a radical political outlook.

Chavan knows how to appeal to this mentality. He has promoted provincial pride without letting it degenerate into chauvinism. He has satisfied the craving for education by building more schools, especially ones with a technical bias, and by providing more teacher-training facilities. He has encouraged Marathas to enter business and professions like medicine, where they have had little representation. Some people think he has gone too far in identifying himself with Maharashtra. The Maharashtra Congress party is now virtually a Maratha caste organization. As the *Statesman* of Calcutta remarked, "The outstanding leaders of the Congress, Mr. Kamaraj Nadar [Madras chief minister] and Mr. Chavan, have adroitly used caste loyalties. With all their ability and acumen, if they had not been born in the strategic castes of Nadars [toddy-tappers] and Marathas, these leaders might have remained among the also-rans of Indian politics." By exploiting caste and provincial loyalties to the hilt, some observers feel that Chavan has disqualified himself for an all-India role. He emphatically denies this. He told me: "My present responsibility is Maharashtra. But my approach, background, everything, is absolutely all-India. As a member of the Congress Working Committee I have to take the larger view. Even my thinking for Maharashtra flows from my thinking about national problems."

Chavan apparently thought he could usefully remain chief minister of Maharashtra until some time in the mid-sixties. Until then he would be consolidating his position and strengthening his ties with Congress leaders in other parts of the country. He was in no hurry to go to New Delhi. Sadiq Ali, the former general secretary of the All-India Congress Committee, said that Chavan would not consider going to the Center for anything less than the Home Ministry. As Ali put it, "He would come only for the assurance of political preferment in the future." There is little doubt that the ultimate preferment Chavan has in mind leads to the prime minister's residence on Teen Murti Marg.

Even while he remained in Maharashtra, Chavan was busy creating an all-India image. He had started making speeches about foreign policy. They were largely a restatement of Nehru ideas, but they established his license to speak on foreign affairs in the highest councils of the party. The care he exercised not to step on Nehru's sensitive toes in the foreign-policy field was glaringly obvious when he droned through a prepared speech to the so-called Seminar on Portuguese Colonialism in October 1961 in Bombay. He usually does not prepare his speeches, but with the seizure of Goa already in the offing he wanted to be absolutely sure that he said nothing amiss.

Whatever Chavan may have said about foreign policy was far less important in creating a national reputation than was his systematic and successful efforts to cultivate the minorities in Maharashtra. Like New York, Bombay is a congeries of minorities. In Maharashtra as a whole, the Marathas account for about 45 per cent of the population. Before Maharashtra was made a separate state, there was talk that Gujaratis, Parsis, Sindhis, south Indians, and other non-Marathas in Bombay would find all doors closed to them and would consequently leave the city en masse. These fears have proved unfounded. The minorities have little political power in Maharashtra, but they still enjoy their traditional position in business, trade, and the professions. Chavan is much more popular with them than was Desai, not because he has done anything outstanding to improve their lot, but because he goes out of his way to demonstrate interest in them. He attends their parties, puts his arm around their leaders, and constantly talks about how much the minorities are a part of Maharashtra.

Chavan's assiduous cultivation of everyone has raised some doubts about his sincerity. As one of his admirers puts it, "It makes you wonder whom he really does like and whether it's all being put on." Chavan says of himself, "I don't give the impression that anyone is my confidant. I don't have an inner circle. But I watch people very closely." A former member of the Rajya Sabha in New Delhi says, "Chavan is not a man of principle. He will do what works." Morarji Desai says, "Chavan is all right. He's done well." He adds with a trace of resentment, "Chavan is interested in himself. This is common in politics. It's nothing to be surprised at." S. K. Patil, who is engaged in an apparently losing fight with Chavan for control of the Bombay branch of the Congress party, calls the Chief Minister an "opportunist" who does whatever Nehru wants.

Such criticism of Chavan is rare. What makes it unique is its comparative mildness. Indian politicians rarely stop short of character assassination in their judgments of a colleague. Political foes whom one would expect to denounce Chavan in the bitterest terms actually come out with encomiums about him. R. D. Bhandare, leader of the radical wing of the Republican party of India, composed largely of untouchables, is savagely critical of most Congress leaders, including Gandhi and Nehru, but not of Chavan. He says, "Chavan has the capacity to be a national leader. He's a socialist by conviction." He says that the Chief Minister at first took seriously the demand of a few extremist untouchable converts to Buddhism for a separate Buddhist homeland and began to express doubt about the loyalty of all former untouchables. But he soon realized his error and sent special police officers to reconcile feuding caste Hindus and untouchable converts to Buddhism in several Maharashtra villages. Bhandare, who, like most leaders of the untouchables, has a chip on his shoulder the size of a boulder, says, "We like Chavan's way of dealing with the [untouchable] problem. He will change his attitude on any particular issue provided we approach him in the right way. We have no mental animus against Chavan."

In the same vein, a respected Praja Socialist party leader in Bombay says, "Chavan's way of handling things has been really remarkable. In almost every other province the Congress has been riven by factions and groups. Maharashtra is relatively free of that. Basically, Chavan is very sound because he is a socialist."

At the other end of the political spectrum, A. D. Shroff says that Chavan is well disposed toward business and only "pretends to be a socialist because everyone in India today has to play up to Nehru." Shroff considers Chavan "a coming man," free of Desai's dogmatism. Like other Bombay businessmen, Shroff credits Chavan with having improved the state administration, kept corruption down, and reconciled conflicting interests.

Praise from such diverse quarters shows that Chavan is a consummate politician, but it does not give a clue to what he really stands for, if anything. His public pronouncements are not very enlightening. Whether he speaks in Marathi, Hindi, or his Indianized English, his words tend to fall into the platitudinous pattern of Congress party political speeches. The clue to Chavan lies solely in his actions. They show clearly that he is a pragmatist, not only on large issues (as Desai is), but in his habits of working and living (as Desai is not). Chavan is no faddist or dogmatist. He began political life as a Marxist and he still uses a Marxist vocabulary. Talking to me in April 1962, he remarked with complete seriousness, "Individually, there are some good industrialists." He is suspicious of monopolistic tendencies in Indian business. When I asked him to clarify a statement he had made to *Blitz* in 1960 about stock exchanges not being necessary in a "grown-up socialist economy," he replied with typical suavity: "That was a theoretical discussion. I was asked if the stock market is necessarily part of our economy. I don't think the stock market is necessarily part of the economic structure, particularly the speculation part of it."

I have never seen Chavan more animated than when he told me, "The young man I admire most in the world today" is President Kennedy. What raised Kennedy's prestige in his eyes more than anything else was the President's firm handling of the steel-price issue in 1962. When Chavan heard that the big steel companies had capitulated under pressure from the White House, he said he felt elated. Half rising from his chair, he told me excitedly, "It was a great victory on the home front for Kennedy." He clearly pictures himself in such a role.

Chavan had never been abroad when he made these re-

marks to me in the spring of 1962. But he has long been fond
of reading American history, both revolutionary and contemporary, and can discuss such figures as Jefferson and Lincoln.
Inevitably, he compares Lincoln to Gandhi. Recently he has
broadened his acquaintance with the American scene by reading novels such as Allen Drury's *Advise and Consent*. He is
almost entirely self-educated as far as American history and the
contemporary world are concerned. Until recent years Indian
universities paid scant attention to such subjects. He often
borrows books from the American Consulate General in Bombay. When he found himself traveling on the same train early
in 1962 with Jane Abel, the Consulate's political officer, he
engaged her in a long conversation about American history
and politics and proceeded to borrow most of the books she
had brought to read on the train.

At diplomatic receptions in Bombay, the peasant-born Chief
Minister moves with assurance and dignity, smiling at everyone, murmuring a few words of greeting but spending most
of the time listening. He is one of the few Indian politicians
I have met who is a good listener and who genuinely wants
to learn. As one American diplomat remarked, "You can stand
with that man for half an hour and come away to realize that
you've been doing all the talking. You don't really know anything more about what Chavan thinks than you did before."

Such talents make the Chief Minister his own best source
of political intelligence. Wherever he goes—to dinner on swank
Malabar Hill or to a night watchman's funeral in the slums
of North Bombay—he is constantly amassing information and
impressions, educating himself and gauging his administration's performance against the complaints he hears. As he
says, "You have to be in touch with public opinion through
different channels. It's a constant process of communication."
The process of communication keeps him on the move eighteen
hours a day. Like Churchill, he prefers to do his brainwork
at night. Days are for meeting and talking to people. Because
he toils until 1:30 A.M. and often much later, the Chief Minister likes to sleep late. And when he does arise he does no yoga
exercises, says no prayers, and performs none of the ablution

rituals most caste Hindus consider inescapable. Yoga would be good for Chavan, because he is seriously overweight, a problem his wife worries about. He is supposed to be dieting, but he relishes good living too much to stint himself or to engage in the puritanisms that so many Congress leaders like to advertise.

Mornings are the only time of day that the Chief Minister has to himself. He likes to gaze out over the calm expanse of the Arabian Sea from Sahyadri (Eternal Mountain), his official residence set among the millionaires' mansions on Malabar Hill. In his air-conditioned sitting room are pictures of the three persons who, Chavan says, have most influenced him: Gandhi (two photographs), Sivaji, and his mother, now well over ninety. She still lives at Karad in a typical peasant house. No one knows her exact age. She says that her son has some job that causes him to move about all the time. Chavan takes care to see that his periodic visits to the wizened old lady are well publicized. Being a peasant boy is no more of a political handicap in India today than being born in a log cabin was in nineteenth-century America.

Visitors who have been lounging around the house since early morning start trooping into Chavan's sitting room at nine o'clock every morning. For an hour and a half he hears their grievances, listens to their complaints, and receives their petitions. Every politician in India is a kind of court of continuous appeal. After one talk I had with Chavan, we walked downstairs to find about thirty disgruntled local politicians waiting on the front porch. Each one wanted to know why he had not been nominated by the Congress party (which in Maharashtra means Chavan) to run in forthcoming district elections. Gesticulating expressively, the Chief Minister explained the situation in Marathi. The office seekers were still irate. Chavan shouldered his way through them and pulled open the door of the 1956 Dodge he uses to get around Bombay. One man would not be put off. He stuck his head through the car window and began haranguing Chavan. The Chief Minister switched to English and finally growled, "I am the boss." With that he closed the car window, practically decapitating the disconsolate politico, and ordered the driver to get moving. As he drove off, the group on the porch settled back to await his return.

After completing his morning audiences, Chavan dons his white Gandhi cap and leaves his home at 10:30 A.M. for the twenty-minute drive to the Sachivalaya, the Maharashtra state government headquarters. This is a functional six-story sky-scraper (by Bombay standards) in the rather insipid style that might be called Indian Modern. In his paneled, book-lined office on the sixth floor, five telephones—four white and one black—cluster by his desk. I do not know the significance of the black one. In any event, he uses them sparingly. Most of his time in the office is taken up with visitors—state officials in the morning, delegations or individual private callers in the afternoon. Except for the Wednesday cabinet meeting and periodic sessions of the Maharashtra Congress Committee, Chavan's days are largely devoted to what one aide calls "public relations." The only time his secretaries can approach him with paper work during the day is when he is eating a box lunch at his desk. From 5:30 to 6:30 P.M. Chavan receives from thirty to forty visitors who come without appointments. The old mogul tradition of public audience persists. In the evening the Chief Minister usually dines out (without his wife) and attends charity shows or meetings of community organizations. He endures long-winded speeches of welcome with cheerful fortitude. By 10:30 P.M. he is back at the Sahyadri. Then his real work begins. He scans several hundred official files, on everything from hydro power to patronage, and jots his decision or comments in the margin as soon as he turns the last page.

The general impression in India is that Chavan's health is excellent. But there are signs that the killing pace he has set himself is beginning to tell. He fell ill in February 1962 during his almost nonstop electioneering. According to one close friend, he had not allowed himself time to recover fully by the end of April.

Even if Chavan had the strength of ten, he could not single-handedly administer a state of nearly forty million people. Maharashtra's population is larger than that of most European countries. Chavan relies on a governmental machine that is good by Indian standards but still far from European or American norms. After the 1962 elections, the Chief Minister appointed an outsized cabinet of seventeen ministers and fourteen deputy ministers, comparable in numbers to Nehru's cabinet in New Delhi. He was not motivated by considerations of efficiency. On the contrary, such ministerial avoirdupois usually encumbers the administrative process. Chavan, who was stoned when he addressed election meetings in one region recently incorporated into Maharashtra, was striving to appease conflicting regional interests and promote what Indians call the "emotional integration" of his state. Whether multiplying cabinet portfolios will in fact accomplish this aim is open to question. Fortunately, Chavan had the wisdom to select as his finance minister a brilliant Brahman and former ICS officer, S. G. Barve, who dilutes the heavy Maratha concentration in the cabinet and can fight Maharashtra's battles with the ICS bureaucrats in New Delhi. This is very important in assuring any state a reasonable share of central government funds, especially for development. Barve's presence is also expected to improve the general tone of the Maharashtra administration.

The most daring step Chavan has taken in his public career is a law that came into force on May 1, 1962, whereby democratically elected district councils are given funds and executive authority to conduct administration, planning, and development at the local level. In Maharashtra, the councils are picked by universal adult suffrage instead of by indirect election, as in several other Indian states. Power is being decentralized so that the government, as the *Times of India* remarked, "is no longer amorphous, remote and inscrutable, but immediate, present and accountable." The ultimate aim is to energize the stagnant countryside and associate Maharashtra's impoverished, sun-blackened rural masses with the quest for self-generating progress. Success in Maharashtra would give powerful impetus to rural regeneration throughout India.

To achieve success, Chavan has surrendered more power— and money—to local bodies than any other chief minister in India. Almost a third of Maharashtra's state budget will henceforth be spent by village and district bodies. The entire land revenue, the traditional backbone of government finance in India, is now allocated to the district councils and the panchayats. Every increment in land revenue will earn a matching grant from the state government. This should encourage the district bodies to overcome their usual reluctance to collect taxes. Each district council, or parishad, will have a specialized executive committee chosen on the basis of proportional representation of all parties and interests in the council. This provision should make it more difficult for landowners, merchants, and moneylenders to stifle free discussion. In recent times panchayats lacked the money to pay even partial wages to the village watchman. Now, to make service on the councils more attractive and to reduce corruption, the state pays 500 rupees a month (about $100) to the president of each district body, and salaries to the members of the executive committees.

Despite the attractive features of the system adopted in Maharashtra, Chavan faces an uphill fight to make local government more than an interesting subject of study for sociologists. As S. K. Dey, India's minister for community development, says, "It is forgotten that the neon lights and the gold rush behind them have seduced the best minds from the countryside. If there is *goonda* [gangster] rule in the village, there is no one to provide the antidote." Starved for brains and money, village institutions have withered in many places, even where they have been revived under official auspices.

The panchayat, or council of village elders elected by adult citizens of a village, is almost as old as India. Under centuries of mogul and British rule these institutions fell into decay as the villagers lapsed into torpid despair. Where they survived, the village panchayats became the plaything of the district collector or the most powerful landlords. Even today district officials tend to be contemptuous of the villagers' ability to handle their own affairs. When the collector or his deputy makes all the decisions, interest in the panchayat soon evaporates. Caste often makes village democracy a sham, and panchayat elections are conducted almost entirely on the basis of caste. I remember visiting a village in Rajasthan where only members of the caste that controlled the panchayat were allowed to benefit from a new irrigation system. No matter which caste runs the panchayat, the untouchables there know they will still be excluded from the main village well and the makeshift temple.

In Maharashtra, Chavan is providing a large number of district officers, technicians, and consultants to serve as the staff of the district councils. It is difficult to say how competent these people are. And the better they are, the more likely they are to dominate the district councils instead of serving them.

Such dangers and difficulties do not make Chavan pessimistic, at least in public. He insists that he is optimistic about the great experiment he has launched. "There is no doubt," he says, "that *panchayat-i-raj* [government by panchayats] will be successful. Very much so. Of course, there will be initial difficulties. But I have faith in the people."

Although Chavan is ultimately responsible for the success or failure of *panchayat-i-raj* in Maharashtra, it is not clear how much, if any, of the basic thinking behind the scheme is his. One respected Praja Socialist leader says flatly, "Chavan hasn't produced a single new idea on panchayats."

Panchayat-i-raj is a long-term challenge to Chavan. The most serious immediate threat he has faced in his public life arose on the morning of July 12, 1961, when the earthen Panshet dam outside Poona gave way under the pressure of torrential monsoon rains. Chavan immediately chartered a plane and flew to Poona with a few aides. He found flood waters raging through the stricken city. Poona was devastated. By conservative official reckoning, 32,000 people were homeless and thousands of others had fled their homes for fear of new disaster. When the dam collapsed, large parts of the city were inundated so quickly by the cascading deluge that at least thirty-one persons were drowned. Those who escaped had no time to retrieve even jewelry or family heirlooms. Poona was a nightmare of chaos and despair. Electricity, water supply, sewage, and communications were disrupted. Typhoid threatened to reach epidemic proportions.

In such crises Chavan is at his best. He immediately took personal command of relief operations. He called together the demoralized local officials and ordered each to survey a

particular problem and report back the next morning. Then
he set out on foot through the water and mountains of debris.
At first he was greeted with sullen looks and angry words
from the dazed populace. For three days and two nights he
never stopped moving. He comforted weeping women, listened
sympathetically to outraged homeowners, and picked up children in his burly arms. Any capable political leader might do
as much. But Chavan drove himself through those grim July
days with a fury that surpassed politics. He waded down every
lane and alley. He set up transit camps for the homeless and
procured food grains and drinking water for the thirsty and
famished. And he listened to the most violent denunciations
of his administration without a flicker of annoyance.

There is little doubt that local officials were negligent in
failing to evacuate low-lying sections of Poona or even to issue
forceful warnings when heavy rains started falling in the
Panshet dam's catchment area on June 25. From that day, the
water level behind the dam rose steadily and menacingly. On
the night of July 10, the executive engineer noticed water
seeping through the downstream rock-toe. A night-long vigil
was ordered. The following day cracks had appeared along
the edges of the settled portion in a direction across the dam
axis. This ominous development was reported to the super-
intending district engineer in Poona. The Army was called in.
At 6:30 P.M. on July 11, 200 army sappers began desperately
stacking earth-filled bags in the sunken portion of the dam.
Throughout the night, as the water surged higher, half-hourly
reports were flashed to the collector of Poona, the highest-
ranking local official. But the residents of the city were allowed to sleep undisturbed, not knowing of the catastrophe
that seemed imminent and was to engulf them.

A few days later an official investigation was ordered. The
disaster at Poona was bad enough in itself, but the fate of the
man appointed to probe it has given rise to insinuations against
Chavan that, as one of his closest advisers told me, have hurt
him more than anything else in his years of public life.

The sequence of events began on October 13, 1961, when
R. S. Bavdekar, a highly respected retired judge of the Bombay
High Court, wrote to Chavan resigning from his post as head

of the commission appointed to investigate the Panshet calamity. He announced that he was quitting because he suspected that an accident report submitted by the dam's chief engineer had been tampered with by officials of the state government. Chavan says that he was unable to see Bavdekar because he was "terribly busy" that week selecting Congress candidates for the state assembly. But the Chief Secretary of the state government, N. T. Mone, was ordered to do everything possible to persuade the old Judge to withdraw his resignation. For the next six days Mone and Bavdekar met repeatedly at odd hours of the day and night at the Sachivalaya. They wrangled bitterly. At one point Bavdekar charged the Chief Secretary with having personally stolen documentary evidence submitted to the commission and substituting falsified documents.

The end came at 9:45 P.M. on October 19, 1961, when the sorely tried Bavdekar plunged to his death from the window of his fourth-story apartment in Bombay. The Judge is alleged to have said earlier that his health was failing and he could not carry on as head of the investigation commission. The police recorded his death as a suicide.

Bavdekar's death was seized on by opposition parties, including the Communists, as an election issue. They whispered that Chavan's government had murdered him after failing to dupe the Judge with forged documents. The accusations were so crude and so obviously political in inspiration that they changed few votes in the 1962 election although the whole episode did leave many questions unanswered. A later report by Justice V. A. Naik, of the Bombay High Court, dismissed Bavdekar's suspicions as "a figment of his overwrought imagination." But, as Chavan himself admits, "this thing must have weighed with Bavdekar."

I have questioned Chavan in detail about the Judge's death. He swears he is sure in his own mind that no one in his administration tampered with evidence given Bavdekar or tried to bring pressure on him. "I'm continuously trying to find out," he says, "what was the real reason for Bavdekar's action. A judge shouldn't act merely on suspicions." He insists that the report Bavdekar believed had been falsified was only an information memorandum to enable the Chief Minister to answer questions on the Panshet disaster in the state assembly. Chavan says that it was never intended for submission to Bavdekar.

As C. D. Deshmukh, the former Union finance minister, who comes from Bombay, says, "The Panshet dam collapse and the Judge's death would have been the end of almost any other government. But Chavan pushed that aside and wasn't hurt by it in the election." A Western diplomat stationed in Bombay is less uncritical. He says that the government's explanation seems "too facile." A well-informed newspaper executive in Bombay told me, "Our feeling is that there is something underhand in Bavdekar's suicide, although I know High Court justices do occasionally go potty." A leading Bombay industrialist whose party opposes Congress says that Bavdekar was inclined to be a "little unbalanced." The mystery remains.

Whatever the final verdict of history, the Bavdekar episode is not likely to retard Chavan's rise to all-India stature. Frank Moraes has written, "Given the very vital element of luck, I venture to predict that some day Mr. Chavan will achieve the office of Prime Minister of India. He has the requisite timber that mellows rather than hardens with experience and keeping. . . . Contemplativeness marches alongside practicality."

At the Bhavnagar Congress session in December 1960, Chavan won more votes for re-electon to the Congress Working Committee that any other candidate except Indira Gandhi. In their private discussions, the editors of the *Times of India* are said to have concluded that Chavan is the man most likely to be the next prime minister. He has youth, ability, and charm, as well as a united provincial party behind him. He has also been remarkably adept at keeping the good will of all factions in New Delhi. Even a brief period of service as a minister in the Union cabinet may dissipate some of this support, but will probably not destroy it entirely. South India would be more inclined to accept Chavan than Desai as prime minister, because Chavan refuses to agitate for the imposition of Hindi as the national language. Uttar Pradesh might accept Chavan because he gives the impression that he would co-operate loyally with the party bosses, most of whom hail from U.P. This impression may well prove mistaken once Chavan is in the driver's seat, but until then it bolsters his standing in the traditional heartland of Congress power. Nehru likes men who are Leftish in thought and elastic in practice. Chavan is both. Like Lal Bahadur Shastri, he has displayed a shrewd pliancy toward anything coming from Nehru, no matter how distasteful it was to Maharashtra. This attitude has earned him the Prime Minister's gratitude. Jayaprakash Narayan, who ordinarily is allergic to party bosses, calls Chavan the ablest chief minister in India. Dr. A. V. Baliga, who managed Krishna Menon's campaign for re-election in 1962, says that Chavan is "one of the few leaders who, like Prime Minister Nehru, sincerely believe in and work for a socialist society." Baliga calls the Chief Minister "truly secular in his outlook," and says, "It is not surprising that many people already think of him as one worthy of succeeding Nehru."

One of the few dissenting opinions about Chavan was voiced by Arthur Schlesinger, Jr., a White House adviser, who scornfully dismissed him as a "fathead" after chatting with him for half an hour in February 1962. Even for a snap judgment, Schlesinger's comment is surprisingly wide of the mark. No one who makes the slightest effort to know Chavan could regard him as a fathead. He is an Indian version of the capable, hard-driving American governor or big-city boss. There is nothing fatuous about Chavan.

Another American observer, whose judgment of Indian politicians presumably carries more weight with Washington than Schlesinger's, says he thinks that Chavan has an excellent chance to become prime minister. He feels that the Chief Minister's only drawback is that he is a "thinner" politician—figuratively speaking—than Nehru or even Morarji Desai. This is probably inevitable in view of Chavan's strictly provincial role until recent years. My own feeling is that the real pitfall he faces is being identified as a caste politician. A purely Maratha figure has little future in Delhi. Although Chavan disavows caste chauvinism, his political machine is now almost entirely Maratha. The test of his ability to control his own followers is still to come. His professed secularism also remains to be put to the test. As long as he ran a one-caste political organization in Maharashtra, he could never prove that he had the capacity to balance caste and communal forces, required of any all-India leader.

Such limitations should not obscure the fact that Chavan has already shown immense talent for self-development. Although he has headed a one-caste machine, he has a far more cosmopolitan outlook than any chief minister in India has had.

Even if he never takes up permanent residence in the prime minister's house, he is bound to play a vital role in Indian politics in the years ahead. He probably represents the new generation more ably than any other leading politician in the country. The smiling man from Satara may lack ideological definition, but he has the executive ability and homespun approach that appeal to younger Congressmen and to the new electorate that sustains them. The world will hear more of Yeshwantrao Chavan.

Indira Gandhi

PLATO BELIEVED that "immortal sons defying their fathers" were the guarantee of progress. Jawaharlal Nehru has no son to defy him, but he has a daughter whose defiance lies in her apparent determination to achieve the things her father only willed.

Indira Gandhi, Nehru's dearest and most trusted disciple, aspires to put his gospel into practice. If she succeeds, she could become the most powerful woman in the world today. If she fails, she will join the ranks of the anonymous offspring of famous fathers. She is different from any of the others sketched in this book, not only because she is a woman, but because her political potential is harder to measure. She has probably been involved in more top-level decisions than any other member of India's present ruling hierarchy except her father. Yet she bears official responsibility for none and can properly claim credit for none. Her power is vast, amorphous, and indefinable. No one doubts that she has easier and more frequent access to her father than any other Indian, but no one really knows the extent of her influence on him. No Congressman dares defy her, yet none openly proclaims his allegiance to her. She holds no official position in the government, but when she goes abroad, President Kennedy and other chiefs of state vie with one another for her favor. No public figure in India disclaims political ambition so insistently and none is more disbelieved.

Such anomalies make Indira Gandhi one of the most fascinating enigmas in India today. Even her looks are a subject of controversy. She is much more attractive than her sinister-looking newspaper pictures, but at first glance there is something forbiddingly regal about this child of the Indian revolution. Her long, thin face and Roman features are severe in repose. I am somehow reminded of a Hapsburg empress when I see her slender sari-draped figure sweeping through the carpeted halls of the prime minister's residence in New Delhi. She enters the little sitting room where visitors are received so swiftly and noiselessly that I am always startled and slightly flustered. It is as if a queenly apparition had suddenly materialized on the couch beside me. But her imperial aura and my confusion vanish as soon as she greets me in a voice so soft that I must strain to hear. Her smile is disarming, almost girlish. The dark eyes are reflective and a bit melancholy. Her white embroidered sari is immaculate. She dresses simply, with little jewelry. Her hair, beginning to turn gray noticeably, is cut short and waved softly, a radical departure from the tight bun most Indian women knot at the back of the head.

There is a note of urgency in the way she talks, in the way she fidgets with her sari and shifts restlessly on the couch. If she is interested or amused, an impish smile keeps tugging at the corners of her mouth. If she is bored or annoyed, her natural reserve can become glacial. But her most striking quality is a passionate sincerity that makes her seem more candid and outspoken than she really is. She has her father's knack for appearing to be modest while saying consistently immodest things about herself. There is a kind of controlled intensity about her that I find appealing, even charming. It is as if she were imploring you to uphold all sorts of good causes in which the powers of light find themselves heavily outnumbered by the forces of darkness. She can be agitated without sacrificing her composure, and emphatic without being strident. Behind the first lady of India I can see the lonely, insecure child who used to admonish her dolls to court arrest when her parents were in jail.

Whatever else I may think about her, I can never forget that she is a Nehru. The chiseled features are the same, as are the seeming hesitancy in the voice, the Brahmanical self-assurance, and the little calculated displays of annoyance. Above all, she is the political projection of her father. Her socialism may be more uncompromising, but it is no less romantic than his. She, like her father, is a case of arrested ideological development, clinging to outworn Fabian dialectics, tilting at vested interests, and forever invoking the utopia of scientific rationalism. She has the reputation of being more radical and incisive than her father, but this is hardly surprising. Youth can afford to be incisive, and radicalism always flourishes best without responsibility. In any event, she disclaims doctrinal orthodoxy. "I don't really have a political philosophy," she says. "I can't say I believe in any ism."

Her detractors are quick to offer an explanation. "Indira Gandhi has no ideas of her own," a former minister in Nehru's cabinet told me. "If you include her in your book, you will be reduced to saying polite things." I have felt no such compulsion. A Western historian who has known the Nehru family for many years calls her a "silly little girl without an idea in her head." One of India's great ladies, a world-famous social worker and disciple of Gandhi, witheringly dismisses her as a "very nice person—genuinely humble."

Such disparagements may be confirmed when Indira Gandhi faces the world without the protection of the parental banyan tree. She may shrivel in the merciless sun of Indian politics. But my own feeling is that she has performed too effectively in too many varied roles for anyone to write her off today. Apart from her father, she may be an unknown quantity; she is certainly not a minus quantity. Even her enemies concede that she was successful in her one-year term as president of the Congress party in 1959-1960. With a political realism lacking in many older Congress leaders, she foresaw the necessity for dividing the old Bombay state on linguistic lines. While

Nehru vacillated on Kerala, she denounced the Communists
for trying to subvert education in the state and urged President Rajendra Prasad to oust Kerala's Communist government. She later helped forge the coalition that defeated the
Communists at the polls in Kerala. When the Tibetan revolt
broke out in March 1959, she took a stronger line than either
her father or Krishna Menon. However she may have modified
her position since then, her bold stand during the Tibetan
crisis proved that she does have the courage to differ with her
father on an important issue.

Indira Gandhi's real forte is organizational and administrative work. Since before independence, she has been the Prime
Minister's official hostess—a job in which she must decide such
diverse questions as who should meet visiting chiefs of state
and what food they should be served. She accompanies her
father on most of his trips abroad and understudies him at
New Delhi diplomatic receptions. When Hindu-Moslem tensions exploded at Jubbulpore early in 1961, she was on the
scene, organizing relief and pacifying the antagonists, long
before other Congress leaders put in an appearance. If the
Indian minority in East Africa is apprehensive about political
developments, she is dispatched to listen to their grievances
and allay their fears. When Indo-American relations show signs
of strain, it is she who undertakes a month-long lecture tour
of the United States. She has been a member of the Congress
party since 1938 and a member of the powerful Congress
Working Committee since 1955. She also belongs to the
party's Central Elections Committee and Central Parliamentary Board. She is president and cofounder of the Women's
Department of Congress. She has organized legislators' seminars, women's work camps, and other training for Congress
members. She has campaigned intensively and extensively in
every major Indian election since independence. She has gone
to jail for the party (thirteen months), fasted as a token of
support for Gandhi, and made walking tours for the party
into the most backward and remote corners of India. Every
Congress candidate for Parliament in the 1962 general election
was approved by her in consultation with her father and
Home Minister Lal Bahadur Shastri. She is the key member of

the special seven-member subcommittee set up by the party after the election to punish rebellious and delinquent Congressmen. In many ways her influence in the party today is more pervasive than when she held the office of Congress president.

Her welfare activities are legion. She is president of the Indian Council for Child Welfare, vice-president of the International Union for Child Welfare, chairman of the National Integration Committee, member of the Executive Board of UNESCO, member of the Central Advisory Board of Education, and founder-president of the Bal Sahyog Samiti, an organization devoted to rehabilitating delinquent boys. She is a trustee of innumerable philanthropic and cultural organizations, and unofficial patron and protector of Indian artists. She may occasionally neglect some of her myriad organizations, but she has never wittingly neglected her responsibilities as the mother of two boys, now in their teens.

The pressure on her time is such that even her father has difficulty seeing his Indoo (moon), as he has called her since she was a child. She keeps two secretaries in perpetual motion. Several years ago she told an interviewer that she had not had a holiday "since I don't know when—in eight years perhaps." When she accompanies her father on what is supposed to be a vacation, she says that people keep telephoning and "are offended if you don't see them." Her health, never robust, has suffered under the strain of relentless work and irregular hours. When she left for her lecture tour of America in the spring of 1962, she told me that she thought she was "going to die," but she felt better by the time she returned to Delhi. She has a recurrent kidney ailment which causes her severe pain on occasion. Some students of Indian politics discount her as a force after Nehru on the grounds of health alone. My own impression is that her frail appearance and well-publicized infirmities are deceptive. They win her sympathy at home and abroad but never seem to prevent her from taking on any job, no matter how arduous, that interests her.

There is something about the only child of Kamla and Jawaharlal Nehru that has always aroused compassion. She was born at Anand Bhavan, the Nehru family mansion in Al-

lahabad, on November 19, 1917, while India groaned under the
burden of a war being fought on another continent. She used
to play around the swimming pool behind the old house and
munch pastries on her grandfather Motilal's lap. "I think I attended my first Congress meeting when I was three," she told
me smilingly when I asked when her political career began.
"I went everywhere, especially when the All-India Congress
Committee was meeting. But the most important meetings
were on our lawn, so there was no question of having to go
attend them." When the party was not caucusing and her
parents were off in prison, she would marshal her dolls in
processions demanding independence for India. Then other
dolls, representing the police, would round them up and take
them to jail. At other times she would collect the servants
around a table top and deliver thunderous political harangues.
"I haven't the remotest idea what I said to them or whether
it made any sense," she says, laughing. "All my games were political ones."

Asked if she had a childhood hero, she said, "When I was
very small I looked up to Joan of Arc." Then she added rather
sheepishly, "But I don't remember this really. Father reminded
me about it. When they'd ask me whom I wanted to be like,
I would say I didn't want to copy anyone. I just wanted to
be myself."

In retrospect she thinks her mother, a frail tubercular
woman, had much more influence on her than her father. "I
think," she insists with a trace of defiance, "I'm very much
more like her than anybody else." She remembers her mother's
determination to do something about women's education
(when not one Indian woman in a hundred could read or
write) and the way she ran the Congress party in Allahabad.
She particularly recalls how her mother helped change Jawaharlal Nehru from an Anglicized and rather foppish product
of Harrow and Cambridge into an Indian patriot over the objections of conservative womenfolk in the family who frowned
on his getting mixed up with Congress.

Her parents' involvement in politics brought more than her
share of heartbreak to their small daughter. She watched for-
lornly as police hustled all the Nehru adults off to prison and

seized cars, carpets, and any other movable property at Anand Bhavan. As Nehru says in his autobiography: "It was the Congress policy not to pay fines. So the police came day after day and attached and carried away bits of furniture. Indira, my four-year-old daughter, was greatly annoyed at this continuous process of despoliation and protested to the police and expressed her strong displeasure. I am afraid those early impressions are likely to color her future views about the police force generally."

Loneliness colored her future views more than anything the police did. One of the few people who came to play with her was Lal Bahadur Shastri. She, however, has no recollection of playing with children, although she later married one boy who sometimes came to Anand Bhavan. She says that it was difficult for a child to make so many decisions that her parents would ordinarily make, including even the choice of her school. "It seemed my parents were always in jail," she laments. For Indira there is the consolation of having learned at an early age to make her own decisions and, as she says, "to stand on my own feet."

Her first taste of schooling abroad was in Switzerland. She returned at the age of ten to find that she was still too young to join her father's party. So she organized a children's auxiliary, known as the Monkey Brigade. The children carried messages for Congress members, helped picket shops selling foreign cloth, and released adults from all sorts of routine party chores. On Sundays she would go to the home of the late Sam Higginbotham, an American Protestant missionary who ran an agricultural institute outside Allahabad, and help his wife sort clothes, toys, and books donated in America for Indian children. During the mass civil-disobedience movement in the early 1930's, casualties were frequently brought to Anand Bhavan because city hospitals would not admit them. Her mother converted one large room into an emergency ward. Indian doctors who were sympathetic to Congress would come at night to treat the injured, many of whom were suffering from gunshot wounds. She remembers one boy who was brought in with such a serious stomach injury that the doctors advised simply making him as comfortable as possible and awaiting the end. "But he was my first patient," she told me, "and I was determined to see him through. I almost staked my faith in God on his pulling through." She should still be a believer, because she met her patient again during the 1951 election campaign.

Indira Gandhi's schooling was constantly interrupted by the exigencies of the independence movement. "When everyone in the family was in jail," she recalls, "I went to school at Poona." There she worked in slum areas among the untouchables to promote Gandhi's campaign for handspun cloth in place of imported British textiles. She also attended Swiss boarding schools and the university at Santiniketan founded by India's Nobel Prize-winning poet Rabindranath Tagore. But her most memorable instruction was a correspondence course in world history given by her father from his prison cell. She was his only pupil. His long, discursive letters to her on the rise and fall of civilizations were later collected in a book entitled *Glimpses of World History*. The glimpses, inevitably obstructed at times by prison bars, were to form the basis of her political thinking.

"What presents can I give you?" Nehru wrote on her thirteenth birthday. "They can only be of the air and of the mind and spirit, such as a good fairy might have bestowed on you—something that even the high walls of prison cannot stop."

When her mother became seriously ill, Indira accompanied her to Switzerland, where Kamla died in 1936. The following year she was admitted to Somerville College, Oxford, where she joined the British Labour party. "I thought if I have to join something," she told me, "I'll join the Labour party." Of course, she found Labour more politically congenial than the Conservatives. She got to know the late Ernest Bevin, Ellen Wilkinson, and other party leaders, and attended Labour rallies. Harold Laski's widow remembers her as a "mousy, shy little girl who didn't seem to have any political ideas."

While she was at Oxford, Indira met Krishna Menon, a man who was often to re-enter her life and to influence it profoundly. "I saw a lot of him, or, rather, a lot of his office," she says, "because I worked for the India League in the afternoons and evenings. In the evenings he was usually away organizing meetings. He was very good at that. Menon gave you the feeling there was something worth-while to do for India. Otherwise there was no outlet at that time. There was no question of helping him personally, although he did have that effect on some of the British students who were very much drawn to him."

Indira herself was drawn to a young Indian Parsi named Feroze Gandhi, who was studying at the London School of Economics. Feroze had been born in Bombay, but his family was from Allahabad. He had been one of her few childhood playmates and was later recruited for Congress party work by her grandfather Motilal. Feroze made much of his devotion to her mother and was at Kamla's bedside when she died. He then went back to England and bombarded Indira with ardent love letters. The two were eventually married, on March 26, 1942, against Nehru's wishes and over the objections of the rest of the family, who opposed a match between a member of their Brahman clan and a Parsi. At that time almost all marriages in India were arranged. But, as Paul Grimes, the former New York *Times* correspondent in India, says, "In the first known test of one strong Nehru will against another, Indira won." Minoo R. Masani, the former socialist leader who was close to Menon in the thirties, says, "Both Indira and Feroze were taken in tow by Menon in England." On their return to India, they joined the new All-India Students' Federation, which later became a Communist front.

Indira Gandhi seems to have made little impression in England. Reginald Sorensen says, "Indira Gandhi didn't impress me except as the reflection of her father. I think she was purely her father's daughter, close to Menon only to the extent that he was her father's friend. But I don't remember her too clearly. She didn't come very much to the India League."

Her stay in England was cut short by illness. Before she could take her degree at Oxford, her father sent her to Leysin, in Switzerland, to recover from the severe pleurisy she had contracted in the English winter. She regained her health quickly but got stuck in Switzerland after France fell to the Nazis. She spent a year trying to get back to India. All the frontiers were closed. "By that time I wanted to get home," she told me. "I felt that the war was more important than my studies."

Back in India, she plunged into Congress politics with Feroze, who was also working at the time as a newspaper editor in Allahabad. Six months after their marriage, they both went to prison for their political activities. At the beginning they were in the same jail, but were allowed to see each other only twice. Feroze had been sentenced to serve eighteen months. Indira was detained without trial and therefore did not enjoy the "A"-class treatment usually accorded political prisoners.

"When I entered prison," she told me with a sardonic smile, "there was nothing on my card to indicate my status except a crude X. So the jail superintendent, who was a pucka Anglo-Indian decided to put me in a new category—X class. That turned out to mean extremely bad treatment for me."

When she heard she was about to be arrested, she addressed a political meeting in Allahabad, because she "wanted to do something to merit arrest." The day she entered the barracks-like prison compound, she was running a high temperature. A government physician sent from Lucknow examined her and prescribed a special diet of eggs, Ovaltine, and fruit. As soon as he left, the jail superintendent jeeringly tore the prescription to shreds before her eyes. When her family sent her boxes of mangoes (for which she has a special fondness), her jailor took delight in telling her, "We enjoyed your family's gift very much. The mangoes were delicious." Of course she never saw them.

She was confined with twenty-two other women in one large barrack with barred windows the size of doors. During the day the sun made the place almost unbearable. Sanitary facilities were primitive and semipublic. Because she did not rate as an "A"-class prisoner, she was not allowed to receive letters or parcels or have the fortnightly interviews allowed other political prisoners. She spent thirteen months in confinement. Nehru remarks in his autobiography that the British seemed to make a point of subjecting women political offenders to particularly harsh treatment in hopes that Congressmen would keep their womenfolk out of the independence movement. Despite the rigors of her imprisonment, Indira Gandhi never considered refraining from political activity.

The only period of comparative domestic tranquillity she and Feroze ever enjoyed was from 1944 to 1946, the interval between the birth of Rajiv, their first son, and Sanjay, their second. The family lived during this time in Allahabad. The coming of independence uprooted them. Nehru moved to a small four-room house in New Delhi when the Constituent Assembly convened in 1946 to draw up a constitution for the future independent state of India. In this house Nehru tried to accommodate fourteen or fifteen people, including Indira, her husband, and their first child. The evening before Sanjay was born, Lady Cripps stopped by and asked Mrs. Gandhi to help her pick out a Kashmir shawl. "There's no one," she pleaded, "who knows just what is right for me the way you do." Indira went along although she felt faint. "That night," she told Barbara Lazarsky, the wife of a former American Embassy official in Delhi, "my second son was born prematurely. We put up a tent, and my husband was put out in that, and the nanny and the baby and I stayed in the bedroom, as we couldn't risk the outdoor chill."

She was still unwell when Gandhi asked her to tour the Moslem areas of old Delhi during the bloody riots that preceded the partition of British India. Cholera had broken out among the terrified Moslems, who preferred to starve in their hovels rather than risk Hindu and Sikh vengeance by venturing out. Indira Gandhi hired a grain truck and brought doctors into the beleaguered Moslem quarter. At first she worked at getting troublemakers arrested, but then she decided she had to have "another angle" and started trying to arrange a meeting of leading Moslems and Hindus. Her efforts bore fruit in typically Indian style when 500 Moslem and Hindu notables mingled at a mammoth tea party in old Delhi. Communal tension eased.

Shortly before partition, the late Pandit Govind Ballabh Pant, then Congress party boss in the United Provinces, asked Mrs. Gandhi to run for the state assembly. She refused, reminding him that she had already declined to run for the

Constituent Assembly. Pant, who was not accustomed to being denied, was furious. He cabled Gandhi asking him to order her to run. She told Gandhi that her children were still small and needed a mother and that she would not be bullied. The Mahatma, recognizing someone of his own inflexible mold, laughed and shrugged his emaciated shoulders.

Since then, Mrs. Gandhi says, she has been asked to run every time India has had a general election. She has always refused, because, as she says with girlish wilfullness, "I don't want to." She insists that in Parliament she would be "limited." She means that as a member of the Congress parliamentary party she would become another cog in the mechanical majority that rubber-stamps whatever Nehru presents. As one of the few important Congress leaders who is not a member of any legislative body, she can escape the slings of ministerial office while she strengthens her position in the party and among the masses.

Despite her refusal to hold legislative office, Indira Gandhi became increasingly enmeshed in politics and statecraft after independence. She became her father's official hostess when he was appointed head of the provisional cabinet before partition. Later she moved with him into the sixteen-room mansion on Teen Murti Marg, traditionally the abode of British commanders in chief in India, that was to become the prime minister's official residence. When Nehru visited China in 1954, she went with him. An English correspondent who covered the trip described her appearance at a Peking reception organized by a Chinese Communist women's group: "When Indira Gandhi entered the clinically furnished room there among the massed blue boiler suits of ideological orthodoxy and the square bobs of liberation, she resembled in some way a lotus flower that had been planted in a bed of broccoli."

A Chinese Foreign Ministry official who observed her in action exclaimed, "It's remarkable; she has a lot of the West in her but, dear me, how intelligent."

The following year she accompanied her father to the Bandung conference, where she was so charmed by Chou En-lai that Western newsmen accused her of having been predisposed in his favor. Her most valuable function at the conference was to moderate her father's outbursts of temper. Purple with rage, Nehru began stalking out of one particularly stormy session until she was overheard to murmur, "Papa, control yourself." Needless to say, no other member of the Indian delegation would have said as much. Later that year she accompanied her father on an official visit to the Soviet Union. She first went to Russia in 1953 on a private visit after attending Queen Elizabeth's coronation in London. She was impressed by what she saw, especially in Soviet Central Asia, but she insists that she could never accept the totalitarian features of the Russian regime. In 1949 and in 1956 she accompanied her father to America.

Such preoccupations did not prevent Indira Gandhi from playing an ever larger role in Congress party affairs, especially in the women's section. Indian women used the independence movement as a vehicle to assert their long-denied rights, and after freedom they continued to agitate through Congress. They were fighting purdah as well as the British. Mrs. Gandhi traveled constantly in the most inaccessible parts of the country, addressing thousands of public meetings, laying dozens of cornerstones, and accepting innumerable garlands.

Such a life was bound to detract from her marriage. Feroze pursued his own career. He was elected on the Congress ticket to the provisional parliament and was a member until his death. He soon made an independent reputation as a crusader against corruption. In 1958 he led the attack on T. T. Krishnamachari, then Finance Minister, in connection with a scandal in the state-owned Life Insurance Corporation. Feroze was a Left Wing socialist, whom I have heard called a "stooge" of Krishna Menon. My own impression is that he co-operated with Menon for tactical and ideological reasons but that he was no one's stooge. It is also widely said in Delhi that Feroze was unfaithful to Indira. Whatever the truth, their marriage was blighted in the decade after independence. At times Feroze lived with his wife at the Prime Minister's house, but when he became a member of Parliament he established separate quarters in New Delhi. Although they had been separated, Indira was deeply affected by her husband's first heart attack. Menon is said to have promoted a reconciliation. Indira and Feroze spent a vacation together with their children in Kashmir, but found that their paths had become too divergent. They agreed to separate again. Rajiv and Sanjay usually stayed with their mother at the Prime Minister's house on vacations from their fashionable Dehra Dun boarding school in the foothills of the Himalayas.

Feroze died in 1960, after another heart attack. He was in his political prime, and was regarded as one of the few bright young men in the aging Congress party. He would almost certainly have attained national stature if his career had not been cut short.

Indira Gandhi had already become a national figure. In January 1959 she signed a manifesto of the Congress party's so-called "Ginger Group" attacking the party for lethargy and failure to carry out its stated policies. This step publicly identified her with the Congress Left Wing, although neither she nor Feroze actually belonged to the Ginger Group. Most members of the group have since been defeated at the polls or in party infighting. The remnants have gravitated toward Krishna Menon.

On February 2, 1959, while Mrs. Gandhi was on a three-day *padayatra* (walking tour) in her father's constituency in Uttar Pradesh, she learned that she had been unanimously elected president of the Congress party, the fourth woman and the third Nehru to hold the post.* She succeeded a party wheel horse, Uchhrangrai Navalshanker Dhebar, who had been imprudent enough to complain to Nehru that the Prime Minister was stifling criticism in the party.

The day a half-dozen Congress state committees (hoping to ingratiate themselves with her father) nominated Indira Gandhi to take charge of the party, Congress seemed headed for a debacle. Never since it was founded in 1885 by Allan Octavian Hume, a Scotsman and former member of the Indian Civil Service, had the party been so divided. Each one of its millions of members (no one knew the exact number because so many members were bogus names on a register) seemed a faction unto himself. Corruption and opportunism

* Her grandfather Motilal and her father previously headed the party.

had robbed Congress of its preindependence luster. In Kerala the party had disintegrated in fratricidal disputes, and the Communists had been voted into power for the first time. Other states threatened to follow suit. The Congress party organization rotted while a parade of self-seekers beat a path to the Prime Minister's door. The job of party president had been correspondingly devalued. At least one state minister had turned it down before Mrs. Gandhi was nominated. When her election was announced, one Indian editor said that she had donned "a crown more of thorns than of roses," adding, "Mrs. Gandhi has been sentenced to hard labor." She knew it. She protested that she had not sought the post, which was true. "I'm not at all anxious to be in this job," she remarked a bit plaintively. But once the crown of thorns was thrust on her head, she set to work with characteristic Nehru diligence to clean up the Congress mess. Even her critics admit that she did a good job during the short term she served. Although her selection was primarily a gesture to her father, she soon surprised the cynics by demonstrating that she had ability in her own right. From being a comparatively minor figure in party councils, she suddenly blossomed as an all-India figure who could more than hold her own with the party bosses. One of her first acts as president was to drop her father from the twenty-one-member Congress Working Committee, a body on which he had served since the 1920's. Lest she be accused of filial ingratitude, she announced that he would still be invited to attend committee meetings. She presided at party conclaves with a rod of iron, silencing long-winded Congress elders, including her father, with the gavel when they exceeded their time.

As far back as 1951, she had shown that she could draw crowds at election rallies in her father's constituency when he was unavailable. Now her speaking gifts were put to the test before mammoth audiences all over India. Dressed in locally made saris and sandals, with her head modestly covered by a shawl in the Hindu style and her forehead smeared with red powder (the villagers' way of showing respect), Mrs. Gandhi preached the gospel of unity and progress.

Her executive ability, if not her political judgment, developed quickly. At her first press conference after becoming Congress president, she proclaimed: "The nation is in a hurry and we can't afford to lose time. My complaint against Congress is that it isn't going as fast as the people are advancing. And that can be fatal for a political organization." She conceded that the outlook and methods of the Communists were different, but predicted with a naïveté that was soon to disappear that they, too, could be expected to co-operate in the "task of national development and reconstruction."

In an interview with the Communist-line weekly *Link*, she even hinted at a kind of popular front in India. "I would like to see active people, nonparty and from other parties, working together with Congress as has happened on the food front. . . . In this way not only would a much larger section of the people be actually involved in constructive work, but party pressures would be less able to obstruct people or programs that didn't agree with their own interests."

This invitation naturally sent shivers of delight through India's Communists and fellow travelers. The pro-Communist weekly *Blitz* noted that Mrs. Gandhi was the same age as her father had been when he was elected Congress president for the first time at the famous Lahore session which took the pledge to win unconditional independence. "Indira will live up to this noble example," *Blitz* warbled, "if her progressive thinking and her will for dynamic action provide a corrective to the compromises her father is sometimes forced to make."

Six months later the Communists were to regret her capacity for "dynamic action." She had contributed significantly to their downfall in Kerala. "Everything the Communists are doing is wrong," she told reporters after visiting the state in the spring of 1959. She found that the state government had actually prepared school textbooks glorifying Lenin and Mao Tse-tung as world heroes and ignoring Gandhi. Her reaction was immediate and decisive. While her father wavered, she went to President Prasad, a staunch Hindu traditionalist, and argued forcefully that the central government should oust the Communists and assume direct control of Kerala, where the state government's efforts to control the schools had already set off bloody riots. Rajkumari Amrit Kaur, a member of

Nehru's first cabinet and a lady of considerable perspicacity, says, "Indira was good on Kerala. She'd been down there, and saw what the Communist government was doing. She came back and insisted on the Center's taking over." The Kerala Communist government was ousted on July 31, 1959, and New Delhi took charge of the state under Article 356 of the Indian Constitution, which empowers the president of India to assume direct control of a state if he is satisfied that its government is not being carried on in accordance with the Constitution. That was the first step. The next was to produce a coalition capable of defeating the Communists at the polls and forming a viable state administration. Mrs. Gandhi overrode strong opposition in Congress to forming an electoral entente in Kerala with the Moslem League, an avowedly communal party. As she told me later, "I don't believe the Moslem League is any more communal than anyone else in Kerala. Everything there is communal. Everything is run by the Nairs, the Nestorians, the Namboodris, or some other sect. You have to deal with communal parties unless you want to forget about Kerala entirely."

Her persistence paid off in the special election in February 1960 in which the anti-Communist electoral front composed of Congress, the Praja Socialist party, and the Moslem League won ninety-three seats in the state assembly, against twenty-nine for the Communists. Ironically, the Communists' percentage of the popular vote actually increased from 35.28 to 43. Their strength in the legislature fell from sixty to twenty-nine because they were no longer able to profit from three-cornered or four-cornered contests.

Kerala and later encounters with the Communists have taught Mrs. Gandhi a respect for Communist organizing ability that is a far cry from her earlier infatuation with the Soviet utopia. "Our people don't work," she says about her own party. "The Communists do very intensive work. They're well organized. They'll do anything if it advances the party. They have more dedication because they are in total opposition. Anyone who isn't dedicated simply drops out of the Communist party." However repugnant she finds Communist lack of scruples, I always have the feeling when I talk to her that she has a sneaking admiration for Communism, which she calls "a kind of fascinating creed that has an attraction for the people that the democratic movement doesn't have." She is no more immune to that attraction than is her father, who still regards the Indian Communists as more "progressive" and therefore less dangerous than even conservative members of his own party. Actually, Mrs. Gandhi is slightly to the left of her father, which leads some Indians to label her an outright fellow traveler. For example, Purshottam Trikumdas, the veteran socialist leader, says unequivocally, "She's been a fellow traveler all her life except for a short phase." The phase he refers to was during her tenure as Congress president, when she took a firm line on Kerala and favored granting asylum to the Dalai Lama and other Tibetans fleeing Chinese oppression. Her enthusiasm for the young god-king has now cooled. When I questioned her on Tibet and the Dalai Lama, she denied that her attitude had changed. "I'm still opposed to what happened," she said mildly.

On the question whether the Dalai Lama should be allowed the same freedom of political expression as refugee Nepalese politicians in India, she was equivocal. "Since we have this trouble with China," she said, "it would complicate our situation. I think Chinese policy is partly motivated by their desire to consolidate Tibet and the frontier with India. They strongly disapprove our giving sanctuary to the Dalai Lama. The Chinese call us American satellites." Asked if she thought they really believed that, she answered, "Yes, I do. I think the Chinese felt the need to consolidate their hold on the border since we were politically 'unreliable.' "

This explanation overlooked the fact that the Chinese had already "consolidated" more than 14,000 square miles of what India insists is its own territory. Nor did Mrs. Gandhi's remarks to me in the summer of 1962 betray any awareness that the Chinese were even then getting ready to assert their claims to a further 36,000 square miles of Indian territory with explosive force. When the blow fell in October, Mrs. Gandhi led the demand for a resolute response by India, but her record as a prophet of Peking's intentions is no better than the worst in New Delhi. When she moved the foreign-policy resolution at the All-India Congress Committee meeting in January 1962, she denounced Western nations for criticizing the seizure of Goa. She ignored the urgent question of Chinese intrusions. The resolution itself made only one passing reference to China, urging a "peaceful settlement" of the dispute.

One important reason for her zigzags on China and the border dispute is undoubtedly Krishna Menon. Indira Gandhi appears to have been in an anti-Menon phase during her Congress presidency. When a Western woman journalist expressed dislike of Menon in a talk with her early in 1960, Mrs. Gandhi agreed and urged the journalist to tell Nehru. She is reported to have said that she no longer discussed Menon with her father "because he won't listen to me on that man." But after Feroze's death, things changed. She was deeply distressed and may have turned to her husband's friend for solace. In any event, Menon oiled his way back into her good graces, lavishing flattery on her, ostentatiously fanning her at public meetings, advising her on which saris and what jewelry to wear, and generally insinuating himself into her life. One close friend of the Nehru family says, "Menon flatters Indira and cultivates her tirelessly." In England I was even told that she and Menon will be married, which would be like matrimony between Rasputin and Florence Nightingale. I think the idea can safely be dismissed; nevertheless, Menon generates the intellectual kinetic energy to move her conventionally "progressive" ideas about socialism and world affairs off dead center. He has long performed much the same service for her father. Mrs. Gandhi's lectures in America in the spring of 1962 bore many traces of Menon's influence, even down to the language she used.

Menon knows how to exploit her weaknesses. He caters to her girlish petulance and helps her give vent to the stultifying frustrations that beset anyone engaged in Indian politics. My impression is that she still thinks she can dispense with Menon whenever it suits her purposes. That may not always be true. But right now, as one Delhi editor puts it, "Indira eats sometimes out of Menon's hand and sometimes out of Lal Bahadur Shastri's hand."

Whatever she really thinks about Menon, Mrs. Gandhi

has often defended him. She praised his "fine brain" and denied that he was a Communist when she was asked to "explain" Menon during a talk to the Women's National Press Club in Washington in November 1961. After the struggle for the deputy leadership of the Congress parliamentary party in 1961, she made it clear that she had favored Jagjivan Ram, who was backed by Menon as a counterweight to Finance Minister Morarji Desai. She told me that only Desai himself thought he had a chance to win. In fact, the opposite was true. Everyone believed that Desai would have won if Nehru had not insisted that the election of a deputy leader be called off.

Indira Gandhi is close to several members of the Menon camp, including the Leftist Oil Minister, K. D. Malaviya, whose radical socialism apparently conforms to her thinking. Her message of greetings to the *Socialist Congressman*, a journal favoring Menon and edited by Malaviya's brother, contained a denunciation of "reactionaries." She condones the strong-arm tactics of Orissa's millionaire Chief Minister, Bijoyananda Patnaik, who is financially and politically linked with Menon. "Orissa," she says with finality, "needs a jolt." And under Patnaik it is getting one.

The notion that Indira Gandhi is her father's logical successor is now being quietly put forward by Congress Left Wingers. Mrs. Violet Alva, deputy chairman of the Rajya Sabha and an avowed Menon admirer, believes that Mrs. Gandhi qualifies because she has "shared her father's secrets" over the years. Mrs. Rajan Nehru, the politically ambitious wife of the Secretary General of the External Affairs Ministry, told me that Mrs. Gandhi's mass following assures her a "brilliant political future." Such expressions reflect her strength in the women's section of Congress, but her support is by no means limited to the distaff side. Among the Congress rank and file her prestige has risen considerably in recent years. There is already an active "lobby" in Delhi proclaiming the virtues of younger leadership of the kind she would supposedly provide. Among state chief ministers she could probably count on Patnaik's support as well as the blessings of Mohanlal Sukhadia, the youthful chief minister of Rajasthan, and Bakshi Ghulam Mohammed, the Kashmir premier, for what they are worth. She would also be backed by Damodaram Sanjivayya, the youthful Congress president, whom she nominated for his present position. I think Y. B. Chavan might accept her as a stopgap prime minister if he could not make the grade himself and feared that the Desai-Patil group might otherwise seize power. The attitude of south Indian leaders like Kamaraj Nadar, chief minister of Madras, and C. Subramaniam, the able minister of steel and heavy industries, is doubtful, but there is nothing to show that they oppose her. In the present Union cabinet, the Right Wingers, including Desai and Patil, are certainly cool to her. However, if it came to a choice between her and Menon, the Right would probably prefer her. Shastri is reported to have said that he would rather work under Mrs. Gandhi than hold the top job himself.

If Menon is balked in his own bid for power, which I regard as almost certain, there is now considerable evidence that he will try to put up Indira Gandhi as her father's political heir. Malaviya, Jagjivan Ram, and the rest of the anti-Desai faction in the cabinet would back this enterprise. Menon's aim would be to play the kingmaker for her, much as Ceylon's coterie of ruling politicians exploits the name of that country's figurehead Prime Minister, Mrs. Srimavo Bandaranaike. But Indira Gandhi is not Mrs. Bandaranaike. She has shown that she has a will of her own at least as strong as that of any member of Nehru's present cabinet. She has had enough experience of practical politics to know when she is being used for ulterior ends. And she now knows what works in India and what is simply doctrinal icing on the cake. In the succinct words of one Bombay editor who knows her well, "Indira is no fool." She may be attracted by Menon, but I doubt that she is duped by him. Minoo Masani, who is not one of her admirers, says, "Indira is not a Menon stooge, but she would go along further with him than any other Congress leader because of her ideological convictions." This assessment corresponds to everything I know on the subject. Indira Gandhi has not just discovered Menon; she knows his faults as well as his strong points. Nor has his flattery yet blinded her to her own limitations. I remember her telling me with some impatience that there were "heaps of people" who could make as good a Congress president as she.

Mrs. Gandhi insists that she has no political ambitions, wants no career, seeks nothing for herself, and threatens no one. Not many people in Delhi are convinced by such professions. As her aunt Mrs. Vijaya Lakshmi Pandit says, "Whatever it was that originally prompted Indira to get into politics, I'm sure she'll continue. She's too deeply involved to get out now." But a high-ranking British diplomat who sees her often says: "Indira is like a soccer player who could have kicked the ball through the goal posts any time she had wanted to. The ball has been at her feet for a long time. If she had wanted to establish herself as the next prime minister, she could easily have done so. I sense in her a genuine reluctance to plunge into politics—a vague feeling that her primary duty is to care for her father and be by his side."

This view is provocative, but I think it overestimates her power and underestimates her ambition. No one, not even a member of the Nehru family, can establish title to the succession without Nehru's public endorsement. The ball has always been at the Prime Minister's feet, and he has always carefully avoided kicking it in the direction of any would-be successor. Indira's eye may now be on her father, rather than on the ball, but once he is gone she is not likely to watch passively while others score the goals. If she feels bound to sustain him in his last years, she will feel even more bound to sustain his policies when he is no longer there to uphold them.

Indira Gandhi clearly wants to make a niche for herself in Indian life. The question arises: Where? Social work, which has never really excited her, provides no adequate outlet for her energies. When I asked her in the spring of 1962 whether she preferred politics or welfare work, her answer was illuminating: "I don't really make a distinction. I have an idea of what India should become. Anything I do I regard as a step toward ensuring what I want India to become. Political stability . . . is the foundation on which everything else is built. I feel strongly enough about it to do something about it."

This feeling will remain the motive force in her life. It will, I believe, overcome all hesitations and uncertainties. Unless her health should deteriorate unexpectedly, there is no doubt in my mind that Indira Gandhi will remain an active performer in the political arena.

All factions might accept her as a compromise prime minister in a national crisis after Nehru, but few Indians expect she would last long. She lacks her father's uncanny talent for being on all sides of every important issue. She is more sharp-edged and less inclined to compromise. In India, perhaps more than anywhere else, politics is the art of the possible. How long could she keep the support of rival groups in Congress?

One difficulty is that, despite her preachments about socialism, no one can really predict what she would do as prime minister. As she told me on one occasion, "I wouldn't say I'm interested in socialism as socialism. For me it's just a tool. If I found a tool that was more efficient, I'd use it." But in India's present semifeudal state she thinks socialism is the "only thing." She rejects the idea of totalitarian control, because India is "too individualistic." But I suspect that her splenetic streak might prompt her to resort to short cuts once she collided head on with Indian reality. Her stand on nationalization is equivocal. She once told a New York *Times* correspondent that nationalization was not practical in India today. When I asked her three years later if she still believed that, she answered, "It depends on nationalization of what. If something is running well in private hands, why disturb it simply for the sake of nationalization? But if they're making a mess of it or have monopoly control, then go ahead and nationalize." She thinks that the government should decide when such a move is necessary. She is equally vague on the relationship between state-owned industry and private enterprise. Should the state sector expand at a faster rate? "A larger public sector certainly," she counters, "but not necessarily at the expense of the private sector." She contends that the public sector versus private sector controversy in India is "unfortunate." She is nevertheless on record as favoring measures such as state trading in food grains (to regulate prices and supplies), across-the-board price control, the fixing of "productivity norms" for state and private industry, formulation of a "national wage policy," and regulation of incomes and salaries, possibly including ceilings on urban incomes. All this fits the socialistic pattern of society advocated by her father since 1927 and grudgingly adopted by the Congress party as official policy in 1955. State trading in food grains has now been largely discarded. Nehru's bid to introduce a ceiling on urban incomes has been rebuffed. The "national wage policy" and the productivity norms are probably destined to remain chimeras. Price control is widespread but ineffective.

If Indira Gandhi is fuzzy on economics, she is clear on the need for making India a nation. She would probably attack the communal demon more zealously than most other contenders for the premiership. Like her father, she would enjoy the confidence of India's minorities, especially of the Moslems. She might do something to rescue Indian education from the morass into which it has sunk. Social welfare would get higher priority under her, but the overlapping and confusion that hamper efforts in this field would doubtless continue. The Civil Service would, I expect, regard her with cool neutrality. The Army might resent the idea of a woman prime minister, but with fifty-one women in the present Indian Parliament it is too late to talk of keeping women out of politics, even the highest politics. Mrs. Gandhi has wisely avoided becoming identified as a red-hot feminist. She has worked for women's rights with considerable success but never to the exclusion of political activity on a broader front. Therefore, the fact that she is a woman is not the first objection you hear when her name is mentioned as a possible successor. The career of Mrs. Pandit, who became the first woman president of the United Nations General Assembly and has represented India in Washington, London, and Moscow, has helped accustom Indians to the idea that women are qualified to hold high positions in government.

Mrs. Gandhi's attitude toward the United States is no more reserved than her father's, probably less. She has visited America six times and gets on well with Americans from Mrs.

John F. Kennedy down to the Gila Bend garden club. In foreign policy, including relations with Washington, she is likely to follow her father's lead more unswervingly than in any other field. The Nehru version of nonalignment would continue unchanged unless she faced drastically different circumstances. India's relations with the Soviet Union would remain friendly, and Mrs. Gandhi would probably make another bid for *rapprochement* with China.

This assumes that Indira Gandhi's father would actively promote her candidacy or at least allow it to be promoted by others. I think this assumption is valid. As Frank Moraes has said, there is no question of Nehru's wanting to create a dynasty of his own; he would find such a suggestion distasteful. But Nehru will do everything in his power to thwart the ambitions of the Congress Right Wing. He may well persuade himself that only his daughter could provide the essential continuity of policy after he leaves office. She is, after all, his only child and the only member of the family capable of holding the torch aloft after he goes.

Her father's active backing would remove many obstacles from Mrs. Gandhi's path. But I do not believe that her father could impose her on the country, even if he were willing to try. Mrs. Pandit says that India would not accept another Nehru as prime minister. Nehru must know how quickly the children of giants are dwarfed, even by ordinary mortals, once the giants depart. An American of some eminence in Delhi answered my questions about Indira Gandhi's future with several questions of his own. "What is Gandhi's son today without Gandhi? Where are the daughters of Sardar Patel and Mohammed Ali Jinnah, who everyone thought would be so important?" Where indeed? The same American calls Mrs. Gandhi "a woman of intelligence but not wisdom, with a facile but conventional mind."

Even now, as Nehru declines in health and strength, his grip on Congress is loosening. How much weaker will it be by the time he goes? Indira Gandhi will cast a shorter shadow when she leaves the Prime Minister's house. It is her misfortune that she will lose her most precious key to power the moment she needs it most—when her father's passing has left an empty room at the top. Without the key, I doubt that Indira Gandhi can open the door to that room unless, of course, it were battered down for her by as yet unseen forces dedicated to the Nehru legend and its political trappings.

Jayaprakash Narayan

"JAYAPRAKASH is the future prime minister of India."

When these words were spoken in 1948 by the first Prime Minister of India, they expressed a widespread conviction. Today neither Nehru nor anyone else familiar with India would make such a prediction without qualifying it. Yet Jayaprakash Narayan, once acclaimed Asia's premier socialist, continues to evoke a deep response among millions of Indians. His contradictory conscience mirrors the anguish of one seventh of mankind. In a disenchanted age he still strives to approximate the ideas and ideals of Mahatma Gandhi. Gandhi called him the greatest Marxist in India. Now many Indians call him the greatest Gandhian. His endless voyage of ideological discovery has made him a wayfarer in politics, but it still ripples the stagnant waters of Indian thought. He is India's foremost dissenter, critic, intellectual nonconformist, and fighter of lost causes that never lose their following. He is a man seemingly destined to be nobly wrong when others were meanly right.

Narayan has never been a minister or a government official.

He has no experience of administration, no talent for organization, and no taste for practicality. Politics as practiced by him is truly the art of the impossible. He is always one ism out of step, one generation too early or too late. His Descartean obsession with first things has led him into the political wilderness and the philosophical void. He is par excellence the character in search of a role. He is, or can be, contradictory, elusive, enigmatic, equivocal, or simply confused. Yet, when contemplating what India can expect after Nehru, his far-ranging mind and fearless conscience may prove indispensable. He could still be prime minister of India.

Narayan has made a round trip from one end of the ideological spectrum to the other, and even broadened it a bit. As a student in Bihar, he began with Gandhi but soon forsook him for Marxism in its many hues. When all shades of Marxism turned gray, he returned to offer posthumous allegiance to the Mahatma. But even Gandhism seemed a pale reflection of Indian imperatives. He is now wandering somewhere beyond the normal political spectrum in a murky region where only his eye detects the nuances.

He still perceives—or thinks he perceives—the evils of Indian society as clearly as when he was an ardent young Communist. But his retreat from all political dogma has become a rout. "For the root," he says, "we will have to go to man himself." He believes that nothing can really change in India until the ordinary Indian villager is changed. The state cannot legislate the new man. In his scheme of things, the government is almost irrelevant. Individuals, he maintains, can only be redeemed from their own folly and ignorance by other, more enlightened, individuals. The apparatus of party politics and the modern state is more harmful than helpful in the remaking of man in India. For Narayan, political platforms have become the impedimenta of virtue. He spurns all parties, but his revulsion at the Left is so strong that he now finds himself closer to the political Right. Today he can even applaud the big-business conservatism of the Swatantra party and the "decent conservatives" who compose it.

Most of his shafts are now aimed at the devotees of Communism, the god that failed him, as well as at those who, like Nehru, incline to propitiate it. Narayan, the implacable revolutionary and underground terrorist has become the prisoner of committee rooms and lecture platforms, a quarry for promoters of good causes in every quarter of the globe. His causes are far-flung: "peace marchers" in Northern Rhodesia, political prisoners in Indonesia, panchayats in Nepal, police firings in Patna, nuclear tests in the Pacific, co-operatives in Uttar Pradesh, and, above all, the salvation of mankind. Some of his enthusiasms are trivial and quickly dissipated. Others, such as his resolute demands for justice in Hungary and Tibet, shook many Indians out of their complacent faith in Nehru's global omniscience long before the Chinese assault awakened the rest of the country. His proposal for arbitration of the Sino-Indian border question was the only fresh thinking done on the subject in the three years between the first major frontier clash in 1959 and the Chinese attack in 1962. But when the real blow did fall, Narayan was characteristically confounded by his own perplexities. As an ardent believer in nonviolence, he said he had been unable to reach any conclusion and had no "positive program to place before the people."

J. P., as he is widely known in India, has the serious, slightly preoccupied look of an American college professor. Half-rim spectacles contribute to the air of sobriety. His complexion is light, and he favors the white dhoti and open sandals. There is, as Vincent Sheehan says, a nobility in his appearance, voice, and manner. He has unshakable self-possession and Gandhi-like serenity. His voice is low, well-modulated, and slightly weary. He is a much more engaging person than his sometimes pontifical pronouncements would lead one to think. He is considerate, generous, and outwardly humble. His sense of the ironic is never far below the surface. Unlike some of his contemporaries in Indian politics, Narayan is a man of taste, refinement, and almost infinite patience. His Gandhian asceticism, unlike Morarji Desai's, is never mechanical and never a burden on others. For example, he prides himself on his knowledge of fruits and makes no secret of enjoying them.

Although he is a vegetarian and a diabetic, he makes no fetish of diet. He is cosmopolitan, as few Indians are, without ever having lost his unmistakable Indianness.

I spent one of the longest days of my life talking to him in Patna, capital of his native Bihar state. Not that J. P. is ever boring; it is the ordeal of sitting cross-legged on a stone floor in his airless little study for an entire day that is exhausting for a Westerner. I was met at the Patna airport by one of his secretaries in a jeep station wagon. In one quarter of that squalid provincial town is a girls' school that J. P. uses as his headquarters when he is in Patna. I walked up a flight of stone steps to the second-floor study, which is bare except for coir mats and a few cushions on the floor and a small desk and one chair in the corner. On all sides yellowing books, papers, and other mementos of his life fill glass-enclosed bookcases. The atmosphere reminded me more of a museum than of a politician's workplace. One tired ceiling fan hardly stirred the air.

The musty torpor of the place suddenly vanished when Narayan entered with his usual preoccupied air and ingratiating smile. He apologized for the lack of furniture and explained that it was his habit to sit on the floor. With professorial precision he told me how I should arrange the cushions behind my back. I asked only one question about his early career, and he began his story in a soft, almost self-deprecating voice. The refreshing thing about him (as compared with most other Indian politicians) is his avoidance of pompous clichés. He can talk for hours without being garrulous. His choice of words makes every sentence a thing of joy. He explains his actions but never tries to conceal his mistakes. He avoids the politician's penchant for self-inflation. He assumes that he does not need to make protestations of his good faith. He is not afraid to voice strong opinions, even to denounce what he regards as chicanery, but I have never detected any bitterness or spite in him. In this he is the antithesis of Krishna Menon, whom he considers a menace.

Unlike Desai, J. P. does not require a Western visitor to renounce all nourishment. He is quick to offer tea and whatever else is available. The difficulty is that not much is available in his kitchen that a Westerner is likely to find appetizing. That day in Patna I drank endless cups of tea and munched the dry Indian pastries that are his staple diet. Since that was all he ate, I was reluctant to ask for anything more. So throughout that long day I sat in his study—hot, famished, and fascinated—while he reviewed his life. I had seen him before, and was to see him many times afterward, but that day in Patna sticks in my mind. What follows is the gist of what he told me.

He was born on October 11, 1902, in the tiny village of Sitabdiara, in impoverished Bihar province. His father was a minor provincial irrigation official. The Narayans are members of the same Kayastha caste that Lal Bahadur Shastri belongs to.

Narayan was eighteen when Gandhi visited his district and urged students to boycott the local high school. His parents were furious when he left school one month before graduation. They tried to enroll him in Banaras Hindu University, but he refused because Gandhi had condemned any educational institution aided by the British. His family had no money to send him to England, but he had heard that it was possible for students from poor families to work their way through college in the United States. He sailed from Calcutta in August 1922, leaving his young wife, whom he had married while still in his teens, with his parents. By the time he reached San Francisco in October, the term had already begun at the University of California, at Berkeley. To earn money while he waited for the opening of the new term, he worked on a ranch near Yuba City. "This was the first time in my life," he told me, "that I had worked with my hands and earned something. It left a deep impression on me. This experience of working in factories and doing odd jobs at college gave me an outlook on life that nothing else could have done. Mere theoretical Gandhism or Marxism couldn't have done it. The equality of human beings and the dignity of labor became real things to me."

Before he left America, he had worked on a Sacramento grape ranch ("God, it was hot"), in a canning plant, a foundry, a Chicago stockyard ("Not killing things"), a terracotta factory, and as a salesman of hair-straightener and complexion cream in the Negro quarter of Chicago. The last job brought him the most money. Indian students were in demand for this work because they could tell the Negroes, "Look at our hair. Look at how light our complexion is." Narayan says, "This was cheating. I don't think I did the cheating part."

He went to Chicago during summer vacation from the University of Iowa, where he had transferred because the tuition was too high at Berkeley. Looking for a job in the year 1926 was an unrewarding experience, and he soon found that he had an added handicap. "We don't want Asiatics," one Chicago factory foreman told him brusquely. He got used to being told, "We don't take colored people," or "We don't want foreigners." "The rooming-house people were more diplomatic than the factory bosses," he recalls with a faint smile. "If I knocked at a house with a 'Room to Let' sign, the landlady would say she'd forgotten to take the sign down or had just let the room when she saw me." In Chicago he finally found lodging with an Indian Christian family.

Narayan is not bitter about this. "I didn't have much direct experience of race prejudice," he says. "Apart from that, I was impressed with the democratic climate in the United States. I noticed how foremen and workers addressed each other by their first names. There was no feeling of being below or inferior or anything like that."

The democratic climate was not warm enough to keep the young man from Bihar from joining a Communist study cell at the University of Wisconsin, the next stop on his academic safari. At Wisconsin he met a young graduate assistant in the German Department named Avrom Landy, who, as Narayan recalls, "gave me lots of his company." Landy began by giving him pamphlets by the Indian Communist M. N. Roy and Trotsky's writings. The group held their meetings at the home of a Russian Jewish tailor in Madison. For the benefit of the study circle, Landy even used his knowledge of German to translate works of Marx that had not yet been published in English. "I read voraciously," Narayan recalls, "and became a Leninist. Landy arranged for me to meet a

Mexican Communist, Manuel Gomez, who was in charge of the Oriental Section of the Communist party, with offices in Chicago. I also met Jay Lovestone, the American Communist. It was arranged with Gomez that I should go to Moscow and join the new Oriental University set up to train foreign students in the science of revolution."

Everything would be furnished free once Narayan reached Moscow, but he was told that he had to pay his own passage to Russia. The Soviet state was less well-heeled in those days. To earn money for the trip, Narayan left Wisconsin at the end of his first term and began knocking at Chicago factory gates. It was winter and bitterly cold. The young Indian was penniless. He lived on two meals a day of rice and sometimes pork and beans. His Indian landlord slipped him coffee. But the strain was too much. He fell ill and almost died. An Indian doctor who practiced in the Negro quarter of Chicago removed his tonsils but left the infected roots. It was three months before Narayan recovered. He was $900 in debt. He cabled his father for money. The elder Narayan was obliged to mortgage his lands. Another member of the family went in alarm to Dr. Rajendra Prasad, who was a Congress colleague of J. P.'s father-in-law, and asked him to try to dissuade Narayan from going to Moscow. The future president of India wrote a letter praising the young man's intelligence and warning him that if he went to Moscow he was not likely to be allowed back in India. Prasad said that the fight for freedom was in India, not in Russia.

"His letter carried weight with me," Narayan says now, "but I think I'd have gone to Moscow in any case if I hadn't fallen ill." The upshot was that he returned to Wisconsin and switched from engineering to a liberal-arts course on Landy's advice. When Landy was given a lectureship at Ohio State University, Narayan went with him. At Columbus, where they roomed together for a while, Narayan finally received his Bachelor of Arts degree, on August 31, 1928. Afterward he studied for his Master's degree on a graduate scholarship and was one of the few foreigners chosen at that time at Ohio State to be a graduate assistant. His thesis was on "Societal Variation." Starting from his Marxian viewpoint, he argued that change in human society is the result of improvements in the tools of production. He also produced copious hand-written notes on such subjects as Zeno's social philosophy, the French Physiocrats, property laws among the Filipinos, and the relation between interest rates and wholesale prices. He wrote gloomy verse and youthful denunciations of human bestiality, especially the sex instinct.

I have perused the comments of his professors at Ohio State written at the time. They make interesting reading. Albert P. Weiss, of the Psychology Department, predicted that Narayan would attain "an outstanding position as a social theorist." F. E. Lumley, of the Sociology Department, said that the young Indian "ranks as high as or higher than any student I've ever had." Naïvely the professor remarked, "I've not yet been able to find out, owing to his Hindu reticence and quietness, whether he has yet shaped up something in the way of a fundamental philosophy of life. He is aggressive in thought but not in action."

Narayan's experience is a frightening commentary on the ability of the Communists to capture the mind of a young, penniless, and insecure foreign student in America. As he says now, "My conception of a capitalist was of the big fat fellow with a cigar." He was intelligent and perceptive enough to rid himself of this stereotype in later years, but he is exceptional. How many other young Asians and Africans who embrace Communism in their student days in the West are able to re-create their intellectual terms of reference? Experience seems to belie the common belief that education in the United States (or another Western democracy) inevitably turns foreign students into admirers of Western institutions. Of course, things are far better for impecunious foreign students in America today, but the fact that Narayan could become a dedicated Communist while he was studying in the richest capitalist country on earth is something to be borne in mind.

What prosperity he saw in the United States, Narayan explained (with the help of Marxist-Leninist dialectics) as the result of the "open frontier" and labor scarcity, which kept wages up. But he says that he did not believe that American industrialists would follow Henry Ford's advice to pay labor enough to enable it to consume the products of machine industry. While at Columbus, he was more than just a study-hall Communist. He participated in strikes and demonstrations organized by the Communists or Leftist-dominated labor unions. He got the line by regularly devouring the *Daily Worker* and *New Masses*. He found Americans, except those at universities, unbelievably ignorant about India. When he told one woman in Chicago that he was a Hindu, she replied, "Oh, you're from Honduras." But in the universities, he found considerable sympathy for Indian freedom.

Narayan ended his seven-year sojourn in America one month before the stock-market collapse of October 1929. He sailed from New York, stopping off in England long enough to meet some British Communists and cable his father for more money; and reached home shortly before his mother's death. He was puzzled to find the Indian Communists refusing to co-operate with Congress and denouncing Gandhi's latest nonco-operation movement. "But what about Lenin's thesis on imperialism to the Second Congress of the Communist International?" Narayan inquired earnestly. The Indian Communists smiled. Stalin had issued different orders.

Narayan joined the Congress party in January 1930, because "it fitted my understanding of a Communist's duty to work sincerely in the national liberation movement." The previous month he had met Jawaharlal Nehru. They immediately felt an intellectual kinship, which has survived all disagreements. Both men wanted to see Congress move to the Left. Nehru appointed the young Bihari to be research director of the Congress Labor Department, a post for which J. P. had no particular qualifications except his work experience in America. Soon promoted to general secretary of Congress, Narayan helped organize the great civil-disobedience movement that swept India in the early 1930's. In 1932 he was arrested and sentenced to Nasik Central Prison, where he met a high-spirited, well-educated group of young north Indian Congressmen who were to join him in launching India's socialist movement. Some members of the group were, like Narayan, Marxists. Others leaned more to British Fabian socialism or a vague kind of "Gandhian socialism." Despite these differences, which were later to prove fatal to Indian socialism, the Congress Socialist party (CSP) was founded on May 17, 1934.

It was a party within a party, part of the Congress party and yet a separate political entity with its own organization and membership. "I thought if the Communists in Congress formed a group inside the party," Narayan says, "we could be more effective. Now I think this was a mistake." It was not his last.

The Indian Communist party was outlawed the same year. The Communists received instructions from the Comintern to switch to a policy of Left unity and to infiltrate Congress. The newly formed Congress Socialist party was the answer to the Communists' prayers. Narayan even spared the Indian comrades the trouble of making the first overture. In January 1936, on his recommendation, the CSP National Executive unanimously adopted a resolution to admit Communists to membership. Before the year was out, E. M. S. Namboodripad, future chief minister of the Kerala Communist ministry, and other Communists controlled CSP units throughout south India. Warnings by the National Executive proved futile. Narayan was still mesmerized by the dream of Marxist unity. By the time Britain had taken India into World War II, the Communists had captured the initiative in the Congress Socialist party and enormously increased their own membership and following.

Throughout this period Narayan sought to appease the Communists by giving them seats on the National Executive and issuing meaningless joint policy statements. The Communists paid off in flattery, hailing him as the "Indian Lenin" and "India's Revolutionary Number One." J. P.'s naïveté about the Indian Communists was matched only by his self-deception concerning the Soviet Union.

"For us who have to do things, who have a task before us," he pontificated, "it is the great principle of a new life which the Russians are so boldly practicing that alone is of value. There is no power or party in India stronger than imperialism and if we humble the latter there will be no one to challenge our will."

To those who argued that there were other roads to socialism than Stalinism, Narayan retorted: "Today more than ever before it is possible to say that there is only one type, one theory of socialism—Marxism. So far only the Communists have vindicated their theory of tactics by their great and remarkable success in Russia. Proponents of other methods are today everywhere in the trough of failure."

No one was deeper in the trough of failure at that moment than Jayaprakash Narayan. His party's vitals had already been eaten away by Communist infiltration. Co-operation was a farce. By December 1939, even J. P. realized the situation and admitted that the Communist party "stood as the sworn enemy of the Congress Socialist party and of every other progressive organization with which it had worked before." Four months later, the CSP National Executive belatedly resolved to expel all Communist members. Large chunks of what the socialists had fondly considered their party broke off and openly joined the Communist party of India (CPI). South Indian CSP units defected en masse to the Communists. As one socialist leader ruefully conceded, the CSP was "all but finished."

Narayan's awakening to Communist aims in India coincided with disenchantment with the country that called itself the Motherland of Socialism. Stalin's purges shook his faith in Soviet achievements. Exposés like Eugene Lyons's *Assignment in Utopia* and the report made on the charges against Trotsky by a committee headed by John Dewey accelerated his rethinking process. "The first breach in the Marxian citadel in my mind," he told me in typically introspective vein, "came with the realization that without democracy there could be no socialism." The breach became a chasm when the Indian Communists obediently dropped all talk of Indian freedom and demanded that the country join the Allied war effort after Russia was attacked in June 1941. Narayan denounced the Communists for playing the imperialist game. He had earlier split with the Congress party when it voted to restrict its followers to nonviolent civil disobedience. He demanded a complete boycott of the government until the British left India. He was arrested and sent to Hazaribagh prison, in a remote part of Bihar.

From there, on the night of November 8, 1942, Narayan and five fellow inmates made what should rank as a historic jail break. Months of preparation went into the effort. They chose a moonlit night during the traditional Diwali celebrations, the most popular Hindu folk festival, when the prison's Hindu warders were off duty and other prisoners and Moslem warders were enjoying a special Diwali feast. At 10:00 P.M., while an inmate accomplice regaled everyone with funny stories, Narayan and his companions scaled a twenty-two-foot wall with the help of a rope made of dhotis. In their haste they forgot to take a package containing money, extra clothing, and shoes. For three days and nights they wandered through dense forest. It was cold. They used their dhoti rope to protect bleeding and swollen feet. With a four-anna piece (equivalent to about six cents) that one of the men found in his clothing, they bought a handful of *chiuda* (parboiled, pounded rice) and some salt and red pepper from the tribal people in the area. But they were afraid to ask directions for fear of giving themselves away. So the little group stumbled on, occasionally dropping in exhaustion under a tree, but fearful of tarrying too long.

On the third day they found a village where friends of a local Congressman then in prison gave them cooked food, old clothes, and—most welcome of all—some old shoes. Narayan had grown a beard. The British were offering a reward of 10,000 rupees (about $2,000) for his capture dead or alive, and 5,000 rupees for each of the others. "Our biggest problem," Narayan recalls, "was the inquisitiveness of the villagers we met as we walked through the back country. Whenever we stopped to draw water from a well, they'd ply us with questions about our caste and subcaste. We finally got fed up answering their questions, but usually we met uneducated people who didn't suspect anything." They were loath to spend nights in the villages, where they could be more easily detected. When they did stop at a tiny country store to buy food and spend the night on the floor, they sensed from the proprietor's questions and his anxious looks that he suspected they were robbers or murderers. The night passed anxiously. Long before dawn the fugitives stole out of the store and disappeared into the forest.

The father-in-law of one of the group was a zamindar, or landlord, who owned a village in the district. Half a mile outside the village, the fugitives halted and sent a small boy to tell the zamindar's *gumashta*, or revenue clerk, that his master's son-in-law had arrived with some friends. The landlord himself lived several miles away. The *gumashta* was incredulous. "If they are there," he grumbled, "let them come into the village." Finally he was persuaded to come out, but his doubts persisted because he had never seen his master's son-in-law. The desperate men were not to be put off. The clerk at length escorted them to his *kucheri*, or village administrative office, and prepared some food for them—"very poor food," Narayan recalls, "because he still suspected we were impostors." But after the clerk reported to the zamindar, he returned a changed man. "The food also changed for the better," Narayan says. "The clerk had orders to keep our presence dark. He thought we had committed some crime."

Three days later the hunted men were on their way again, moving on foot, concealed behind gunny bags in a bullock cart, and feigning illness, to avoid prying questions, on third-class railway coaches. In passing near one town where British and American forces were based, the driver of their hired bullock cart was closely questioned, but he answered blandly that he was taking a load of grain to market. The fugitives had separated into two groups by this time to minimize chances of detection. Narayan's objective was Banaras Hindu University, where he had friends. The first one he approached —a chemistry professor *—had trouble recognizing the bearded rustic who knocked at his door. Then, obviously fearful, he stammered something about having guests who would be suspicious if Narayan holed up in the house. Narayan finally found refuge with another university teacher in Banaras. He

---

* It is characteristic of J. P. that when he mentioned the professor during our talk he asked me not to use his name "because he behaved rather badly."

got in touch with underground headquarters in Bombay, where Mrs. Aruna Asaf Ali, who later joined the Communist party, was working. The underground sent him money and instructions on where to go.

When he arrived secretly in Delhi, he wrote the first of his famous "Letters to Fighters for Freedom." One of them was an appeal to American servicemen stationed in India not to co-operate with the British, "who are waging a fascist war against us." He asked them to consider him a fugitive prisoner of war. "Whoever among you may become a prisoner of war will consider it his duty," he wrote, "to escape from the enemy's prison as soon as he has an opportunity. . . . I want to dedicate myself at the altar of the liberation of our country." The document was covertly distributed in American barracks. One can imagine the puzzled interest it excited among readers who had never heard of Jayaprakash Narayan.

Narayan was assigned to set up a terrorist headquarters and training center for saboteurs in neighboring Nepal. The underground Azad Dasta, or Freedom Brigade, was made up of ten-man sabotage squads. Most of its recruits were deserters from the Indian Army. Nepal's Rana regime winked at Narayan's activities until he set up a clandestine broadcasting apparatus that enraged the British. Under tremendous British pressure, the Nepalese finally sent armed police to surround the underground headquarters and arrest Narayan and six others, including Dr. Ram Manohar Lohia, who now leads the splinter Socialist party of India. As they were being conveyed to the Indo-Nepalese border, Narayan managed to slip a message to an Azad Dasta volunteer whose identity was still unknown to the Nepalese. Four nights later, while the prisoners were waiting at a Nepalese frontier post for British authorities to take charge of them, they were awakened by rifle fire. A haystack in an adjacent field was set afire. The Nepalese guards rushed toward the flames, only to find themselves under a hail of bullets from thirty Azad Dasta attackers. A stray bullet struck a gong in the guardhouse where the prisoners were lodged. Narayan leaped to his feet and made a break for it. He was followed by the others, including Lohia, who kept objecting that no one seemed to care about his safety. "It's every man for himself," Narayan snapped. The fugitives and their liberators fled together through the night. Before dawn they had crossed into Indian territory. Afraid to ride the trains, they asked a village boatman to ferry them across the Ganges. The boatman agreed but said he could not leave until his mother pounded some rice for him to eat en route. "We'll buy you food," Narayan implored. But the boatman was obdurate. From the looks they were getting, Narayan realized that the villagers thought his group was a gang of thieves. Slowly the fugitives began walking along a railway embankment, hoping to slip away without attracting further notice. But when they looked back, they saw they were being followed by seven or eight villagers armed with lathis. Then their pursuers started running after them. Suraj Narayan Singh, now general secretary of the Praja Socialist party in Bihar, whirled and trained his revolver on the villagers. He shouted, "Look, we are fighting for the freedom of our country. Is this the way for you to act? If you don't turn back, I'll shoot as many of you as possible." The villagers turned back.

In September 1943, as famine swept Bengal and India came increasingly to resemble an armed camp, the underground high command decided that Narayan should go to Kashmir to rouse the chronically rebellious Pathan tribesmen against the British. Narayan had escaped detection so long that he had grown careless. He had shaved his beard, taken to wearing European clothes, and adopted a Punjabi pseudonym— Mehta. On September 16 India's most wanted underground leader boarded a sleeper train at Delhi for the long journey to Rawalpindi, on the northwest frontier. He was mildly surprised to find his pseudonym on a reservation slip on the compartment door, together with the name of a "Major Khan and family." Underground chiefs are not in the habit of booking reservations, even under their pseudonyms. He was even more surprised when no one appeared to share his compartment. When the train stopped at a wayside station, he got out and walked on the platform with his hat pulled low. "There was a man on the platform whose eyes seemed to burn into me," he recalls. "I should have broken the trip then, but I dismissed the strange feeling and got back on the train." As the train pulled into Amritsar early the next morning, Narayan rolled up his bedding on the upper berth and opened the compartment door to ask for tea. "In those days," he told me with typical Indian irrelevance, "the tea service on the trains was much better than now." He was surprised to find three men, including an Englishman, standing outside. He closed the door and started getting dressed. A few moments later there was a sharp knock.

"Come in. I'm alone," Narayan said courteously, thinking the strangers were looking for berths. At this point the Englishman asked to see his ticket.

"Are you a railway official?" he asked.

"No," the Englishman replied, "but I'd like to see your ticket." He scrutinized it for a moment, then asked, "Are you Jayaprakash Narayan?"

"I don't know what you're talking about," Narayan lied. "I'm Mehraj Mehta."

"All right," the Englishman said. "I don't believe that. We'll search your things." Then his eye lighted on the rolled bedding in the upper berth. "Where is the second man?" he inquired.

"I'm alone, as I told you," Narayan answered.

"Look here," the Englishman exploded. "This is not Nepal. This is the Punjab. I have orders to shoot. If there's the slightest suspicious move, I'll fire. Now you get dressed."

Narayan, still in his pajamas, realized the game was up. Outside Lahore he was taken off the train in handcuffs. The Englishman, who was Lahore's senior superintendent of police, kept warning him against trying to escape. As they drove into the grim Lahore Fort, he told Narayan, "We have 1,600 armed police around here. This is not Nepal. Don't try anything." For the first month, Narayan was never allowed outside his cell in solitary confinement. He was permitted no newspapers or books. Food was shoved under an iron bar into his cell by guards who had orders not to speak to him. A month after his arrest, teams of three or four police inspectors began interrogating him from early morning until late at night. He was allowed back into his cell only to use the latrine.

The police told him they had arrested Mrs. Ali, Dr. Lohia, and other underground leaders. They pretended to read from written confessions, which sounded genuine because the police had usually been just forty-eight hours behind him after his escape from Hazaribagh jail. One set of inquisitors adopted the "soft sell." They told Narayan that he was the most important man in India after Gandhi and Nehru. They begged him to co-operate by giving them the names of other members of the underground. They even said that they would lose their jobs and their families would go hungry if they failed to persuade him to make a statement. The other team was abusive and menacing. They handcuffed him to a chair and slapped him on the face to prevent him from falling asleep. They threatened to take him to the basement dungeon and resort to the long neem tree twigs that Hindus use to clean their teeth. Their words were punctuated by screams from other parts of the fort. "I don't know if these screams were genuine or staged for my benefit," Narayan remarked to me offhandedly.

The last ten days of the ordeal were the worst. He was allowed no sleep at all. After all-day questioning, he would be told at 9:00 P.M., "That's all for today. You can return to your cell and have a good rest." But just as he was sinking into an exhausted sleep, another team of interrogators would enter his cell and take him out for all-night questioning. He ate practically nothing during this time. "My head buzzed like a beehive," he says. For a week he was locked in a foul little cell in the basement dungeon. "But I think they would have had to put me through much more to make me talk," he says stoutly. "In any case, there really wasn't much to tell. People imagine this underground business is very sinister and important. The fact is, you spend most of your time just trying to save your own skin."

Suddenly the nonstop interrogation ended. By this time stories were circulating all over India that Jayaprakash Narayan, the lion of the underground, was being brutally tortured in Lahore Fort. A Bombay attorney who tried to obtain a writ of habeas corpus for him in Lahore was unlawfully arrested. A storm broke over the Punjab government. Three police officers who were responsible for arresting the lawyer were later censured severely by a Lahore court. The Punjab Home Secretary visited Narayan in prison to ask if he had "any complaints." "Yes, I do have a few," the prisoner replied with a trace of a smile. "I'll put them in writing if you give me paper and pen." Thereafter he was allowed to cook his own food and take exercise in the prison courtyard. He was produced in court sixteen months after his arrest. He had spent the entire period in solitary confinement and had been questioned fifty days and nights. As a result of his petition to the High Court, he was transferred to Agra Central Prison, where conditions were much better. "Even in those days," he recalls, "the Punjab police had a reputation for brutality."

But he found the best of prisons galling. The day he learned that Paris had been liberated by the Allies, he wrote a moving account of his feelings. "It was a great day for Europe when Paris was liberated. But Europe is far away and beyond my world. A sealed-off, walled-off, barred and bolted, 15 by 12 bit of space—that is my world, set in a cosmos of similar planets. A cosmos that is not of God's but man's creation. When I hear the howls [of prisoners] I find myself turning into a brute. Raging, tearing, brutal vengeance wells up within my being. I fight hard to keep my humanity. It is difficult, very difficult. And I am not sure I quite succeed."

The only action Narayan could observe in his little world was the love life of Churchill, the prison tomcat.

His political comments were bitter. On August 4, 1944, he wrote: "The Atlantic Charter has shrunk to the dimensions of the English Channel. The liquidation of empires and imperialist policies cannot come from the top, that is, on the volition of the imperialist powers which, one should remember, include the USA, which has a not inconsiderable economic empire in Central and South America. China's regeneration, if it is allowed full scope after the war, will be the second [after India] powerful nail driven into the coffin of world empires. As for the UN, it is a tremendous hoax. The postwar world is going to be dominated by Anglo-America and the UN will be only the bandboys."

Despite his bitterness against the Western powers, Narayan had little use for Stalin and Stalinist methods. He was contemptuous of Soviet apologists in the west. But as late as November 1944, he could still speak of "my lingering faith in Stalin's socialism," but complained that "the head of a professedly socialist state talks like the imperialist and capitalist rulers of the world."

At this time Narayan denigrated the village-based economy he now advocates. "Village self-sufficiency," he wrote from his cell on April 19, 1944, "had been the basis of Indian society in the past. Its political result was the civic and political isolation of the village. . . . In free India the state will have consciously to endeavor to break up the remaining self-sufficiency and isolation of the villages and make them coherent economic units in a united and interdependent national economy."

Narayan was finally released on April 12, 1946, long after most other Indian freedom fighters had been set free. He plunged back into the freedom movement and was again chosen to serve on the Congress Working Committee, for which Nehru had first nominated him in 1936. He resolved, as one American student observes, "to eschew doctrinaire political thinking in favor of pragmatic and empirical analyses of India's problems as a necessary first step in evolving a new 'democratic socialism' related to Indian realities." But, as before, realities proved less congenial than theorizing on the nature of man and society.

The socialists in Congress were more divided than ever. They rejected an offer of seats in the Constituent Assembly called to write India's future constitution. Less than seven months before Britain gave India its freedom, Narayan was writing in the socialist newspaper organ: "The soothing talk that the British have made up their minds to quit is calculated merely to deceive the people and quieten their fears that, instead of eliminating obstacles in our path, we might compromise with them and thus jeopardize freedom and democracy. In the fire of revolution alone can be burnt down the edifice of imperialism together with the supporting edifices of feudalism and communalism. We have to exert the utmost pressure on Congress from within in order to persuade or compel it to accept a revolutionary course of action."

The fires of revolution were to be lighted by some 10,000 armed guerrillas said to have been maintained by the socialist underground. Narayan continued to function within Congress because he believed the socialists could eventually capture the party. He was encouraged in this delusion by Nehru's radicalism and Gandhi's shrewd tactic of promoting socialist leaders to positions beyond the strength of their support. In 1947 Gandhi proposed Narayan for the presidency of the Congress party, probably expecting that the office would moderate or discredit the socialist firebrand once and for all. Gandhi's plan was thwarted by the party's increasingly powerful Right Wing, led by Sardar Patel. On January 30, 1948, Gandhi was assassinated in New Delhi and the road was open for the Rightists to drive the Congress socialists into the political wilderness. The Patel group pushed through a resolution outlawing political parties within Congress. In 1948 Narayan led a battered band of followers out of Congress. A number of his former cohorts in the underground had already joined the Communists. Many moderate socialists opted to remain in Congress. The knell had sounded for the independent Indian socialist movement.

Narayan did not hear it. He still dreamed of militant mass struggle against social and economic injustice. He foresaw an aging and increasingly reactionary Congress on one side and a discredited Communist party on the other being swept aside by the swelling tide of "democratic socialism." In the aftermath of Gandhi's death, he reread the Mahatma's works. He no longer dismissed him as a "bourgeois reformist" mired in "a bog of timid economic analysis, good intentions, and ineffective moralizing." The problem of means and ends troubled him, and Gandhi had much to say on this score. When hardcore socialists accused him of trying to escape from political reality by talking about spiritual regeneration, Narayan replied: "I have no knowledge of matters spiritual if the term is understood in a religious or metaphysical sense. I have not suddenly come to acquire faith in something called the spirit or the soul or Brahman. Such philosophy as I have is earthly and human."

By mid-1950 Narayan had begun doubting even socialism. Where socialist parties had come to power in Western Europe, they had failed to transform society. Stalinist Russia was a growing nightmare. The ills of society seemed to dwarf and defy the power of any regime. Like Banquo's ghost, the specter of totalitarianism kept returning to haunt Narayan. He lashed out angrily at those who dubbed him a "reformist," accusing them of still living in the age "when one contrasted the failures of European social democracy with the brilliant successes of Lenin." He told his detractors: "But years have rolled by since then, years of poignant and tragic history, of lost dreams and of the very God that failed. . . . The new enthusiast . . . assumes that the theories will inevitably lead to the values; so, when the theories become a state religion he assumes that the values have been realized and socialism established on earth. The phenomenon is common in the history of religions."

So also was the phenomenon of one man's progressive disillusionment. The 1951 Indian elections relegated the socialists to third place, behind Congress and the Communists. The socialists sought to bolster their position by merging with a small party formed by disgruntled Gandhian ex-Congressmen. The result was the Praja (People's) Socialist party (PSP), which still exists. But at the very moment he was embracing his new Gandhian colleagues, Narayan felt compelled to say, "One does not know whether there is anything like an integrated Gandhian philosophy." He acknowledged that history had "falsified" his stand on the necessity of violence for obtaining India's independence. Trying to escape from the "amoralism" of Soviet Communism, he began championing the Yugoslav brand. In January 1953 he told an Asian socialist conference in Rangoon that the Yugoslav Communists were "anxious to bring to an end as speedily as possible this one-party rule. The Yugoslav Communist party has decided it is for the people themselves to rule over themselves." Eighteen months later he was still convinced that the Yugoslav comrades were "the one and only Left party which has analyzed this new disease [Soviet totalitarianism] and is trying to find out how this new monster is developing further." But continued one-party rule and periodic reversions to the "hard line" in Yugoslavia have cooled J. P.'s ardor for the gospel according to Belgrade.

The turning point in his postwar thinking came in 1952 when he met the aged and venerable Acharya Vinoba Bhave, a Gandhi disciple then in the second year of his Bhoodan (land gift) movement. "He impressed me as a person in dead earnest," Narayan told me of their first meeting in the Uttar Pradesh hinterland of north-central India. "He really wanted to go to the root of the question. It wasn't a question of just collecting a little land to blunt the land hunger of the revolution. His program was really socialistic."

Bhave had conceived the idea of Bhoodan on April 18, 1951, during a visit to the strife-torn Telangana region of Hyderabad, in south India. The Indian Communists were then using Mao Tse-tung's guerrilla tactics to establish a Red pocket in the area, from which they hoped to expand until all India was communized by force. They had armed and organized the peasants for systematic attacks on the landlords in Telangana. When Bhave arrived at the village of Pochampalli, he was approached by a deputation of untouchable families who lamented their poverty and landlessness. The old man asked them how much land they would need to be self-supporting. One untouchable blurted, "One hundred acres," but the others said they could make do with eighty. Bhave turned to the wealthier peasants and said, "There must be among you someone who can fulfill this request." One local landlord stood up to announce that he would give the untouchables one hundred acres. Bhave interpreted this episode as divine guidance to devote the rest of his life to soliciting voluntary donations of land to alleviate the plight of India's huge landless rural population. He collected more than 12,000 acres in Telangana. From September to November 1951, Bhave was given almost 20,000 acres as he trudged from Telangana to Delhi. His movement, like so many other evangelistic efforts, caught the country's imagination—for a time. During an eight-month stretch in Uttar Pradesh, Bhave met Narayan. There is no record of their talk, but Narayan says that he asked Bhave if he should resign from leadership of the PSP. The Acharya advised him not to take the step then. Two years later—on April 19, 1954—Narayan announced dramatically that he was quitting "party and power politics" to dedicate his life to the Bhoodan movement.

Despite the best efforts of Bhave and Narayan, Bhoodan has not fulfilled its early promise. The goal of fifty million acres in five years—enough to give five acres to every family of landless agricultural laborers—is far from attainment. In fact, after 1951, only about five million acres had been collected in a decade of dedicated effort by an army of *sarvodaya* workers. The *sarvodaya* (literally, uplift of all) ideal was championed by Gandhi and promoted by a loosely organized movement of his followers, including Bhave, after the Mahatma's death. One American study describes the *sarvodaya* objective as "an ideal social order based upon nonviolence and envisaged in terms of harmonious, casteless, classless society with equal opportunity for all." When *sarvodaya* is achieved, society will also be stateless. Bhave conceived of Bhoodan as the perfect instrument for attaining this blissful order of things.

As Bhoodan lost momentum, Bhave launched other *dan* (gift) movements: Sampattidan (gift of wealth), Gramdan (gift of entire villages), and Shramdan (gift of labor). "I tell people," Narayan says, "'If you don't like Bhoodan, try Gramdan.'" The movement comes in all flavors.

Under Bhoodan, as originally conceived by Bhave, the landless were supposed to decide by unanimous agreement or by drawing lots who would get donated land. Under Gramdan, all land is given to the village community. From 5 to 10 per cent is set aside as common land to be cultivated free of charge by the villagers. The produce of this land goes to the village store for common purposes in accordance with the decisions of the village panchayat. The rest of the land is redistributed on the basis of the villagers' "needs" and the size of their families. Thus, a family of ten, regardless of its ability to make improvements or work the land productively, would receive twice as much as a family of five. Cultivators in Gramdan villages are prohibited from selling or mortgaging the land they till. In the light of the Indian peasant's passionate attachment to his land, it is not surprising that many of the more than 5,500 villages that originally adopted Gramdan have now reverted to the old system. In many places the villagers were swept up in the revivalist atmosphere of the Bhoodan-Gramdan movement without having any clear idea of what they were getting into. Mrs. Kusum Nair, the able Indian sociologist and writer, reports that many of the Gramdan villagers are primitive tribal people who joined the scheme simply because they were told their debts would be canceled.

Distribution of Bhoodan land has been even more haphazard than its collection. Fewer than one million acres of the five million deeded to Bhave had been given away to landless laborers by the end of 1961. The rest was lying fallow or had reverted to the former owners. In most cases, donated land is of such poor quality that it is only marginally productive when farmed as part of a larger holding. Bhave has now implicitly acknowledged Bhoodan's disarray by appealing to landlords to make collective, rather than individual, land donations and to distribute their largesse themselves among the landless of their choice. I doubt if such patent buck-passing will appeal to landlords.

With the fervor he once reserved for Communism, Narayan told Nehru in 1953, "Bhoodan is the seed of love that is to grow into the tree of world peace. Even Vinoba is merely the instrument of the Time-spirit." But the Time-spirit seems to have misused its instrument. As Narayan admitted to me, "Bhoodan is now in a state of stalemate. We've not been able to break that." He now feels that Bhoodan is "too cut and dried." Instead of propagating Bhoodan, or any of its sister movements, he believes that the 35,000 full- and part-time *sarvodaya* workers "should go to the people and try to find out what's troubling them, what their grievances are. We should never act as brokers between the people and the state."

All during that day in Patna, as we sat cross-legged on the floor, Narayan had talked with almost clinical detachment about his most poignant experiences. But when he began

Mrs. Indira Gandhi with the Dalai Lama at the Prime Minister's house in New Delhi

Central Newsphoto Service, New Delhi

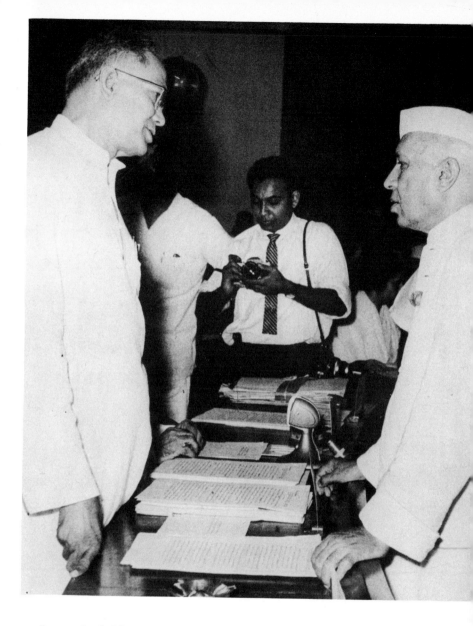

Jayaprakash Narayan with Prime Minister Nehru at the National Integration Conference in New Delhi, October 1961
Press Information Bureau, Government of India

At left, Mrs. Indira Gandhi with her father, Prime Minister Jawaharlal Nehru
Central Newsphoto Service, New Delhi

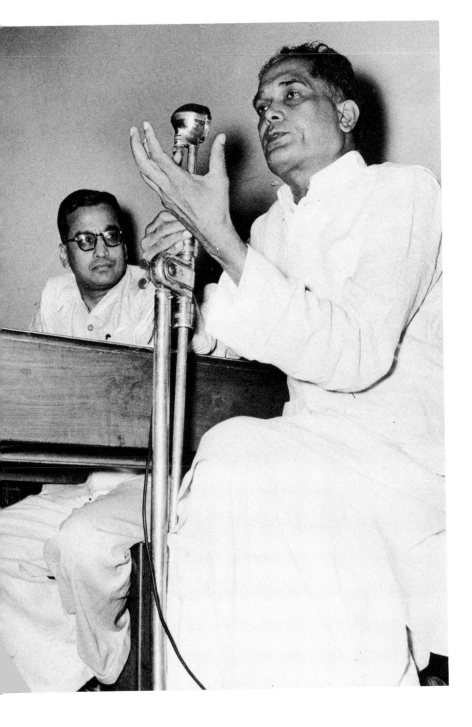

Minister of Food and Agriculture S. K. Patil addressing a meeting of traders in Delhi
Central Newsphoto Service, New Delhi

At left, Jayaprakash Narayan addressing a meeting at Delhi University
Central Newsphoto Service, New Delhi

S. K. Patil with Secretary of State Dean Rusk in Washington,
June 1961
Press Information Bureau, Government of India

At right, General B. M. Kaul with Krishna Menon and Prime
Minister Nehru at Ambala, 1958

General K. S. Thimayya and General B. M. Kaul (third from left) watching Krishna Menon laying the foundation stone of the Defence Pavilion in New Delhi, August 1958

Armed Forces Information Office, New Delhi

speaking about the plight of the Indian villager, his usually
serene face clouded with a kind of suppressed anguish. For
the first time he seemed troubled. His expressive gestures became more emphatic. He remarked that Indians are "basically
no different" from Germans, Japanese, or Chinese. "But a long
period of foreign rule has atrophied them completely," he
said. "They are in the position of a fractured limb that's just
been taken out of a plaster cast." As he made this comparison,
he gripped his right forearm and moved it slowly back and
forth as if he were trying to rehabilitate India's wasted rural
limb. Then, switching metaphors, he said that India's
peasantry is a "sleeping Leviathan" whose immense potential
strength is nullified by "despair, hopelessness, and a peculiar
kind of lifelessness." The giant can never be aroused by
pinpricks from Delhi or the state capitals. Subordinate officials,
such as the government's so-called village-level workers, are
"largely corrupt," according to Narayan. They resent outsiders like the *sarvodaya* workers entering the villages, "because we may prevent them from getting something out of the
people." Narayan was still physically present in the stifling
little study, but I could see that his mind was now somewhere in that bottomless cavern of misery called the Indian
countryside. He was grappling with what is for him the
supreme problem of India today. "On the other hand," he
went on, "the villagers automatically distrust any official or
middle-class person. Then there is the caste system. It maintains a veritable devil's workshop of idleness because it ordains that certain castes may not perform any honest manual
labor."

Narayan fell silent at this point and stared somberly into
space. I wanted to ask more questions, but to break the silence
just then seemed almost blasphemous. I don't know how long
we sat there without uttering a word. It was a lizard that
finally brought Narayan out of his reverie. "Open the bookcase immediately," he ordered his secretary in a tone of command I had not heard before. "I wonder how long the poor
thing has been in there." The secretary, a rather flustered
young man, hastily unlocked the glass door of the bookcase
where a small lizard had just appeared. Such animals are com-

mon in any house in India, and are usually welcomed because
they keep down the insect population, especially during the
monsoon. Lizards, being intelligent, rarely get trapped, and
the one in the bookcase struck me as being well fed and
healthy. But Narayan was concerned. "Leave the bookcase
open," he said. "Be sure she doesn't get caught in there again."

What is it about India that makes the once iron-willed
revolutionary start with horror at the sight of a lizard behind
a bookcase door? I sometimes feel that Indians care more
about animals than about other humans. But this is not true
of Narayan; he cares about everything, which is one of his
difficulties.

Turning back to me after a last anxious look at the lizard,
he reverted to the subject of caste as if nothing had interrupted him. "Appeals to caste were very open and widespread
in the last election," he said. "Caste is the most persuasive
platform."

The setback to Bhoodan has turned his restless mind to
other outlets. As president of the All-India Panchayat parishad
and the Association of Voluntary Agencies for Rural Development (AVARD), he now advocates drastic constitutional reforms that would abolish India's parliamentary system and
replace it by a multitiered arrangement based on village
panchayats. He argues that the present "inorganic" system,
based on individual voters and political parties, inevitably
causes power to be concentrated at the top. Local organs of
administration wither and centralized bureaucracy pro-
liferates. He insists that political parties should be excluded
from panchayat elections at village and district levels. How
this is to be accomplished he has never convincingly explained.
He says that there is no "collective will" in the caste-ridden
Indian village today. In this situation, elections on party
lines simply embitter caste and factional antagonisms.

"Party quarrels over socialism, the public sector, and foreign
policy have no relevance to village problems," he says. "The
village is concerned with growing more wheat, building a new
school, or digging a drainage ditch. These are not things on
which the parties differ."

Narayan wants candidates for Parliament and state legislatures to be chosen by an electoral college composed of two delegates from each village assembly in the constituency. Then each village assembly would vote on these candidates. This system is akin to Pakistan's indirect elections under "basic democracies."

Narayan's insistence on sweeping constitutional changes was one reason for the breakdown of his talks with Nehru in 1953 for a PSP-Congress alliance. Nehru had taken the initiative in proposing co-operation at all levels between the two parties. As usual, Narayan overbid. He presented a sweeping "minimum program" calling for constitutional amendments, nationalization of banking and key industries, and other drastic measures that would have driven the Congress Right Wing into open revolt. Nehru backed off. He suggested that they drop the idea of "formal" co-operation.

Narayan believes political decentralization requires economic decentralization. He now advocates "agro-industrial" communities that would be largely self-sufficient. They would process wheat, rice, fruit, and vegetables, as well as cotton or sugar cane. He also envisions their manufacturing such consumer goods as radios, bicycle parts, and sewing mechines. Economic activity in the village would be on the owner-worker or co-operative pattern. Such a "small-machine, labor-intensive" rural economy would, in his judgment, be neither "bureaucracy-ridden nor exploitative." He urges villagers to offer *gram-samkalpa*—a resolution to make their villages self-sufficient as soon as possible in clothing and other necessities that they can produce for themselves. At the same time the villagers would pledge to use only goods made in their village or neighboring villages. Narayan's reversion to Gandhian nostalgia for village industry is of a piece with his new-found regard for ancient Hindu Ayur-Vedic medicine.

Another cause that he now espouses is the Shanti Sena (Peace Brigade). It is affiliated with the World Peace Brigade, of which he is cochairman with the Reverend Michael Scott. The Shanti Sena is mainly employed to counteract Hindu-Moslem tension. In the spring of 1962 Narayan expanded the brigade by relaxing regulations that virtually restricted membership to full-time *sarvodaya* workers. His aim is to have brigade members in every major Indian city in sufficient numbers to intervene when communal tensions threaten to erupt in conflict. The Shanti Sena would be a kind of internal-security auxiliary force. He has also taken an increasing interest in the World Peace Brigade. In May 1962 he attended a rally in Tanganyika where the brigade debated sending volunteers on a nonviolent march into Northern Rhodesia to offer *satyagraha* (force of truth) against racial discrimination. Happily, the idea was dropped.

The pursuit of the quixotic has not made Narayan a narrow-minded zealot. He may sometimes sit cross-legged on coir mats, but he is equally at home in London drawing rooms and New York lecture halls. He has a broader knowledge of the outside world than any other Indian leader except Nehru, and possibly Krishna Menon. Many causes are inscribed on his banner today, but he has given up his long search for solutions. I remember the look of weariness and resignation on his face as he remarked one night at dinner in Delhi, "Now I only try to do what's right. The rest must take care of itself." It would have sounded pompous coming from anyone else. He was not trying to dramatize himself. We were dining at the home of Indian friends who were distressed to see him in low spirits. Sensing their concern, he tried to turn the conversation to lighter subjects. He joked about his fondness for melon and urged all of us to eat more, although he himself ate almost nothing. But whenever the flickering candlelight caught his face in repose, I realized that the old revolutionary is a sorely chastened man. His pursuit of "what is right" means doing whatever appears useful without calculating the chances of ultimate success. His approach is now to projects and programs, rather than to ultimate truths and all-embracing doctrines. But his addiction to sweeping and often contradictory judgments persists. I remember one speech in which he talked about giving the rich an opportunity to "correct" themselves because "We all know that wealth cannot be amassed except by exploitation." But in almost the same breath he can proclaim, "A decent conservative is a decent person because he provides the ballast in the ship of state and prevents it from being blown over in a storm."

Today Narayan falls midway between Nehru and Gandhi. Like Nehru, he is still a romantic socialist and a rational humanist. But unlike Nehru, he lacks political acumen and ability to manipulate men. Like Gandhi after the Mahatma retired from the Congress party in 1934, Narayan continues to exercise wide influence without formal responsibility. Gandhi always tailored his ideas to Indian realities. Narayan has often landed in the void. With a convert's zeal, he has embraced nonviolence and the Gandhian dictum that social progress is impossible without individual moral regeneration through *sarvodaya*. But he has never equalled Gandhi's uncanny understanding of the Indian mind, nor his luminous spirituality.

J. P.'s present role is almost as hard to define as his views. Nehru accuses him of "playing hide-and-seek between the pillars of politics and Bhoodan." India's Communist and fellow-traveling press labels him a Western stooge. *Blitz* accuses "Bhoodani-Jeevandani * Narayan" of conspiring with reactionaries and "fossilized Gandhians" against Indian socialism and the country's nonalignment policy.

Despite his announced retirement from "party and power politics," Narayan says, "I am engaged in politics from head to foot, trying all the time to change its entire complexion. The type of politics I am engaged in is different from the politics which aims at securing power for the fulfillment of narrow partisan or personal ends. I am engaged in a deeper and wider kind of politics."

He admits, however, that he would return to the crasser sort of politics to "answer the call of duty in an emergency." He is available for a draft. "One can't go around asking for Bhoodan in a crisis," he told me matter-of-factly, adding, "At present I wouldn't say there is a crisis. But there is lots of talk in Delhi about a military coup as Nehru shows signs of failing." Narayan now wants the PSP to merge with Congress to bolster the ruling party's weak "socialist core." This is necessary, he says, to save Congress from reactionary communal forces on the Right and infiltrating Communists on

* From Jeevandan, dedication of one's life to a cause.

the Left. "But if I join Congress now amid all this succession talk," he says, "they'll say I've become a contender for the premiership. They'll say I stayed out until I saw that Nehru was failing and then jumped back in." And so they would.

In April 1962, when Nehru was seriously ill for the first time in twenty-six years, Narayan publicly expressed the view that the Prime Minister should have retired from office and "taken up the leadership of the people, like Gandhiji." The succession could then have been settled while Nehru was still vigorous. If Nehru is physically unable to lead the country when the 1967 elections are held, Narayan fears that "violent forces" may extinguish Indian democracy. Most Indians who give his views any thought resent this suggestion. They prefer to rest in the shade of the Nehru banyan. J. P. had helped, however, to shake the comfortable Indian myth that Nehru is immortal.

Nowhere has Narayan's myth-shattering been more valuable than in the realm of Indian foreign policy. In a scathing speech in Bombay on November 11, 1956, he denounced the Nehru government's "perverse and false" view of the Hungarian uprising. The audience in the hall sat spellbound. Commenting on Krishna Menon's attempt to depict the slaughter in Budapest as Hungary's "domestic affair," Narayan said, "As an Indian I hang my head in shame that a spokesman of my country should have gone so far in cynical disregard of truth and the fundamental principles of freedom and peace that are said to guide our international conduct." He pointed out that India's vote in the U.N. General Assembly against the second resolution on Hungary (with only the Soviet bloc and Yugoslavia) was the logical consequence of Nehru's speech to the All-India Congress Committee a few days before, in which he largely parroted the Soviet line on Hungary. With something of his old polemic zest, Narayan exploded, "It took him [Nehru] two weeks to make up his mind about an event the significance of which should be clear to any person acquainted even slightly with the situation in Eastern Europe. . . . It is too sad for words. To apply one set of rules to Egypt and another to Hungary is to make use of a double standard which, to say the least, is unworthy of this country. The sooner we renounce this double standard the better for India's honor, for the peace of the world, and for good will among nations."

Narayan's "double standard" speech echoed throughout India. He had given pointed expression to the educated Indian public's dissatisfaction with Nehru's equivocations on Hungary. His was the voice of the loyal opposition. There could be no higher tribute to his success in this role than Nehru's long-winded attempts to justify India's original stand on Hungary even as he modified it to conform more closely to the facts. The Prime Minister had grossly underestimated his own public.

The Tibetan revolt of March 1959 produced a similar situation. Nehru sought to minimize the struggle as merely "a conflict of wills." As the Chinese systematically crushed Tibetan resistance, he quibbled over the question of China's "suzerainty" or "sovereignty" in Tibet and finally concluded that there was no real difference between the two terms. In either case, he said, Tibet was China's affair.

Narayan led the outburst of protest. He rejected the "moth-eaten imperialistic formula" by which Nehru sought to portray Tibet as a purely Chinese concern and asked: "Overseas empires are perhaps easy to spot, but why should it be so difficult to discern the reality behind the land empires whose contiguous territories create the illusion of a single nationhood?"

He cited the historical record. China, he said, had not exercised suzerainty, sovereignty, or any other form of control over Tibet at any time from 1912 to 1950, when Chinese Communist forces invaded the country and compelled the Dalai Lama to accept the so-called Seventeen-Point Agreement. At this time India told the U.N. General Assembly that Chinese troops had halted some 300 miles from Lhasa and that the Indian Government was "certain that the Tibetan question would be settled by peaceful means." After Peking broke its pledge to respect Tibet's autonomy, the Dalai Lama's government repudiated the Seventeen-Point Agreement on March 11, 1959, thereby provoking a full-scale Chinese assault. India maintains a consul general in Lhasa and trade representatives at several other places in Tibet. No other country except

China itself has comparable access to information about Tibet. But Nehru complained constantly that he was in the dark about what was happening to India's northern neighbor and could, therefore, never express a clear judgment. Narayan called the Prime Minister one of "the worldly-wise, who, by their lack of courage and faith, block the progress of the human race, not towards the moon but towards humanity itself. These persons have a myopic view and forget that nothing stands, or can stand still in history—not even the Chinese empire."

Narayan has been less successful but no less diligent in his efforts to correct the impression always left by Nehru's speeches that Soviet Communism and Western democracy are equally amoral technological civilizations. The Prime Minister finds great difficulty in distinguishing between the two systems (at least in public) and usually implies that Communism is more "progressive" than anything the West can offer.

Narayan, the one-time Communist, makes a searing rebuttal. "History will soon prove that Communism, instead of being the final flowering of human civilization, was a temporary aberration of the human mind, a brief nightmare to be soon forgotten. Communism, as it grew up in Russia and is growing up in China now, represented the darkness of the soul and imprisonment of the mind, colossal violence and injustice. Whoever thinks of the future of the human race in these terms is condemning man to eternal perdition. It is not the cold war or the economic war that will spell the ultimate defeat of Communism; it is, rather, the working of the human spirit."

He has also provided a valuable corrective to Indian chauvinism on Kashmir. His plea for understanding between India and Pakistan has earned him the gratitude of moderates in both countries. He is now trying to get in touch with what he calls "like-minded persons" in Pakistan in hopes of starting a "dialogue on the Kashmir problem in the spirit of non-violence." He feels that India has nothing to lose and much to gain by a friendlier approach to Pakistan; and that such an approach would evoke a similar response from the Pakistanis. He thinks that India has a good enough case in Kashmir to make some concessions, and he favors talks at the highest level on the whole range of problems that now bedevil Indo-Pakistani relations. Pakistan's President, Field Marshal Ayub Khan, has said that he wishes Pakistan had more men like Narayan—a statement that made J. P. the target of violent abuse from Indian Communists and Hindu zealots.

Narayan's reaction to the Indian seizure of Portuguese Goa in December 1961 was considerably less free of chauvinism. He first echoed Nehru's line about India's having been "compelled" to take Goa by force. He went even further, by asserting that India's action was "wholly due to the refusal of the NATO powers, particularly of Britain, to discharge honestly their responsibilities to the ideals of freedom they have so loudly professed as leaders of the so-called 'free world.'" He accused Britain and the United States of having "betrayed their lingering love for colonialism" by publicly deploring India's use of force. But in the same statement, issued December 19, 1961, in Calcutta, he admitted that the taking of Goa would damage Indian prestige in the world and lay New Delhi open to the charge of inconsistency. Then, in a last Olympian leap into confusion, he concluded, "More particularly and pointedly, the blame [for Goa] lies on Vinoba's head, the commander of the Shanti Sena, and us, his soldiers." It was wrong for the Peace Brigade to think in terms of solutions for international problems, "which are hidden in the lap of the gods," but something positive and nonviolent should have been done to prevent the Goa issue. Less than six months later, he told me, "If force was justified anywhere, it was justified in Goa, but on the basis of the principles of the U.N. Charter it was wrong to use force. From the viewpoint of nonviolence it was 100 per cent wrong." Some of this mental tightrope-walking is a quest for truth. But most of it is probably an effort to accommodate to domestic Indian opinion and retain his popular following.

The size of Narayan's following is difficult to determine. He is an all-India figure, one of the last of the old charismatic leaders like Nehru and Gandhi. His name is still a household word in north India, but the younger generation in Bombay, Bengal, and the south is less familiar with him. A Bombay newspaper executive says, "If you asked people in the south who J. P. is, they probably wouldn't know. He has been out of the political limelight for fourteen years." On the other hand, Dr. Ram Subhag Singh, the agriculture minister (under Patil) and one of India's bright young men, told me, "J. P. is a pure man, widely respected for his ideals. He's now concentrating on Bhoodan, panchayats, and the Peace Brigade, but he could be drawn back into Congress at any time. He has wide national influence." A poll conducted in 1961 by the Indian Institute of Public Opinion reported that Narayan outranked all other contenders as the public's choice to succeed Nehru. It should be emphasized, however, that Indian polling techniques are still unreliable, and even in this poll more than half those interviewed had no opinion when they were asked to express their preference for the next prime minister. The percentage favoring Narayan, although higher than that for any other contender, was only 11.1. He was favored by 14.1 per cent of the urban dwellers and 10.5 per cent of the country folk.

Whatever his popular support, there are other factors that are likely to be more immediately important in deciding his political future. His standing with the Congress leadership after Nehru goes will be the most important single consideration. Lal Bahadur Shastri, S. K. Dey, and some other "Gandhians" in Congress are sympathetic to him. They are not likely to back him as prime minister (at least in the short run), but they would probably favor his inclusion in the Union cabinet. Congress machine operators like S. K. Patil and Kamaraj Nadar regard Narayan as a dangerous maverick. Morarji Desai, with whom one would think Narayan would have much in common, is hostile. Desai says that J. P. is a swinging pendulum that does not inspire confidence, and asks, "Why does Narayan always attack Congress in his public statements and always support the PSP if he is out of politics and unconnected with any political party?" Desai insists that J. P. became a fanatic anti-Communist "more out of disappointment and frustration than conviction." Echoing the view expressed many years ago by one of Narayan's professors at Ohio State, Desai says, "He is a good man, but weak in action." Even those who sympathize with Narayan wonder if the aging titan of Indian radicalism has the stamina to take on the premiership and its crushing burdens.

The best-educated guess in India today is that he has no chance of succeeding Nehru directly and little hope of doing it later unless a series of ineffectual Congress machine appointees should destroy the country's faith in a party stalwart as prime minister. If the party bosses cannot rule with one of their own kind, they might feel compelled to draft Narayan back into the party as a symbol of national unity and a living reminder of the freedom struggle. This possibility presupposes conditions of extreme distress in India, aggravated by the failure of successive Congress governments. By that time, of course, a conservative army clique might well decide that Congress was incapable of governing the country. Narayan might then be summoned to New Delhi to provide a respectable civilian façade for military rule. His increasingly Right Wing pronouncements, coupled with his known dedication to Gandhian nonviolence, could make him seem attractive and harmless to an army junta in search of a "reliable" premier.

My own view, however, is that Narayan is not likely to win or be given the leadership of the government of India. Even if he were, I think his dissenter's soul would soon take him off the high road of power. His probings of the human spirit are not likely to stop short at the prime minister's desk, however much he may covet the office. The old revolutionary who now shudders at the plight of a lizard locked in a bookcase is ill-fitted to apply the kind of coercion that is the ultimate sanction of government, especially in Asia. Reality is his greatest regret, and there is no escape from it at the summit. The gadfly of the Indian elephant can hardly turn himself into its driver. Jayaprakash Narayan, who has built and razed more temples of the mind than any other Indian of his generation, must say with Omar Khayyam:

"Myself when young, did eagerly frequent
Doctor and saint, and did hear great argument,
About it and about,
But evermore did leave by the same door wherein I came."

S. K. Patil

BOMBAY IS INDIA'S MANHATTAN. It began on a cluster of seven
tiny islands (which Ptolemy called the Heptanesia) separated
at low tide by putrid malarial mud flats which prompted the
saying, "Two monsoons are the life of a man." The seven
islands were made one by the reclamation efforts of the English
East India Company. The resultant island of Bombay is about
the size of Manhattan and roughly the same shape.

There are other similarities. Bombay is the commercial
capital of India. It professes to look down on Delhi, as New
York looks down on Washington. To an Indian, Bombay
means vitality, big business, overcrowded suburban trains, and
a stroll along Marine Drive as the sun sets in the Arabian Sea.
No Indian is ever lost in Bombay, because he is sure to find
others from his caste or district settled in some quarter of the
city. It is the one place in India that could never be called
provincial. Hindus, Moslems, Parsis, Jews, Jains, Christians,
Sikhs, and agnostics all call Bombay home. Bankers and bootleggers (since prohibition) find profit there. Artists, writers,
and movie actors find Bombay as congenial a refuge from

Indian reality as do the pimps and prostitutes who make it the country's most notorious sin bazaar.

The Maharashtrian coolie in his driftwood shack and Sir Homi Mody, the Parsi financier, surveying the city from his air-conditioned mansion, is each a Bombay booster in his own way. No other Indian city inspires such loyalty.

Even the smell of poverty is different in Bombay. The usual cow-dung smoke, garlic, and spice odors are compounded with Bombay's own grit and fumes, and the whole is soaked in the most oppressively humid air that I have ever encountered. Its florid Victorian gothic architecture is more outlandish than anything else in India. Its harbor is more congested (with the exception of Calcutta's), its politics is more boisterous, and its evening parties (perhaps as a reaction to prohibition) are more frenetic. One of Louis Bromfield's characters says of Bombay: "There was nothing like this in the world, no city so fantastic. Baghdad in its heyday was no more absurd and mixed-up and fascinating."

Bombay is not the largest Indian city (4,152,000 compared with more than 6,200,000 in Greater Calcutta), or the oldest, cleanest, or most beautiful. But it is the one city in India that has the self-assurance of knowing it is a city. Bombay makes no apologies for itself. I suppose that is why Indians from Amritsar to Tuticorin always talk of going "back" to Bombay even though they may never have been there, and why there is always a kind of suppressed excitement aboard an Indian plane bound for Bombay.

No one mirrors the ebullient character of Bombay more faithfully than its political overlord for well-nigh thirty years, Sadashiv Kanoji Patil (pronounced with the accent on the first syllable). Since April 1957, he has been a member of the Union cabinet in New Delhi, but his heart and the roots of his political power are still in Bombay. If this man of immense energy, infinite patience, and vast organizing ability ever reaches the top, Bombay, not New Delhi, will be the real capital of India.

I first met S. K. Patil (as everyone knows him in India) in the fall of 1959, soon after he had become Union minister of food and agriculture in Nehru's cabinet. Since then I have talked with him more often than with any other major figure in this book. I always see him at his big ministerial "bungalow" at 5 Dr. Rajendra Prasad (formerly Queen Victoria) Road, in one of the shadiest and most tranquil sections of New Delhi. The procedure is always the same. I am ushered in punctually (a rarity in Indian ministers' offices) to find Patil sitting behind a plastic-topped, boomerang-shaped desk in his small study, where several air conditioners keep the temperature near freezing. Patil wears a white buttoned-up *achkan* coat like Nehru's, but without the red rose in the buttonhole. His face is heavy and blunt, but the black eyes are lively, even mischievous. His English is unmistakably Indian, but his voice is deep and resonant, a pleasant relief from the piping sing-song of so many Indians. There is something bearlike and elemental about him. His directness and lack of verbal circumlocutions remind me of a busy American politician. He is blunt without ever being discourteous.

"What can I do for you?" he intones as soon as I sit down. I ask my questions, and Patil is off, not garrulously, but with some forthrightly expressed ideas. As he talks, secretaries scurry in and out of the little office with penciled notes. Sometimes he will take a long-distance call from Bombay, but most of the time he gives undivided attention to a visitor. He is an organizer who knows how to use time economically. When a half hour has passed, he booms, "Well, thank you very much," and rises to indicate the end of the interview.

Despite his nonchalance, Patil is much less at home behind a ministerial desk in Delhi than in the rough-and-tumble of Bombay city politics. The "uncrowned king of Bombay," as one former Congress party president calls him, has little use for the bulging files so dear to Morarji Desai's heart. Patil is a boisterous, exuberant extrovert in a country where the mighty are expected to cultivate a certain remoteness. As one Indian newspaperman remarked, "Patil is widely liked because he is human. Unlike some of his Congress colleagues, he trails no sanctimonious coat behind him. Not for him the incense and myrrh of virtuous perfection."

One Indian who has never been attracted to Patil is Jawaharlal Nehru. The Prime Minister kept him out of the cen-

tral government for ten years after independence because
Patil was the chief lieutenant of the late Sardar Patel, the last
Congress leader who refused to bow to Nehru. Finally, in
1957—seven years after Patel's death—Nehru agreed to let
Patil join the Union cabinet as a concession to the Congress
Right Wing, which Sardar Patel had headed. He retains him
in the cabinet for the same reason and because Patil has
demonstrated executive ability of a high order in three central
ministries.

It would be hard to imagine two more antithetical personalities than the fastidious aristocrat in the prime minister's
seat and the long-time Tammany Hall-like boss who covets
his place. Nehru has a subtle, often devious, mind, addicted
to theorizing and allergic to compulsion and other crudities
of politics. Patil has no taste for theory and no qualms about
upholding authority by forceful methods. He prides himself
on being tough and direct, although he can also be cunning
when the occasion demands. Nehru abhors the mentality of
the market place. Patil relishes it. Ironically, both men are
Brahmans. But Nehru is a high-caste Kashmiri Brahman,
whereas Patil (whose family name is derived from a word
meaning village headman) comes from a lower subcaste of
Saraswat Brahmans who worship the goddess of learning and
were traditionally looked down on by other Brahmans on the
west coast of India.

The Prime Minister and his Food Minister are the senior
Congressmen in the central government today in terms of
length of service with the party. Patil might also share seniority
of service in the cabinet with Nehru if he had not been excluded for so long because of his association with the Sardar
Patel faction.

When he finally did come to Delhi, Patil found himself
saddled with some of the toughest and least glamorous technical jobs in the cabinet. First he had the Irrigation and
Power Ministry for a year, then the Transport and Communications Ministry for sixteen months. In August 1959 Ajit
Prasad Jain resigned as Union minister of food and agriculture. He had failed miserably to solve the problem of India's
chronic food deficits. The country's agricultural imports were

larger than ever. Food prices were spiraling upward. Jain was not the first food minister to choke on his portfolio. The job had long been considered a graveyard of ministerial reputations. When Patil was sworn in as food minister in September 1959, it was widely assumed that Nehru was looking forward to the minister's early interment.

Patil proved to be a lively corpse. He quickly set about dismantling the cumbersome system of government controls aimed at regulating distribution of food grains. He abandoned wholesale trading by the government in such staples as wheat and rice. He removed zonal restrictions on the movement of wheat within India. He opposed Nehru's industry-centered approach to economic planning, and extracted more money for agriculture in the third five-year plan, which began in 1961. He exhorted, wheedled, and cajoled Parliament and the state governments into underwriting his policy of internal free trade in foodstuffs. Above all, he sought to harness the farmer's profit motive for the country's benefit instead of trying to stifle it under government controls. His aim was always the same: more food and the political blessings to be derived from it.

The Indian peasant cultivator is long-suffering. He expects to be exploited, victimized, cheated, and ignored. Historically, he has had no alternative but to submit, to withdraw onto his own land (if he had any) and produce just enough to satisfy the landlord and provide for his family's subsistence. Often he failed even to do that. Patil realized that the incentive of higher prices was urgently needed to break the inertia of hopelessness in the countryside.

"What I am saying," he told the Lok Sabha, "is that this mute man, this helpless man, the farmer, must be given the honor and dignity to which he is entitled. Seventy per cent of this country is made of farmers and by denying him the rights of his produce or by denying him even the place or position to which he is entitled, we shall never succeed, neither in agricultural production nor in any branch of development that we are going to take up."

To drive home the lesson, Patil ordered every official in his ministry to spend at least fifteen days a year on a farm "whether they know farming or not." Of himself he said, "Unless I soil my hand with mother earth and smell it also, I am not a food and agriculture minister."

Patil's most spectacular coup came on May 4, 1960, when he strode into the White House to conclude the largest agreement for American aid since the Marshall Plan. For the next four years India could receive an average of one shipload a day of American grain to relieve hunger and build up vital food stockpiles against famine. The agreement signed by Patil and President Eisenhower provided for sixteen million tons of American surplus wheat and one million tons of rice —worth $1.3 billion—to be sold to India for rupees under Public Law 480. Eighty-five per cent of the proceeds are returned as grants and loans to promote India's economic development. The *Times of India,* which rarely finds virtue in American policy, exclaimed, "No government has ever been more generous." The deal Patil had negotiated gave India desperately needed time to step up its own grain output and to build more grain-storage capacity. It also gave Patil his biggest political boost since he had gone to Delhi. But the Communists objected that Patil was tying India to America's coattails. Other critics said that the massive infusion of gift food would kill the very incentive to produce that the Food Minister was trying to create.

With the oratorical instincts acquired during long years of ward politicking, the square-shouldered, chocolate-faced man from Maharashtra rose in Parliament to rebut the charges. "I am not very fond of depending on other countries. I have as much self-respect as any other honorable members in this house. This country of ours being predominantly agricultural, it is folly, it is a hundred times folly, to go to other countries for food. But what can I do? What we are doing is merely to tide over the difficulties. I have said repeatedly if this house co-operates with me, if the country co-operates with me, I have said that at the end of the third five-year plan [1966] there will be no necessity to bring anything, not even one maund of wheat or rice from any other country."

Such was the challenge and the pledge that Patil offered India in the spring of 1960. He showed that he had a knack for the daring and the dramatic. His optimism might over-reach his discretion, but his spirited performance in the food crisis contrasted sharply with the general lassitude and indecision in New Delhi. With mountains of American wheat and rice ready to funnel into Indian ports, Patil could undercut the speculators who drove up grain prices. "If somebody wants to play a trick by raising prices or anything like that," he growled, "I can blow all that grain like hot air into that particular state when I know that it is necessary in order to hold the prices." Grain prices stabilized and in some places actually declined.

Patil turned next to mobilizing the forces of the market place. "Controls have got to go," he said in accents that would be familiar on Washington's Capitol Hill, but that sounded strange in the Parliament of socialist India. "Controls are bad," he told Parliament. "You know what these controls are. They make our lives artificial. When there is control, it is followed by ration cards." His attack on marketing controls was coupled with a new program—old hat in America, but revolutionary in India—for supporting farm prices. "When the prices are falling beyond the level where it is advantageous for the farmer and they are not remunerative," he declared, "then it becomes the duty of the state to run to the rescue of the farmers and buy the produce at a minimum price." By the spring of 1962, he had set a support price for wheat of thirteen rupees a maund. He called it "the greatest thing that has happened in this country in recent years." In the fall of 1962, he was laying plans to set similar floor prices for rice and other farm products. At the same time the weather gods finally relented. India harvested an all-time record of eighty-two million tons of food grains despite destructive monsoon floods in the summer of 1961 and 1962. The main result of the grain deal with the United States had been its psychological effect in curbing speculation on Indian markets, although shipments were stepped up after the Chinese attack in 1962. By the end of 1962, between 5.6 and 5.7 million tons of P.L. 480 wheat and about 450,000 tons of American rice had actually been imported under the Patil-Eisenhower agreement. One reason for the slow rate of imports was lack of storage capacity. But the situation on the food front had improved so markedly that the conservative *Statesman* of Calcutta sighed, "At last organization of the food supply is beginning to be effective."

Patil's natural optimism reached dizzy heights. En route home from a fourteen-country tour in 1961, he boasted that India had solved its agricultural crisis and was now in a position to export food. He announced that government policy would henceforth emphasize cash crops such as jute, tea, and copra. He added pontifically, "I will not produce more food." Later, in Bombay, he reverted to his theme and insisted that India had "turned the corner" on food.

He was immediately challenged by Indian and American authorities. The *Times of India* said, "It is one thing to deny that there is famine anywhere and quite another to claim, as Mr. Patil seemed to do, that the food problem of this country has been very nearly solved." It warned that complacency could only breed indifference. Patil insisted that the third-five-year-plan target of "self-sufficiency" in food grains would be attained, but he admitted that the goal of eighteen ounces of food grains per person per day had been scaled down to seventeen and a half ounces in accordance with the upward revision of population estimates. He argued that even sixteen ounces a day is adequate if wheat or rice is supplemented with other food. But the other food is not yet forthcoming. Per capita milk consumption in India is lower today than twenty-five years ago. While Patil boasted of increased rice yields, final official estimates for the 1961-1962 season showed a decline in the average yield from 909 pounds to 900 pounds per acre. Total rice production also dropped despite an increase in acreage. Indian productivity of the land continues to lag far behind that of other countries. No optimistic statistics can conceal the fact that most Indian farmers still use wooden plows of the kind already discarded in pre-Christian Rome. Even if irrigation water is available, they often do not know how to utilize it or they do not want to make the extra effort required to dig the necessary channels. Fertilizer and improved seed are in chronically short supply, and even when they are provided, they are frequently wasted.

An Iowa farmer still grows almost five times as much corn and six times as much grain sorghum per acre as his Indian counterpart. And the Iowan's hens lay almost four times as many eggs. Despite the existence of almost 3,000 state seed farms, less than 1 per cent of India's total corn and grain sorghum acreage is planted with hybrids. In the United States the proportions are exactly reversed.

Fertilizer production has been a soft spot in all of India's five-year plans. Everyone admits that it is the crucial element in raising farm output, but production of nitrogenous fertilizer in 1961-1962 amounted to only about 300,000 metric tons (in terms of nitrogen), against the third-five-year-plan-production target of one million tons by 1965-1966. The rate of increase of India's fertilizer production was disastrously slow. Output at the big state-owned Sindri fertilizer plant in Bihar actually declined, although the staff was increased. In 1961-1962 India imported 80,000 tons of fertilizer (in terms of nitrogen) to supplement domestic production, but effective demand by the farmers was estimated at 670,000 tons, about double the supply. In May 1962 Patil admitted that "hundreds of thousands of tons" of sodium sulphate, a crop poison, had been fraudulently sold by dealers to farmers as the popular fertilizer ammonium sulphate.

Only slightly less serious than the failure to achieve fertilizer targets was the lagging progress of construction of grain-storage capacity. Late in 1962 Patil announced that he was almost two million tons short of the target of five million tons of storage capacity set for that year. The target has now been moved ahead to 1966.

Not all these difficulties could be laid at Patil's door, but they hardly justified his bumptious optimism. His approach to food, as to everything else, is essentially political. He seems more concerned with the appearance of success than with any real change in Indian agriculture. The pursuit of political success on the food front does, of course, entail changes and improvements in production and distribution, but my feeling is that these are largely ephemeral. The basic problem remains.

The pursuit of success has been the leitmotiv of Sadashiv Kanoji Patil's life almost since it began on August 14, 1900, in the tumble-down provincial town of Savantvadi, not far from India's west coast and on the edge of former Portuguese Goa. He was the eldest son in a family of three boys and three girls. His father was a minor police officer, on special duty in the area. The family owned some land. Young Patil was only ten years old when both his parents died. His admirers now tell how he "tasted hunger" in his youth, but when I asked him about this, he replied brusquely, "I wasn't actually hungry, but I didn't have very good meals either." He looked after his three sisters and two younger brothers, but he managed to attend high school in the west coast town of Malvan and get a scholarship to St. Xavier's College, a mission school in what he calls "that grandest city, Bombay." He distinguished himself in the school's debating society and made a good record in studies, but he was never graduated from St. Xavier's. In 1920 he joined Gandhi's nonco-operation movement and led a student boycott of the school. In talking to me about his early life, he has always refrained from trying to paint himself as a youthful hero. He told me candidly, "I had nothing to lose by following Gandhiji." Few Congress leaders would concede as much. Patil's debating experience stood him in good stead as he harangued his schoolmates on the glories of *swaraj,* or independence.

A year before, at the age of nineteen, he had married an eighteen-year-old girl of his own subcaste. He says now that his marriage was "too early." His wife rarely appears in public and never accepts invitations to official functions. She can converse comfortably only in Marathi. In many visits to the Patil home, I have never seen Mrs. Patil, although I once talked with one of their daughters.

For four years after leading the student boycott at St. Xavier's, Patil conducted so-called schools of national education, the Congress-sponsored nationalist institutions designed to replace what Gandhi called "satanic" British-run schools. The national-education movement collapsed in 1924 with the end of that phase of Gandhian nonco-operation.

Patil had already been admitted to the University of Missouri, where he intended to study for a Master of Arts degree in journalism, but he had to wait six months for his visa to

America. He says that he was the first student to go from India under the 1924 immigration act. During the three-week voyage from Bombay to England, he was perpetually seasick, and by the time he reached England his whole body craved an interlude on dry land. He spent a fortnight there, "to get on my legs," and by that time the semester had already begun at Missouri. "I couldn't afford to waste another six months waiting for the new semester to start," he says. "So I went to school in London." There he was one of thousands of Indian students who studied under the late Harold Laski at the London School of Economics. He also attended the London School of Journalism. Laski had less impact on the bushy-browed young man from Savantvadi than the writings of Bertrand Russell and H. G. Wells did. The whole socialist ethos of the Bloomsbury intellectuals seems to have been largely lost on him. He acquired none of the English habits of thought, speech, and dress adopted by so many of his future colleagues in the Congress party. Three years in London were not enough to divert his thoughts from Bombay.

When Patil returned to India in 1927, the nationalist movement was at low ebb. He had decided to take up journalism, and became what was then called a political commissioner (equivalent to a political reporter) on the now defunct Bombay *Chronicle*. He held the job five years, gaining a valuable ward's-eye view of Bombay politics. In 1929 he was elected general secretary of the Bombay city committee of the Congress party. The following year Gandhi launched his great civil disobedience movement, and Patil was jailed for the first time for his part in the disturbances that shook Bombay. In 1931 he resigned from the Bombay *Chronicle* to devote full time to the Congress, and to jail-going. But he still regards journalism as his "only heaven," and his passport still describes his profession as "journalist." "Often," he says with a faraway look in his eyes, "I think I should go back to journalism."

From 1930 to 1945, Patil went to prison eight times, for a total of more than ten years. His record in this department is as good as Nehru's. What Laski and the London School of Economics failed to give him in the way of political education,

Patil imbibed in jail. He read a great deal and lectured fellow inmates, as he says now, on "socialism, communism, and other theories." I suspect there was a heavy admixture of practical politics with the theory. Political prisoners made up some 90 per cent of the jail population in those days. At least a quarter of a million Indians learned political theory (usually Leftist) at government expense during this period when the British allowed Congress leaders to turn the jails into universities. Patil says that most of his following in the country today, "which is pretty deep-rooted," is made up of former inmate-students and those whom they have influenced.

During an interlude of freedom in 1937, he was elected to the All-India Congress Committee, a body on which he still serves. He was already a power in the Bombay Congress party when he was elected to the AICC. When World War II broke out, he felt no moral scruples about demanding Britain's withdrawal from India. He supported Gandhi's Quit India movement from the beginning, without the soul-searching that Nehru and Chavan went through. He insists that he also backed the Mahatma in opposing violence of any sort in connection with the wartime movement. "I was the most vocal critic of the underground movement," he recalls, "because it went against the moral philosophy of Gandhi's civil-disobedience movement." During this period Sardar Patel was consolidating his grip on the Congress party in Bombay and nearby Gujarat. The Sardar was a genius at political organization, imperious, ruthless, and indefatigable. He needed a chief of staff in Bombay. Patil was his man. "What little I know of organization and administration, I have learned from this great man," he once wrote, with seemingly genuine reverence for his former master. He imitates the Sardar's frowning exterior and his air of total self-possession. He even manages to look a bit like Patel. When the grand old man of the Congress Right died on December 15, 1950, leaving Congress and the country to Nehru, Patil called it "the darkest day for India."

The Sardar was an individualist and a conservative who openly scorned Nehru's socialist theories. During the independence struggle, he was remarkably successful in coaxing financial contributions from Indian businessmen, especially from the Bombay and Ahmedabad industrialists. He felt no hostility toward private enterprise and thought it should be given wide scope in the economy of independent India. Helen B. Lamb, in her chapter on "Business Organization and Leadership in India Today," in *Leadership and Political Institutions in India,* suggests that Indian business may feel isolated and bereaved since Patel's death. Business contributions to campaign chests are as eagerly solicited in India as elsewhere, but business endorsement carries less weight in Indian elections than it does in many American and British races. Helen Lamb has pointed out that Indian business lacks the prestige and general acceptance accorded business in the West. The Indian financial and industrial community is narrowly based and divided against itself on communal and family lines. The prevalence of black-marketeering (in peace as well as war), tax evasion, and adulterated products has tarnished the image of India's "private sector." Although Indian business emits the usual cries about socialism and government regulation, most firms are assured of fat profits because they operate in the world's second-most-populous closed market. There is little incentive to modernize antiquated textile or sugar-refining machinery or to compete in the export market. Indian business is generally content to criticize Congress policy and governmental procedures without offering any practical alternative to Nehru's "socialist pattern of society." Despite the imperfections of Indian private enterprise, I have always felt that Nehru could have harnessed its undoubted energies in the work of modernizing the Indian economy instead of encumbering business with a bewildering maze of regulations and restrictions.

Bombay business houses and many in other parts of the country appreciate Patil's readiness to do favors for them, but they are increasingly dubious of his political prospects. A Bombay financier who is a leader in the Swatantra party, told me, "Patil's heart is with us. If he came and asked me for anything, I'd give it to him even though he's in Congress. I'm a great admirer of Patil, but I don't see any future for him."

These doubts are well founded. Since he came to Delhi in 1957, Patil has not only failed to grow in stature under the

Nehru banyan tree, but his political roots, stretching back to Bombay, have been seriously loosened by the emergence of Y. B. Chavan as the new Congress powerhouse in that part of India. It is ironic that Patil's political fortunes should have declined while he was winning—at least temporarily—India's battle for food. But such is the way of politics, an ungrateful mistress. It proves again that in India personalities and political organizations are far more important than the most outstanding performance in office.

Many Indian and foreign political observers now insist that Patil is out of the running for the prime ministership. Former Union Finance Minister C. D. Deshmukh says, "Patil has good managerial ability, but so far as his popular influence is concerned, it's practically nil except for what he can obtain by logrolling with the mercantile community in Bombay. He is distrusted and disliked by the people at large, who think he's too much of a machine politician. Patil gets things done by making deals with the money boys in Bombay."

I doubt that Patil has so completely lost his following in Bombay, but there is no doubt that he lacks an all-India mass following. Only .5 per cent of those polled by the Indian Institute of Public Opinion in 1961 favored Patil to succeed Nehru as prime minister. Even a late-comer like Chavan, with no experience in the central government, outpolled Patil. Seventy-three per cent of those questioned had no opinion about Patil's performance, while only .8 per cent rated him "very good." However crude such gauges of public opinion in India, it is apparent that Patil must depend on support from the Congress machine rather than from the electorate at large. His own machine—the Bombay provincial Congress committee—is now in danger of being absorbed into the larger Maharashtra provincial Congress committee, which is controlled by Chavan.

Patil knows that Chavan is undermining his position in Bombay, but he is reluctant to make a frontal attack on the powerful Chief Minister of Maharashtra. Of Chavan he says warily, "It takes two to make a quarrel. I tell people I'm not going to quarrel with Chavan."

To bolster his waning power in Bombay, Patil flies there

from Delhi almost every weekend. He goes on Thursday or Friday and returns on Monday. He cuts ribbons, lays corner-stones, inaugurates seminars, addresses luncheon groups, and appears wherever a crowd can be assembled. As an American resident of the city says, "Bombay is Patil's Brooklyn. He loves it. Whenever he gets up to speak, he murders the English language almost as badly as Casey Stengel. He opens and closes everything. But the longer he stays in Delhi the more shadowy I feel he's becoming for these people." As the only man ever elected mayor of Bombay for three terms, Patil is far from conceding defeat. "I've served that city for the last forty-two years as no other man in history," he told me when I asked about Chavan's inroads. "In the 1962 election I got 64 per cent of the votes cast in my parliamentary constituency—an all-time record. For the last thirty-eight years I've been elected in some shape or form from the Bombay city south constituency."

The test of who runs the Congress machine in Bombay came during the bitterly contested race in 1962 between Krishna Menon and Acharya J. B. Kripalani. Patil has never concealed his hatred of Menon and, despite intense pressure from Nehru, he never explicitly endorsed Menon during the campaign. Chavan, on the other hand, campaigned for Menon in the closing stages and also ordered Congress workers to go all out to re-elect the Defense Minister. Menon's landslide victory was owing considerable part to Chavan's dominance in the Bombay party organization. Menon tried to avenge himself on Patil after the election by urging Nehru to drop him from the cabinet. Nehru demurred, thereby saving Patil from political extinction. Patil admits that his position is precarious. "If I leave government," he says grimly, "I'll be forgotten. That's the way things work here."

Even on the managerial and organizing side, Patil's role has been curtailed. He took little part in directing the Congress campaign in the 1962 election. Although he has proved over the years to be the party's ablest fund-raiser, he was stripped of most of his power in this field when party fund-raising was decentralized to the state organizations.

Patil's weakened position makes him chary of expressing

views at variance with Nehru's. Except on the affairs of his own ministry, he keeps silent in public. Even in private his opinions seem to be based more on expediency than on conviction. He insists that an "indigenous" brand of socialism is inescapable in impoverished India, but never explains what it is. He says that the state should intervene in the economy when private capital is not forthcoming. But he clearly favors a broader role for Indian business. He takes credit for opening the badly muddled fertilizer industry to private firms and for enabling the Tatas, India's largest private producers of electric power, to expand their capacity. He wants private operators to undertake a program of crop insurance, but thinks the job is probably too big for anyone but the government. When Nehru wanted Congress to campaign in 1962 on a platform calling for a ceiling on urban incomes, Patil objected in the Congress Working Committee. In the end the platform contained only an innocuous reference to "some limitations on high urban incomes through taxation and other means."

Like other conservative members of the cabinet, Patil is privately critical of Nehru's handling of foreign policy. He asks why India must offer advice on every international question, whereas Japan, "a much richer and more developed country than we," takes a stand only on questions of concern to itself. He objects to the way the cabinet was bypassed when Nehru and Menon decided to seize Goa and to negotiate for the purchase of Russian MiG-21 supersonic fighters. Patil thinks that Menon's anti-American diatribes are a disaster for India. If he were in a position to influence Indian foreign policy, I think he would support nonalignment but without its present pro-Soviet bias.

Disunity is one reason for weakness in the Congress Right Wing. Patil, Desai, and other conservatives have long eyed one another suspiciously. It has been easy for Nehru to play off one against the other. There are also personality conflicts among the Right Wing leaders. Patil, for example, has no use for Desai's asceticism. He frankly seeks power and makes no secret of enjoying the good things of life. I remember asking him if he thought that he hurt his chances by failing to conform to the Indian image of leadership. His answer was revealing. "Isn't the Indian image of leadership changing? It's true I'm not an ascetic. You can't reflect something you aren't. I want to serve the people, not just reflect asceticism. The people are very happy if their lot improves. That's the important thing to them. But if you mean by ascetic that a man must be religious and God-fearing, then I'm second to none in those things. But as for frugal living, avoiding motion pictures, wearing khaddi—that kind of thing—I don't practice and I don't ask any man to do that. Desai even turns off the ceiling fan when he goes to sleep. I can't live without air conditioning. He wears the dhoti. I don't because I don't believe a dhoti is necessary in the modern world where in an hour's time I may be asked to go to London."

Patil admits that he is "not exactly religious," but says that he has a "religious temperament and background." He thinks that Nehru makes a mistake by proclaiming his "paganism" and decrying all organized religion. He talks glibly about "rationalizing" religion, but it is clear that for him religion, like most other things, cannot be separated from its political context. He believes that being religious is good politics as long as most Indians are deeply influenced by religion. When I asked him about such drawbacks of latter-day Hinduism as the caste system, he replied bluntly, "There are positive disadvantages to Hinduism. It would have been best for people who can think for themselves. But the masses can't think for themselves. So religion became associated with rituals and superstitions."

Patil has done little to combat one of the most pernicious distortions of Hinduism: the refusal to slaughter diseased and useless cattle. India now has more than 225 million cows, bullocks, and buffaloes—one fourth of the entire world population. These animals resemble skeletons covered by tarpaulins. They compete directly with humans for India's limited food and living space. The imbalance between man and animal is so glaring that an official report estimates that India's national income would rise by the equivalent of $140 million if only 10 per cent of the unserviceable cattle were destroyed. Surplus livestock leads to overgrazing, with resultant soil erosion and further reduction of arable acreage. Stray cows wander through the streets of Delhi and other cities, blocking traffic and causing accidents. They break into fields and destroy crops and irrigation ditches. Although Hindus profess to regard the cow as the "mother of humanity," nowhere else in the world is livestock so neglected as in India. Devout Hindus often endow cow shelters, but the number of animals far exceeds such facilities. The vocal Gosamvardhan (literally, development of cow wealth) movement is more concerned with preventing the slaughter of cows and bulls than with improving livestock conditions. One result of their agitation has been to remove water buffalo "steak" from the menu of New Delhi's largest hotel, which caters largely to American and other meat-eating tourists.

Patil admits in private that the agitation against cow slaughter is "wrongly connected with our religion." But in public he protests his devotion to the Gosamvardhan Council. He once told Parliament: "Honorable members know my views. So far as cow protection is concerned, I am one with them and I know what really the cow wealth can mean for us. Not only is it necessary that the cow must be protected; it must not be killed."

When I pressed Patil to reconcile his statements, he finally retorted, "Everyone can't be Jesus Christ. You have to win elections. My deputy said something in favor of cow slaughter and almost lost his election. I had to rescue him. It's a very delicate matter and must be dealt with delicately. You can't offend against the sentiments of millions of people at once." I have always felt that few issues cast a more melancholy light on the workings of Indian democracy than the refusal to halt the livestock explosion.

Political opportunism also threatens one of the most ambitious programs ever launched to overcome India's perennial food crisis. The intensive agricultural-district program, commonly known as the package program, is a $100-million Indo-American effort to raise farm production in seven naturally favored districts covering six million acres in different parts of India. Fertilizer, hybrid seeds, improved farm implements, supervised credit, and trained extension workers are being poured into the seven areas in hopes of revolutionizing farm methods, obtaining at least two million more tons of grain, and setting a dramatic example for the rest of the country. The program is the outgrowth of a report called "India's Food Crisis and the Steps to Meet It," written in 1959 by an Indo-American team of specialists under Ford Foundation auspices. Despite the vagaries of an Indian printer who first published the report under the title "India's Ford Crisis and the Slips to Meet It," the document had considerable impact. It awakened Indian leaders for the first time to the gravity of their food situation. It gave Patil the opportunity he needed to focus attention on the Food and Agriculture Ministry. He led the way in getting Indian government approval for the team's proposals for urgent steps to increase food output.

He warned that if the package program failed, the consequences would be "too terrible to contemplate." He told district workers engaged in the program that "any thought of defeatism cannot be tolerated and there is no room for dilatory or halfhearted measures." His zeal for the intensive district program did not deter him from making it extensive for political purposes. Under pressure from state leaders, he agreed to add nine more "intensive" districts to the original seven selected by the Ford Foundation. To Parliament he explained lamely, "I thought that there will be unhealthy rivalry between a state and a state if seven states get them and the other states do not get them. They would feel that their farmers could not go to the other states to see." The upshot has been the spread of an already inadequate staff even more thinly. The Ford Foundation is restricting its financial aid to the seven original districts, but has reluctantly agreed to provide technical assistance to the other nine. Like the much-advertised Community Development program (launched in 1952), the package plan is threatened with death by dilution. The temptation in India is always to stretch a good idea so far that it is indistinguishable from a bad one.

A Ford Foundation executive who works closely with Patil remarks bitterly, "I see no evidence that Patil is personally and emotionally interested in what he does in the Food and Agriculture Ministry. He's in Bombay every weekend from

Thursday or Friday until Monday. He's a politician. He feels he's done his job by ensuring that the country won't have any more famines. How has he done this? By P. L. 480. But that's no solution. Moreover, he's giving no leadership on the package program. If you asked him, he probably wouldn't be able to tell you what the package program is. The good thing about Patil is that you can push and prod him and he doesn't get angry."

Patil is more complacent about the package program today than he was in 1960 because two good grain harvests have given an appearance of abundance. The food-grain target of 105 million tons annually has been scaled down to 100 million tons in line with his insistence that Indians already eat too much grain in relation to other food. More money is earmarked for dairy schemes in the third five-year plan than in the first two five-year plans combined. There is also somewhat more emphasis on raising pigs and hatching fish. But an American authority says flatly, "India has made a bad show in agriculture outside food-grain production."

The worst show has been in sugar, now suffering from a glut, and cotton, which is in critically short supply. Although India's domestic sugar consumption has been almost static since 1958, Patil raised the price of cane as an incentive to growers. He first termed the resultant 300,000-ton increase in sugar stocks "something very excellent indeed," but later admitted that it was anything but excellent. India is a high-cost, low-yield sugar producer. Patil exported some sugar to the United States and bartered 50,000 tons for urgently needed American cotton. The cotton shortage resulted largely from low yields per acre and low prices paid to growers. When cloth prices began rising ominously in the spring of 1962, the government finally consented to raise cotton prices.

Sugar and cotton illustrate the extent of government intervention in India's agriculture and the problem of administering complex controls under pressure from powerful lobbies. Despite his mistakes, Patil has shown far more skill than most Indian politicians in exploiting natural market forces for the country's benefit.

He has also brought political oratory to a high degree of

perfection. His gestures are almost as eloquent as the movements of a classical Indian dance. He exudes euphoria. Reporting one of his speeches on sugar in Parliament, the *Hindustan
Times* observed that he "allayed all fears, raised all hopes, for-
gave the ignorant, complimented the knowledgeable, soothed
the mills, consumers and cane-growers, and by the time he had
finished he had managed to convince the house that there was
not only no 'sugar problem' but that, if anything, India was
on the top of the world as regards this commodity."

Patil's humor is as pervasive as his euphoria. In telling
Parliament about a rat invasion that damaged flowering
bamboo trees in the eastern province of Assam, he intoned:
"This is a wonderful phenomenon. This is a wonderful rat.
. . . This rat has its visitation once in thirty years. When this
particular bamboo flowers, it has got such an influence on
these rats. The flower must be very tasty. But when the flower
is destroyed, the rat also is destroyed. Where it goes nobody
knows. It has no habit of traveling. Otherwise, I think, the
Tourist Department would welcome it."

Patil's exuberance and betel-nut-chewing informality have
also endeared him to American officials accustomed to dealing with more sedate Indians. He visited the United States for
the first time in 1948 as mayor of Bombay and studied munici-
pal administration in forty American cities. In 1950 he discovered Hollywood in his capacity as chairman of the Indian
government's Film Enquiry Board. He says that his job involved "the same type of work Eric Johnston did." He visited
America for the sixth time in the summer of 1961 in search
of a quota for Indian sugar. On the same trip he visited
Russia and several eastern European satellites for the first time.
He was unimpressed.

His frequent forays abroad, especially during Delhi's hot
season, have been criticized as "ministerial globe-trotting." His
fondness for movie actresses, home-grown or foreign, is viewed
less indulgently in traditionalist India than it would be in
most Western countries. His most obvious weakness is his
insatiable appetite for movies, preferably enjoyed in the air-
conditioned comfort of a Bombay preview theater. Bridge is
his principal outlet in Delhi. His rear porch is cluttered with

bridge tables, to which he vainly tries to entice other cabinet ministers. I think they stay away because they fear they may be beaten and possibly because they feel Patil's star is waning.

Patil knows this. But he is not prey to panic. He knows he is still the most effective campaign manager in Congress and the potential architect of victory for the party's Right Wing. He may have no all-India following, and some politicians may shun him today, but his name still carries weight in the marigold-scented rooms where Indian party bosses take off their garlands and haggle over tickets. Over the years he has done enough favors for enough Congressmen and businessmen to ensure that he will not be forgotten if the Rightists divide the spoils. By the yardstick of Indian politics, he is comparatively young. His energy is inexhaustible. His political wisdom is unmatched, although his political appeal may be deficient. Today he talks of "collective leadership" after Nehru. He says with apparently genuine confidence that he will figure in that leadership. He predicts a "great split" in Congress after its banyan tree is finally felled. "Nothing can prevent a split in Congress after Jawaharlal," he says incisively. "It won't be a bad thing. It will be the genesis of a two-party system." But it will take as much as twenty-five years, according to him, before a real two-party setup has evolved in India. S. K. Patil cannot wait that long, but he will be around when Indian democracy faces its supreme test in the aftermath of Nehru. And the broad-faced man from Savantvadi intends to be heard from.

Brij Mohan Kaul

THE BRAHMANS are supposed to be the highest caste. But there is in India today a supercaste—a privileged, articulate, homogeneous, and highly disciplined power elite that towers over all other castes like Everest over the Ganges plain. It is the officer corps of the Indian Army.

The supercaste commands the largest army in Asia outside Communist China, and the fourth largest in the world. The Indian Army has doubled in size in the last five years and now numbers almost 600,000 men, all volunteers. They are deployed from Katanga to the Karakoram and from Gaza to the jungles of Assam. The traditions of the Indian Army go back seven generations. Once the guardian of the brightest jewel of the world's largest empire, the Indian soldier now serves one of the "new" countries that champions the cause of anti-imperialism. The Army is in India but not of it. It remains something apart from the main currents of Indian life and thought.

I am never so conscious of the British Empire as when I visit an Indian officers' mess. It is really the empire's last outpost. The mess will certainly be the last institution in India to be Indianized. It echoes with Sandhurst accents (real or acquired) and bristles with martial mustaches and polished swagger sticks. The talk runs to regimental cricket and the sporting thing to do on a tiger shoot. I always expect to find Kipling scribbling somewhere in the corner and Gunga Din serving up a tot of whisky. The officers' mess is in fact a museum of Anglophilia. Its ethos has permeated every nook and cranny of the Indian Army. The Indian officer's Sandhurst accent is matched by his British weapons, British-style uniform, British drill manuals, and the British table of organization of his unit. Even the signs on an Indian Army base look as if they had been lettered in England. The regimental sports trophies have a musty English respectability. English is the language of command, and the Royal Military College the fountainhead of strategy.

Colonel Blimp's Indian imitators are as clannish, suspicious of innovation, and goutily conservative as the old gentleman himself. Even the non-Blimps, the able officers who have saved the Indian Army from suffocating in its own professionalism, come from the same landed families as do the Blimps. The Army has been a closed corporation during most of its history, a fraternity of the privileged as much akin to the rest of India as the Union League Club is to America. When Mahatma Gandhi and Jawaharlal Nehru defied the British Raj, the Indian Army stood primly aloof or actually joined in suppressing the independence movement. When the flag of freedom was hoisted by the insurgent Indian National Army during World War II, it was trampled in the dust with the help of Indian troops led by Indian officers under the Union Jack. When India gained independence in 1947, the flag became Indian but the Indian Army did not. The British officers quickly departed, but their mentality lingered on. Indians, including army officers, found it inconceivable that the Army now belonged to them. The Congress party faithful regarded it with understandable resentment and suspicion. The Indian officers carried on as before. It took a trip to London, more than two years after independence, to convince General K. S. Thimayya, the future chief of staff, that the

Army was, as he puts it, "no longer a private preserve of the British." I have found many Indian officers who still do not really believe it.

However crustily British the Indian Army may appear even today, subtle changes have taken place. There are now only nine Sandhurst-trained generals on active duty. The new officers are graduates of the Indian Military Academy, Dehra Dun. Most of them have never served under an Englishman or seen Britain. They are a different breed from the old landed aristocracy that once monopolized the officer's uniform. The young officers are poorer, more urban, more political, more bourgeois, and infinitely more Indian than their senior colleagues. They include many more non-Brahmans. They tend to be Indian-nationalists first and professional soldiers second. They have never played polo and have no estates to which they can retire at the age of fifty-five. The oldest members of the new breed were recruited from Indian universities during the desperate early years of the war. They are now majors and colonels, the Indian chassis of their country's British-model military machine. They have the Sandhurst accent and know the right things to say in the officers' mess, but their thoughts are tinged by ambitions and frustrations the old breed never knew. The new generation of Indian officers is the first to realize that they have the power to change the course of Indian history with one blow.

The archetype and exemplar of the new Indian Army is, ironically, a product of the old. Brij Mohan Kaul, the chief of the general staff at army headquarters, is a Kashmiri Brahman, scion of a wealthy family, graduate of Sandhurst, opening bowler on the East Surrey regimental cricket team, colonel in chief of the Jat Regiment, and holder of the Vishisht Seva Medal (Class I) for distinguished service of the highest order. But such hallmarks of orthodoxy are no clue to the transcendent ambition and ability of the officer who more than any other controls the fate of the Indian Army today. Lieutenant General Kaul has no time for small talk in the mess; he is hurrying to keep an appointment with destiny. He is the only Indian general I have ever met who neither smokes nor drinks. All his habits are spartan. He moves like a cyclone from one end of India to the other. Sleep seems to be the only thing that tires him. His interests range from Himalayan cartography to Emily Dickinson's poetry. He is a lover of the theater, a mountain climber, and a student of military history. There is something self-consciously Napoleonic about the simple camp bed in his study. He is a twentieth-century soldier, but he has an Indian's respect for horoscopes, and his foretells that he will one day rule India. Being related by blood and marriage to Nehru (whose family name was originally Kaul) seemingly reinforces the augury of the stars.

It is fashionable in Delhi to belittle Kaul as a military "house-builder" who lacks combat experience and does not come from one of India's traditional martial castes like the Sikhs or the Marathas. He is dismissed as a stooge of Krishna Menon, a dupe of the Chinese Communists, and a flashy self-seeker. "Comrade Kaul," the pundits sneer, could not even lead a mutiny of the Quartermaster Corps, where he achieved his highest distinction before reaching his present position. After he fell ill soon after taking command of a new corps on the northeast frontier with Tibet in October 1962, Kaul's enemies spread the rumor that he was malingering for fear of being at his post when the Chinese attacked.

The first time I went to see Kaul, I expected a bemedaled dandy who would fit his cocktail-circuit epithet of "Stopgap." The man who rose quickly from behind a sea of files to greet me in his office was no dandy. Even in a lounge suit (which he wears frequently on duty), Kaul looks military. High-voltage energy ripples through every fiber of his shorter-than-average frame. He seems to find repose unbearable. His clean-shaven face, with its strong features and steady gaze, is a study in animation.

I began with what I thought was a fairly innocuous question. "Could you tell me something about your program for forming units composed of men from different castes?" I asked. General Kaul was off before I had finished speaking. He began by deprecating the idea of eliminating the old one-caste regiments. Then he turned to a lightning review of the history of the Indian Army. He swiveled in his chair, half rose to emphasize a point, brought his fist down hard on the desk. It was as if he were arguing to save his troops from annihilation. For half an hour he discoursed persuasively, often eloquently. His voice rose to peaks of fervor as he recalled old campaigns. But he was no old soldier recounting musty exploits. His reminiscences were carefully chosen to support his conclusion.

"The British called us loyal, devoted, good chaps," he said, giving a contemptuous ring to the last two words. "But our compatriots told us we were the tools of foreign oppressors. This created doubts in the minds of the soldiers." But never, I soon realized, in the mind of General Kaul, who has always known what he wants.

"After independence," he went on, "was the first time no one tried to detract from the Indian soldier. He's no longer suspect. The soldier now feels he's redeemed."

India remains to be redeemed. "Individually," Kaul says, "India has some of the greatest painters, poets, administrators, and soldiers, but collectively—well, it doesn't work. Look at the universities. Individually, we have some brilliant students, but the universities are in a mess."

Collective action, he believes, must be disciplined if it is to be effective. The armed forces are the only valid example of collective discipline in India today. The conclusion is evident. Kaul is no nonviolent Gandhian. He makes no secret of his sympathy with what the military has done in Pakistan and Burma. He thinks the Army is mistaken to leave power in civilian hands in Indonesia.

At the height of the Hindu-Moslem-Sikh communal slaughter in 1947, Kaul suggested privately to Jayaprakash Narayan that a "strong" government was needed to prevent India from drowning in blood. Narayan interpreted this as a suggestion for army rule and he rejected it. Kaul might find more sympathetic listeners if India were again plunged into chaos. He has made clear in private talks recently that the Army should not hesitate to seize power if the civil government were incapable of ruling or India were about to fall prey to Communists, foreign or domestic. He is not worried about doing something without a popular mandate, which he regards as largely fictitious in an underdeveloped and illiterate country.

"Biji" Kaul (the nickname craze is as strong in the Indian

Army as in the American) is unlike any other person in this
book or in India today. A Western military attaché in Delhi
says that he is the most un-Indian Indian he has ever met. Kaul
has something of Menon's brilliance, Nehru's guile, Desai's
asceticism, and Chavan's charm. He is ruthless but intensely
human. He inspires loyalty. He has an un-Indian abhorrence
of red tape. Delay and timidity infuriate him. He is proud
and profane in the best Indian Army tradition, but he spurns
the garrulous small talk so dear to the old breed of officers.
When the right side of his face was temporarily paralyzed a
few years ago, he felt a rare impulse to pray. But he disdained
praying to be spared and muttered simply, "Lord, give me
strength to bear whatever is being inflicted on me."

One affliction from which he has never suffered is lack of
self-confidence. His aplomb is nearly unshakable. There is no
task that he will not undertake. To handle the mass of work
that comes his way, he toils sixteen to eighteen hours a day.
He works harder than any other man in the Indian Army,
sees dozens of callers every day, and disposes of official files
at night. He has none of the Indian officer's traditional distaste for politics. He is political to the end of his swagger
stick. He is the new kind of Indian officer, who wears his
patriotism as well as his rank on his shoulder. He is not inclined to hide either. Selfless anonymity is not his notion of
what he is destined to achieve. He delights in conflict and
controversy. No bugler need announce General Kaul's regal
entrances. Like many another would-be man of destiny, he
may feel Bonaparte's bicorn hat on his head and the imperial
mace in his hand so vividly that he forgets his actual accouter-
ments. But at least if destiny does keep its appointment with
General Kaul, he will not be tardy.

The remarkable thing about him is that his most knowledgeable enemies concede his importance. The custom in India
is to belittle an antagonist as if he were a crawling infant or
an institutionalized lunatic. Only those who have never met
Kaul are really contemptuous of him. General Thimayya, who
professes contempt for his erstwhile deputy, told me that he
actually thinks Kaul is "smarter and more dangerous" than
Menon and may be using the former Defense Minister. Other

officers, including Western military attachés in Delhi, now credit Kaul with having infused new drive and efficiency into the Army. No one doubts that it is he who runs the Indian Army rather than General Pran Nath Thapar, the amiable figurehead who succeeded Thimayya as chief of staff in May 1961. There is also general agreement that Kaul's gifts qualify him for bigger things. An old schoolmate, now a well-informed Delhi editor, says that Kaul "probably thinks he could be prime minister of India." A Western officer who knows him well says, "Kaul's ambitions certainly don't stop short of being defense minister, probably prime minister."

Like many generals, the Chief of the General Staff (CGS) of the Indian Army likes to dramatize himself. "I must have been born," he told me once, "under some star that's never given me the normal run of things." He has a gambler's reverence for signs and portents. "My whole life has been built around gestures," he observes.

When Brij Mohan Kaul went on active duty in this life on May 1, 1912, he already ranked high in Indian society. The Kauls were prosperous Kashmiri Brahmans who had established themselves near Lahore, in what is now West Pakistan, the breeding ground of Indian generals. But Kaul takes little account of his actual birthplace. "The first thing," he says emphatically, "is that I come from Kashmir. That is an important biological fact." His father, a civil servant, owned land and other property. In his first ten years of schooling, young Kaul attended a Christian missionary school, where he says he learned the Bible "by heart," a Moslem school, where he studied the Koran, a Sikh school, where he read the Sikh scriptures, a Hindu school, where he learned the Veda, and, finally, a secular government school. He says that this early exposure to different faiths has imbued him with respect for all India's diverse religions. Later, when he was commanding troops in the Punjab, he copied the mogul emperor Akbar and built a Hall of All Religions, where Hindu, Moslem, Sikh, and Christian religious services were held.

His mother died when Kaul was six. His elder sister succumbed to tuberculosis five years later. And his father died when he was sixteen. Soon afterward, Kaul turned over the family estate to his stepmother and her three children and began "struggling with life."

His struggles with the British had already started, according to his account. At fifteen, he had had his first taste of the independence movement. He had joined student demonstrations in 1928 against Sir John Simon's all-British commission, which came to investigate India's political grievances. He had escaped unscathed from several police firings. He says that he happened to be sitting in the visitors' gallery of the Central Assembly in New Delhi on April 8, 1928, when two young terrorists hurled homemade bombs at the Government front bench during debate on a bill providing for detention without trial. The bombs caused no fatalities, but their echo was heard throughout India. Kaul was arrested and questioned along with many others in the gallery, but was released. Later he stood outside the Lahore district jail when one of the terrorists who had been convicted in the famous Lahore conspiracy case of murdering a British police officer was hanged and his body cut in four pieces. "That had the most tremendous effect on me," he says.

Kaul engaged in some minor underground activities of his own. He pasted up nationalist posters and helped deliver explosives that were used to dynamite the Viceroy's train (the Viceroy and his staff escaped unhurt). But military life attracted him more than the underground did. His nationalist record would have kept him out of Sandhurst if he had not been related to some prominent local officials. When a British deputy commissioner told him that his views were "all wrong" and asked why he wanted to join the Indian Army, Kaul retorted with typical spunk, "Naturally I want to join the Indian Army because it's my country's army. Would I want to join the French or German Army?"

Kaul says that he disliked the British before he went to Sandhurst, but found them a "sterling race" at the Royal Military College. Cricket and track appealed to him. Drinking and smoking repelled him. When other Indian cadets told him that he could never "get on" unless he knew how to down his whisky, the young Kashmiri exploded, "Who are you pygmies to tell me how to run my life?" When thousands of men stood up in the academy banquet hall to toast the King in port or sherry, Kaul would drink a glass of soda.

After Sandhurst, Kaul joined the East Surrey regiment, where he learned cross-country running (he had been a quarter-miler at Sandhurst) and achieved the distinction of being opening bowler on the regimental cricket team.

He saw action for the first time against Pathan tribesmen in the Northwest Frontier Province of India. One of his commanding officers in the early days was an eccentric and controversial British soldier, Major (later Major General) T. W. (Pete) Rees, whom he calls "the biggest architect of my military career." Rees clashed with General Montgomery and other British commanders in North Africa in World War II and finally retired under a cloud after the border force he commanded in the Punjab failed to stop communal pogroms in 1947. Kaul, whose own career has been as stormy, says he will always uphold his old commander against charges of being pro-Pakistani.

Kaul's role in the Burma campaign against the Japanese is a matter of dispute. The Japanese had overrun Burma in 1942 and had entered Kohima, in eastern India. They were threatening a full-scale invasion of India. Thimayya, one of only three Indian officers to command a brigade under the British during the war, says that Kaul never saw combat in the Burma-India theater. "In fact," Thimayya says, "he was CO of an Army Service Corps regiment that was supplying us rations from one hundred miles behind the fighting line." He says that Kaul had switched from the infantry to the ASC because "even then" he could not get along with his commanding officer. Kaul insists that he saw front-line action in the Buthidaung-Maungdaw area of the Arakan front with the 33rd Corps, part of General (now Viscount) William Slim's Fourteenth Army. No matter where Kaul actually spent most of his time, it is likely that he saw a fair amount of action. The Burma-India theater was not designed for comfort or safety, even for rear-echelon troops.

Indian troops were fighting on both sides in the Burma campaign. The Bengali nationalist leader, Subhas Chandra Bose, fled from India early in the war and lent his support to the so-called Indian National Army (INA) organized by the Japanese. INA troops advanced with the Japanese into Burma. Their loud-speakers blared propaganda across the front line to Indian troops fighting with the British. Kaul says that "quite a number" of Indian troops responded to INA appeals to desert. General Joseph W. ("Vinegar Joe") Stilwell, the American commander in the theater, angered the British by saying in effect that Indian officers under their command were so demoralized that Indian forces could not fight properly. When Thimayya's battalion captured an important hill at the beginning of the British-Indian counterattack, Lord Louis Mountbatten held him up as an example of high Indian morale. Kaul's own feelings were mixed. He felt that it was wrong to call members of the INA traitors. He respected Bose as a man who had "done a lot for my country," but opposed his movement because it would have meant exchanging British overlords for Japanese.

Kaul remained with the Fourteenth Army until July 1945. After a short tour of duty at army headquarters in New Delhi, he was picked by his newly powerful relative Jawaharlal Nehru to go to Washington as free India's first military attaché. "America took me by storm," Kaul exclaims. "There were so many things happening there. Temperamentally that suits me." Kaul now goes to elaborate pains to repress the notion that he is or ever was anti-American. Whatever his motives for now giving vent to his admiration for things American, I have always felt there was something genuine in the enthusiasm that creeps into his voice when he talks about the United States. In many ways he reminds me of General Maxwell Taylor (whom he greatly admires) or any of the other more intellectual American generals. He himself takes pride in such affinities.

The young Kashmiri colonel worked with demonic energy in Washington. "We've been bellyaching for a thousand years about being slaves," he told an overworked secretary in the Indian Embassy, "so I can't go home in the evening. I must sweat blood." He did. But not all the blood was his. He became the *enfant terrible* of the military attaché corps in Washington. He demanded—and eventually received—permission to spend more than the single day usually allowed foreign attachés at West Point, where, he says, "everything impressed me." He did not conceal his resentment at Lieutenant General John W. ("Iron Mike") O'Daniel's highhanded treatment of foreign military attachés on a visit to Fort Benning, Georgia, but he says that he later got on well with the tough old soldier.

Kaul traded on a wartime meeting in India with Louis Johnson (then acting as President Franklin D. Roosevelt's personal representative) to ask for bombers in January 1948, when Johnson was Secretary of Defense. The Kashmir fighting had broken out, and the Indian Air Force was sorely in need of planes.

"We've got into a scrap with Pakistan," Kaul told Johnson. "We need bombers."

"How many do you want?" Johnson is said to have replied.

Kaul named a figure. Johnson made a long-distance call, then turned, according to Kaul, and said, "That's okay. It's a deal."

But it was not. The State Department objected strongly when it heard of the scheme. At the time, Kaul had been detailed by Nehru to serve as military adviser to the Indian delegation during the U.N. Security Council debate on Kashmir. Warren Austin, the chief American delegate, called the young Indian officer in to explain to him why the bomber deal could not go through. Kaul was indignant. Austin asked him to appreciate the reasons for America's reluctance to appear to take sides in Kashmir. Kaul was unmollified.

"We're mad," he blurted. "We're fighting a war. I can't help being bitter about it."

Despite the bomber fiasco, Kaul says, "Psychologically, I was very well treated in America. I was extremely open with them. It went like a house on fire." He was given a double promotion six months after going to Washington, and he put his elder daughter in school there and started giving lectures on the development of the Indian Army. He asked to return to India in October 1947 when word came that the officer originally destined to have his post as military attaché became the first Indian casualty in the Kashmir fighting. "When this news came over the ticker, I fell off my chair," he says. He told Asaf Ali, the Indian ambassador, "I can't justify my conscience. If he had come here, he wouldn't be dead now. I have to go back." This is the kind of story Kaul delights in telling about himself.

Whatever the circumstances, he did not get home until March 1948, when he was assigned to organize a guerrilla force to fight along with the Indian Army in Kashmir. He raised 10,000 irregulars in record time and "led them everywhere," according to his account, until he had "some differences" with Sheik Abdullah, the Indian-backed premier of Kashmir.

Kaul had already become a quasi-political figure in the Army. And he was to become even more deeply implicated in politics five years later, when Nehru sent him back to Kashmir to oversee the midnight arrest of Sheik Abdullah, who had alarmed the Indians by toying with the idea of an independent Kashmir. Kaul's account of his role in the affair strikes me as completely disingenuous. He told me the story as we sat one evening in his study surrounded by seven model planes and dozens of books. "Nehru sent me in my personal capacity," he said, "to assess what was going on. I found Abdullah preparing to declare Kashmir independent." The Sheik's pro-Indian lieutenants (including the present prime minister of Kashmir) then arrested him on their own initiative. "I sensed it coming," Kaul confided, "but didn't interfere. Nehru had told me the situation was very delicate."

In fact, Kaul appears to have been the initiator of the most unpopular thing India has ever done in Kashmir. Abdullah was released briefly in 1958, then rearrested. He and fourteen codefendants are still being tried on charges of plotting with Pakistan to take Kashmir out of the Indian Union. Abdullah will soon have passed more than a decade in prison.

The real turning point in Kaul's career came when he was assigned to be chief of staff of the U.N. Neutral Nations Repatriation Commission, which handled the ticklish problem of 170,000 Chinese and North Korean prisoners of war, a third of whom refused to go home after the Korean war. The chairman of the commission was Thimayya, who had just been promoted to lieutenant general. Kaul clashed repeatedly with him during what he calls a "tough, perplexing time."

Americans who knew both men in Korea say that Kaul was frightened of Thimayya. Kaul denies this and says that Thimayya actually apologized to him for showing classified telegrams to the Americans. On the major problem, Kaul admits that he "could not believe" that thousands of prisoners from China and North Korea did not want to be repatriated, while Thimayya, though he bent over backward to show impartiality, had no trouble believing it. The latter mixed socially with American officers, got on well with them, and had little but formal official contact with the Chinese and North Koreans. Kaul, on the other hand, was courted by the Chinese, who sent him chickens and eggs when he was hospitalized in Korea and invited him to make an official visit to China.

On this visit he was impressed by the People's Liberation Army and the guerrilla-warfare tactics devised by Mao Tsetung. He was also struck by the new regime's drive and the discipline of the Chinese people. But he insists that he did not go to China because he was sympathetic to Communism. He says that he was ordered to accept Peking's invitation by Nehru, who thought it would be impolitic to refuse. His answers to reporters' questions on his return from China were misinterpreted, he contends. "I didn't say I liked the bloody Mao system or Communism," he growls. "But Thimayya told the Americans I had been brainwashed by the Chinese. They made a complete cuckoo out of me on this. On this bloody thing all my difficulties arose."

Thimayya's version is different. "Kaul came back from China singing their praises," he says. "That's when I sacked him. He offered me his resignation. I refused and urged him to take a long leave in India. We were all under pretty heavy strain in those days. The other officers thought I was a fool not to have accepted Kaul's resignation. Now I'm inclined to think they were right."

When he left Korea, Kaul was named commander of the Fourth Division, the famous "Fighting Fourth," on the Indo-

Pakistani frontier in the Punjab. He held this command for three years.

He might never have risen above the rank of division commander had it not been for the appointment on April 17, 1957, of Krishna Menon to be defense minister. The new minister was deeply suspicious of the old-line Indian generals. He wanted to bring up younger men, who would be more responsive to his wishes, especially in demonstrating the economic capabilities of the defense establishment. His eye lighted on Kaul, then chafing in enforced anonymity in the Punjab. He was impressed by the military housing colony of Jawanabad, which was built during off-duty hours in five months in 1949 by Kaul's troops of the 11th Infantry Brigade. Kaul says that his aim was to provide shelter for men who had lost their homes in the partition riots. Later, as commander of the Fighting Fourth, Kaul built Amar, another showpiece military housing project. The ruthless efficiency that went into these accomplishments appealed to Menon, who was also intrigued by Kaul's record in Korea and may have assumed from it that the young general was far to the left of other high-ranking Indian officers. Kaul did nothing to disabuse his minister. On the contrary, he seems to have shrewdly exploited Menon's susceptibility to flattery.

Menon waited for the right moment to have Kaul promoted. The opportunity came in 1959, when Thimayya proposed that a third star be awarded to Major General P. S. Gyani, an outstanding artillery officer who had become the first Asian commander of the U.N. Emergency Force in Gaza, which had a large Indian contingent. Menon demanded that Kaul should "come up" at the same time. Thimayya balked. Menon insisted. The matter went to Nehru, who, as usual, upheld Menon.

Kaul was promoted to lieutenant general in June 1959. At the same time, he was named quartermaster general and put in charge of a crash program to build thousands of miles of roads in Himalayan border areas threatened by the Chinese. The program was actually the basis of India's whole defense effort on the northern frontier, because without roads the outnumbered Indian troops could never hope to counter the Chinese. Kaul tackled the job with his customary frenzy, but the Chinese offensive in October 1962 came long before the road network was due to be completed.

Relations between Menon and Thimayya worsened steadily after Kaul's promotion. In August 1959 Timmy, as Delhi knows him, submitted his resignation to Nehru in protest against the Defense Minister's interference. Thimayya told friends, "This whole thing between me and that man [Menon] is about Kaul." Nehru talked him out of resigning and defended Menon against the bitter criticism in Parliament after the story was leaked to the press. The Prime Minister ascribed Thimayya's resignation to "temperamental differences" with Menon, dismissed his charges of interference as "rather trivial and of no consequence," and reproached him for wanting to quit in the midst of the Sino-Indian border crisis. The Menon-Thimayya feud was papered over but, as Thimayya said, "Things were very bad after that."

On May 8, 1961, Thimayya retired at the end of his two-year tour as chief of staff, the highest uniformed position in the Indian defense services. He was succeeded by Lieutenant General (now General) P. N. Thapar, then in charge of India's Western Area Command. Kaul had already moved up to the position of chief of the general staff at Army Headquarters in Delhi. He superseded at least half a dozen more senior generals. Menon's object in promoting Kaul seemed to be to pave the way for him to succeed Thapar as chief of staff, either directly or after one intervening term had been served by Lieutenant General Joyanto Nath Choudhri, who ranks next to Thapar in seniority. This suspicion was voiced in an anonymous letter to Nehru in the spring of 1961 from a group of army officers who accused Menon of practicing "black magic over the mind of the prime minister."

The juggling of generals provoked an anguished outcry in the Indian Parliament. Menon was accused of undermining the country's defenses at a critical moment by playing favorites in the officer corps and disregarding recommendations of the promotion boards. Again Nehru came to Menon's rescue and assumed personal responsibility for every major appointment in the services. Rebutting charges that Kaul was nothing but an Army Service Corps "house-builder" without combat experience, Nehru told Parliament that he was "an officer who has been in the infantry for twenty-five years out of his twenty-eight years of service," adding, "I say with complete confidence and knowledge that he is one of our brightest and best officers in the army." For his part, Menon recalled that Kaul had been commissioned in the East Surrey regiment, an infantry unit, and that, "His period in the Army Service Corps during British times amounts to somewhere around eight or ten years out of twenty-eight years of service."

The discrepancy arises from the fact that Kaul has held a variety of staff jobs that cannot precisely be assigned to the infantry or the Service Corps. He says that he spent only three years with the Service Corps as such. Many observers were misled by Menon's defense of Kaul into assuming that the CGS was simply a stooge of the Defense Minister. This is untrue.

My information indicates that Kaul opposed Menon on the purchase of Soviet AN-12 turboprop transports for use on the northern frontier. I understand he also urged Menon to consider American and French supersonic fighters before concluding the MiG deal with Moscow. Infuriated at Kaul's interest in American weapons, Menon once exploded, "Why don't you take out American citizenship?"

Kaul insists that he did not know Menon well before he was promoted to be CGS. Early in 1962 he told me testily, "I stand up to Menon ten times a day. It can be difficult." I know from other sources that Menon and Kaul were increasingly at odds before Menon resigned as defense minister in October 1962. My impression is that the Menon-Kaul alliance was a temporary marriage of convenience that could be broken off or renewed at any time, depending on circumstances. I can hardly think of two more dissimilar men in temperament and political outlook.

One significant issue on which I know Kaul outmaneuvered Menon is the "forward" strategy adopted by the Indian Army in the summer of 1962 against the Chinese in Ladakh and on the northeast frontier. Kaul went to Nehru and persuaded him to let the Army establish advance check posts to outflank Chinese posts set up on Indian territory. "The Army has to have self-respect," Kaul insisted. Menon was hamstrung. He could not openly oppose a policy aimed at reclaiming lost Indian territory. Menon's long-standing orders that Indian patrols should not engage the Chinese under any circumstances were revoked. Indian troops were told to hold their ground and open fire if the Chinese sought to dislodge them from any position on Indian soil.

Kaul's "forward" strategy evoked a violent Chinese response that culminated in the general attacks launched at both ends of the frontier on October 20, 1962. Inevitably, his enemies in the Army and outside accused Kaul of having heedlessly jeopardized Indian defenses for the illusory gain of some desolate mountain tracts, but Nehru, who had personally approved the new tactics, refused to disown him.

If Kaul depended exclusively on Nehru, he would be little better than a military counterpart of Menon. But the CGS is not content to rely on the patronage of his powerful relative. For many years he has cultivated a larger circle of friends outside the service than has any other Indian officer. His one-story pillared home on New Delhi's shady Motilal Nehru Marg (formerly York Road) is frequented at all hours by a motley collection of friends, hangers-on, favor-seekers, job-hunters, and the simply curious. "I make it a practice," Kaul told me proudly, "to see everyone who comes here and help everyone I can. Widows, orphans, saints, murderers, thieves, policemen —all—come here every day. I never say no to anyone in trouble."

I know that Kaul personally borrowed heavily to start a charity store for servicemen's dependents. He went out of his way to persuade the American Embassy to hire orphaned children of servicemen as guides in the American pavilion at the 1961 Industries Fair in New Delhi. One military attaché in Delhi says, "This is the politician in Kaul. But he also has a genuinely human side." For example, he made elaborate but unpublicized arrangements to send an ailing Indian general to America for medical treatment. Another example is the story that en route one day to a meeting of the cabinet's

Defense Committee, Kaul noticed a man who had collapsed in the road. He ordered his driver to stop and alighted to find out what was wrong. The man was suffering from tuberculosis of the bone. He had been forced to sell his tiny stall shop and was now penniless. "By that evening," Kaul says, "I had collected 2,000 rupees [about $400] for his treatment. He eventually made a full recovery. I paid another 2,000 rupees to get his shop back for him. I've never seen him again."

At another time Kaul says he harbored a murderer in his home until arrangements could be made to rehabilitate the man. When the son of a Defense Ministry messenger died of a broken back, Kaul paid for a dignified Hindu cremation. My impression is that such acts of benevolence give Kaul genuine satisfaction as well as enhance his reputation in Delhi. He constantly borrows money to lend to the needy and rarely seems to worry about repayment.

It would be naïve, however, to regard Kaul as a kind of uniformed angel of mercy. He is ruthless toward anyone he suspects of opposing him. The attempted plot to accuse Major General S.H.F.J. (Sam) Manekshaw, former commandant of the Defense Services Staff College, of impugning constituted authority, was ordered by Menon with Kaul's connivance. Several officers were persuaded to bring trumped-up accusations against Manekshaw after his third star had been announced but not yet conferred. The actual reason for trying to get rid of this brilliant Parsi officer was his outspoken opposition to Menon. Manekshaw was ready to resign, but Thimayya persuaded him to call his accusers' bluff. In the end, a three-man inquiry board dismissed the charges against Manekshaw and recommended that some of his accusers be made to answer for their conduct.

Kaul's family ties with Nehru gave him an early taste of politics on a high level. He met most of the important Indian politicians and government officials long before he would have done so in line of duty. When his younger daughter was married in May 1962, he invited 2,000 of Delhi's elite to a lavish wedding feast in his garden, replete with Indian orchestral accompaniment and long tables laden with delicacies. I remember Kaul furiously striding around that rainy night in a loosely wound maroon turban, cream-colored *achkan,* and knee breeches, shouting orders at what seemed to be half the Indian Army. The General was irked because the rain had disrupted the elaborate strings of colored lights that festooned his house and the wedding *shamiana,* or tent. The Kaul wedding was as big a social event in Delhi as the inaugural ball is in Washington.

From the time he was in Korea until early in 1961, Kaul shunned Americans in Delhi. Then about February he began showing marked cordiality to them. He never missed a dinner invitation from the American Ambassador, John Kenneth Galbraith, and began visiting other American homes in Delhi. He suddenly became accessible to American correspondents. He explained that he wanted to show that he was not anti-American and had been misrepresented. When Menon chided him for accepting Galbraith's invitation without being equally convivial with the Russians, Kaul is reputed to have answered, "I know the British and Americans. They speak my language. They're my friends. I don't know these other people."

When General Herbert Powell, then commander of the continental U.S. Army, and several other senior American military men passed through Delhi at various times in 1961 and 1962, Kaul was usually present when they called on General Thapar. He asked for private meetings with them and urged the United States to allow India to buy American military equipment on a deferred-payment basis or on other terms that would meet Menon's objections to spending scarce foreign exchange on arms. At several of these meetings he complained bitterly against Menon and asked the Americans to do everything possible to maintain Western links with the Indian Army. As one Western attaché says, "Kaul definitely does want to buy American, but he's a nationalist and if he can't get the equipment he needs from the West, he'd turn to the East bloc without a moment's hesitation." I have had indications that Kaul has dissuaded Menon from buying more Communist-bloc military equipment despite the attractive payment conditions offered by those countries.

When the Chinese attacked in October 1962 Kaul helped persuade Nehru to request American and other Western arms on an emergency basis despite Menon's last-ditch objections. Kaul submitted a tentative list of Indian military needs to Galbraith even before Nehru had taken the decision to turn to the West in India's hour of peril.

Kaul says that he knew nothing of the impending MiG deal until he happened to hear that Air Vice Marshal Ranjan Dutt, head of the state-owned Hindustan Aircraft, Limited, was going to Moscow in the spring of 1962. When Kaul insisted that American and French fighters should also be considered, Menon told him, "You know nothing about this." Kaul had earlier told Galbraith that only Nehru and President Kennedy could work out arrangements for India to purchase supersonic Western fighters. He also raised the subject with Chester Bowles, a former American ambassador to India and an old friend.

While he awaits the day when he will be the acknowledged military chief of the Indian Army, Kaul is quietly moving his backers into key positions at headquarters. Brigadier D. K. Palit, Kaul's hand-picked director of military operations, is an extremely competent infantry officer, author of a number of books on tactics, and prime architect of Operation Vijay, the seizure of Goa. The director of military intelligence is another Kaul protégé.

"Every sepoy in the army," according to Thimayya, "knows Kaul has never been a combat soldier. You can't hide that sort of thing in the Army. The officers don't respect Kaul." Less partisan observers question this view. A Western military attaché with considerable experience in India reports that many Indian officers who were hostile to Kaul before he became CGS, and who are still opposed to Menon, now say that Kaul is brilliant and extremely able. Their regard for Kaul appears to be genuine. Under his direction, the Army was expanded by about one fifth in the first eighteen months after he became CGS. Efficiency has certainly not declined, and may well have improved. Opportunities for promotion have increased—something bound to benefit Kaul in the eyes of his juniors. His vainglory and flamboyance may evoke smiles in Delhi, but they add zest to barracks life on the outer fringes of the Indian empire. My own feeling is that

Kaul reflects the impatient nationalism and many of the other strivings of India's younger officers.

He may have seen much less combat than Thimayya and other senior officers did, but he has proved on more than one occasion that he possesses unquestionable personal courage. In November 1955, when forty soldiers whom he had sent for winter training on the Tibetan border (against the advice of experts) were caught in the snowbound Rohtang Pass, Kaul set out on foot with an aide to rescue them. Buffeted by 100-mile-an-hour gales on the way up the pass, they lost practically all their kit, including food. Their porters vanished. Two hundred feet from the top of the pass the exhausted climbers collapsed in ten-foot snowdrifts. "After a little while," Kaul says, "we felt as if life were oozing out of us. We wrote a message in hopes that it would be found on our bodies the next morning. It was addressed to the stranded men and said simply, 'We did our best to reach and rescue you but, sorry, death is cheating us.' "

This flourish proved premature. Shortly after midnight, two of their porters returned with some tea which they managed to heat over a kerosene burner. Kaul says that he gave the first cup to the porters, although it was "bloody difficult" not to drink it himself. The four men managed to live through the night. When morning came, the storm abated and the skies cleared. By this time, two other porters originally attached to Kaul had reached the forty soldiers stranded farther up the pass and told them their would-be rescuers had frozen to death. Two members of the stranded group went in search of the bodies. When they ran into Kaul (who was wearing no insignia), one of them asked, "Have you seen two army chaps who died coming up here?" Kaul feigned ignorance for a time, then finally identified himself. At that point, he says, they all started laughing hysterically and ended by weeping. The next step was to lead everyone to safety. Only ten soldiers out of the original forty were fit to walk. The others were suffering from frostbite, pneumonia, or exhaustion. Kaul made each able-bodied man responsible for three others. For the next fifteen hours they worked their way down the pass, lashed by angry winds as they plodded through the snow. When they reached the bottom, Kaul noticed that one man was missing. He asked for volunteers to accompany him back up the mountain. One benumbed figure tottered forward to offer his services. He and Kaul started climbing back up. Fortunately, they had gone only a short distance when they found the missing soldier unconscious under a tree.

Four years later, when the Chinese Communists occupied the tiny Indian border settlement of Longju, in the east, Kaul trekked hundreds of miles on foot to the nearest Indian post. He wanted to see the situation for himself.

Such episodes may not always reflect credit on Kaul's judgment, but they help endear him to the Indian *jawan,* or common soldier, who loves nothing better than a legend of heroism.

On December 2, 1960, when Kaul was quartermaster general, he figured in an escapade that had international repercussions. He flew with a Soviet pilot and two Indian airmen in one of India's newly acquired Russian MI-4 helicopters to a point near the Karakoram Pass, in extreme northern Ladakh. The MI-4 is reputed to be able to climb to 21,000 feet, but American authorities doubt that it has ever flown higher than 16,500 feet. Kaul says that Menon insisted there was no need to test the Soviet machines because they had already been tested in Russia. While Menon was attending a U.N. meeting in New York, Kaul overrode the objections of Russian technicians and pilots and ordered the MI-4 to fly north through the fog-shrouded mountains. When they neared the Karakoram Pass, more than 18,000 feet above sea level, Kaul told the Russian pilot to land. The pilot objected that there was no level ground and that he might never be able to take off again. "If you people say you can land on the moon," Kaul exploded, "you can bloody well land on that spot down there. If not, it means you can't land anywhere." The Russian landed. Then Kaul told him that they were a twenty-one-day march from the nearest post. "If we can't take off," he threatened, "we'll all freeze into nice ice cream for someone." With such a fate in prospect, the Russian got the machine off the frozen ground and headed back. Thirty minutes out of Leh, the Ladakhi capital, the pilot announced that he had fuel for only seven minutes more. They set down in a snowdrift beside a stream bed. Kaul climbed out and hiked to the nearest hilltop, where a half-frozen Sikh lookout was startled to meet the Quartermaster General of the Indian Army. Kaul and the others were later picked up by a Dakota, which managed to land on the glassy streambed. The helicopter was abandoned to the Himalayan winter. Kaul says that Menon later "ticked me off" for flying the MI-4, but in Parliament the next spring Menon defended Kaul's action and said that he was the only person who had volunteered to test-fly the machine.

Kaul came under fire on the northeastern frontier on October 10, 1962, when the Chinese launched their largest probing attack preparatory to the October 20 offensive against Indian positions in several sectors of the frontier. He was at an advance company headquarters at the time, having trekked over most of the area in the previous week. Early in October he had been named to command a new corps on the northeastern border with the specific assignment of ejecting Chinese troops that had entered this sector the previous month. He escaped unhurt from the Chinese fire but later contracted pneumonia as a result of his exertions at altitudes up to 14,500 feet.

Such examples of bravura have given Kaul the reputation of being a flashy operator. I think it would be a mistake, nevertheless, to write him off as an Indian edition of General Custer. He has a Kashmiri's native guile, which conditions his impulsive nature. Moreover, Kaul has frequently demonstrated his administrative ability and his sagacity in things political. Even his detractors have difficulty finding fault with his performance as quartermaster general and as co-ordinator of the Border Roads Commission, set up after Chinese incursions threatened the whole Himalayan frontier.

The bane of Kaul's existence is the global dispersion of his army. A reinforced brigade is committed to the U.N. force in the Congo. Smaller but still sizable units are serving in Gaza. The equivalent of a full division has been tied down in Nagaland since 1954 fighting underground insurgents who want a separate Naga nation. Most hurtful of all, from 50 to 60 per cent of the Indian Army is committed along the Kash-

mir cease-fire line and other parts of India's 2,800-mile frontier
with Pakistan. This leaves Kaul with the logistic capacity to
support the equivalent of only three brigades in Ladakh. "We
could take care of the Chinese," he laments, "if it weren't for
the need to watch the Pakistanis."

Kaul fears that Pakistan will launch an Algeria-style guerrilla war in Indian-held Kashmir. He suspects that Pakistani
troops may be disguised as tribesmen and sent into Indian
territory with arms furnished by Communist China. Such misgivings reflect no deep hostility on Kaul's part to Pakistan
or its military leaders. On the contrary, he knows and likes
many members of the present Pakistani regime. He says, "I'm
constantly trying to bring these two countries [India and
Pakistan] together. The army people in Pakistan understand
me. They agree, but the others don't." With what sounded
like real regret in his voice, he told me once that he thought
India could have been "really great, first-class, if we hadn't
fallen victim to our own disunity."

He is enthusiastic about his men. He loves giving them
rousing pep talks. Indian troops, he tells them, are "the best
damned soldiers in the world." Addressing a group of his Jats
bound for Ladakh in the spring of 1962, he reminded them
that one of their number had been decorated for knocking
out a German machine-gun post in World War II. "The Germans are a hell of a lot better fighters than the Chinese," he
shouted at the top of his lungs, "but we beat the Germans.
So don't listen to anyone up there in Ladakh who tells you
how tough things are going to be. Unless you come back in
a couple of years with two or three VC's [Victoria Crosses]
among you, I don't want to see you. In that case you can just
bugger off." This typically profane peroration was greeted
with cheers and arm-waving by the impressionable Jats.

Kaul's faith in Indian troops is more than bravado. He is
really convinced that they are better trained (despite the cut
in basic training from forty-eight to thirty-two weeks), better
motivated, and in better physical condition than their more
numerous adversaries across the Himalayas. He discounts the
common notion that the Chinese have an easier supply problem because they have to climb only 3,000 to 4,000 feet from

the Tibetan plateau, whereas the Indians start 6,000 to 7,000 feet below the Himalayan passes. "The Chinese," he insists, "have twenty times the difficulty we have in resupplying their troops. Their supply line may not be so steep as ours, but it's a lot longer."

Despite these difficulties, the Chinese were able to concentrate large masses of troops and equipment at both ends of the frontier for their offensive in the fall of 1962. Their performance surprised Western military authorities as well as the Indians.

Given adequate equipment and supplies, Kaul believes his men are more than a match for the Chinese. India's forces are all volunteer. China's is a conscript army. Indian troops get mail from home air-dropped with their supplies. They also get regular leave, even in Ladakh, and they are periodically rotated to more hospitable billets. The Chinese told Kaul in Korea that their men never got leave. Their troops receive mail infrequently and after long delays. Other military observers generally confirm Kaul's estimate of the two armies despite reports of a minor mutiny among Indian Gurkha troops in Ladakh in the summer of 1960.

The Indians' most serious deficiency in Ladakh is motor transport. They have to climb steep hillsides, while the Chinese move in trucks over a network of military roads and feeder tracks they have built across Aksai Chin's barren soda plains. The Chinese have at least eighteen major military supply dumps in Tibet, and seven of the fourteen airfields they plan for Tibet are already completed. The Chinese are able to reinforce more quickly than the Indians.

Kaul moved two extra battalions—1,800 men—into Ladakh as part of the Indian build-up in the spring of 1962. Roads leading north were clogged with military vehicles. Kaul kept as many as twenty-four C-119's (acquired on easy terms from the United States in 1959) in the air at a time, ferrying supplies to forward posts. Nehru said later that this movement had enabled Indian troops to secure possession of 2,500 square miles in Ladakh that were previously considered under Chinese control. Unfortunately, their gains were short-lived.

India's real weakness in facing the Chinese is not the numerical inferiority of its forces, but the equipment muddle caused by Menon's obsession with producing arms domestically or buying them from the East bloc in preference to India's traditional Western suppliers. When the Chinese attacked in October 1962, the Indian Army still lacked a good rifle. Indian infantrymen used a ponderous local version of the World War I bolt-action .303 British Enfield, which has a strong recoil. Indian-made automatic rifles almost invariably develop a malfunction after three or four rounds in test demonstrations. The locally produced 4.2-millimeter mortar has a range of only 4,700 yards, compared with 7,900 yards for a U.S. weapon. The much-advertised Indian-made turboprop transport, the Avro-748, is the butt of ridicule because of repeated delays in its production and the plane's very low payload. Production of the HT-2 trainer was discontinued at the Hindustan Aircraft plant at Bangalore after only 160 planes had been made.

Menon boasted in 1961 that India was perfecting an air-to-air missile, but he later admitted that by the time anything of the sort could be supplied to the Air Force, it would be hopelessly outdated. The fiasco of the HF-24, touted as the first supersonic plane made in Asia, led directly to the quest for MiGs.

When Indian troops overran Goa in December 1961, many marched in canvas shoes because a contract for boots had been switched from the Bata company to a small Indian firm, which failed to deliver.

While the old Ishapore rifle factory near Calcutta is still unable to make a modern rifle, it did turn out, between 1958 and 1960, a total of fifteen *espresso* coffee machines at a cost of 4,500 rupees (about $900) apiece. None of these not-so-violent weapons could be sold to the public, but one was given away to the late Dr. B. C. Roy, then chief minister of West Bengal and a confirmed tea drinker.

Armed with *espresso* coffee machines and canvas shoes, even the finest Indian troops are ill-equipped to guard the country's 8,200 miles of land frontier (including some of the most difficult terrain on earth) and 3,500 miles of sea frontier. The Army consists of ten regular divisions, including one armored division with an independent armored brigade and several independent infantry brigades. The armored units must get along with British Centurions, American Shermans, and French AMX light tanks. Sometime in the future, the first Indian-assembled tanks will roll out of the Avadi plant near Madras. They will be produced under license from the British Vickers-Armstrongs firm.

These ground forces are aided by a small Air Force equipped with a mixture of British, American, French, and Russian planes. There is no effective ground radar net. The Indian Navy acquired a refitted British aircraft carrier in 1961 to team with its two Ajax-class light cruisers and destroyer flotilla. The Navy's first antisubmarine reconnaissance squadron, equipped with French Alize aircraft, was commissioned in March 1961. The appointment of Rear Admiral B. S. Soman, a sailor with little sea experience for the last eleven years, as chief of the naval staff in April 1962 caused almost as loud a furor as the supersessions in the Army. Rear Admiral Ajitendu Chakraverti, then the Navy's senior directing staff officer at the National Defense College in New Delhi, resigned because his seniority and longer sea experience had been disregarded.

Despite their relative newness in the military picture, both the Navy and Air Force are much more homogeneous than the Indian Army is. Diversity in the enlisted ranks is the Army's worst handicap next to its inadequate equipment. In British days the Army was a caste organization, with units organized on strict caste lines. Infantry regiments were recruited separately from the so-called martial classes—Jats, Rajputs, Punjabis, Dogras, Garhwalis, Gurkhas, and Marathas. South Indian Madrasis, adept with their hands, provided most of the sappers. Sikhs predominated among noncommissioned officers. There were vegetarian and nonvegetarian messes and other concessions to religious feeling. The officers were relatively homogeneous. They all communicated easily in English. Noncoms used a kind of basic Hindustani or the regional language of their unit.

To get away from caste divisions, the Nehru government has repeatedly brought pressure on the generals to create mixed units. Enlisted ranks are now open to all comers, re-gardless of caste or region, but in practice the old martial castes still predominate. The best fighting formations are still close-knit one-caste outfits. Kaul insists that nothing can ever replace the martial spirit and centuries-old traditions of the one-class regiments.

In another effort to promote "integration," the government is trying to popularize Hindi as the lingua franca of the armed forces. Officers are now supposed to pass an examination in Hindi. But the enlisted men's newspaper, *Sainik Samachar*, is still published in nine languages. A truly national army does not yet exist at the enlisted level in India.

The fragmentation of India's military establishment (pri-marily the Army) is often cited by those who insist that a military coup is impossible in India. They contend that Sikhs, Jats, Dogras, Gurkhas, and others in Indian uniform can never be welded into a coherent force willing or able to sustain an officers' junta in power. I have never been able to accept this comfortable view. Everything I have seen of the Indian Army indicates that its officer corps is the most homogeneous and well-integrated all-India group in the country. The *jawans* take their cue from the officers, not from the politicians back home. Military discipline and tradition, as Selig Harrison rightly points out, help insulate the Army from regional and communal pressures. The Indian Army is an oasis of order in a national desert of indiscipline. The Army boasts an *esprit de corps* unknown in any other Indian institution, including the Congress party and the present Civil Service.

I therefore think it naïve to assume that the Army will necessarily be paralyzed in a crisis by its own diversity, which is not the same thing as disunity. If the civil power collapses, the Army is not likely to stand aside passively while India disintegrates. It is true that the Army has traditionally been a nonpolitical force on the British model. But the professional character of the British Indian Army applied as much to its Moslem officers, men like Ayub Khan, as to the non-Moslems. Yet Ayub and his fellow Pakistani officers did not hesitate to seize power in October 1958 when Pakistan's civilian poli-ticians had demonstrated their incapacity. The same thing could happen in India if Congress shows itself incapable of ruling without Nehru. The Indian officers are as conscious of their own power as the Pakistani officers were. I do not expect for a moment that the Indian Army will try to overthrow a functioning and reasonably efficient civilian regime even after Nehru goes. The Congress and Civil Service tradition is too deeply imbedded in Indian life to be uprooted by the caprice of the officer corps. But what could well happen is that the Army will come to regard itself as the only source of redress in a period of national calamity.

If such evils do befall India, I think it would be impossible to overlook Brij Mohan Kaul. He far outranks other Indian generals in knowledge of the nonmilitary world, especially of foreign affairs. His experience in Washington and Korea and at the U.N. has given him an insight into international politics possessed by no other Indian officer. He is a man of bottomless self-confidence. He has the added advantages of youth, good health, and extremely influential family connections. If he fails, it is likely to be owing to what Metternich called an "excess of zeal." He could as well turn out to be a Boulanger as a Bonaparte.

The key question is whether Kaul could command the support of enough of the Indian Army (and possibly elements of the Air Force and Navy) to dominate the country in a period of upheaval. A Delhi editor who professes to know says flatly, "Kaul is a house-builder, not a military man. He couldn't pull a coup because the Army wouldn't follow him." This is probably true today and for the next year or two. Kaul would have no chance before he became chief of staff. But after that, his position, already good, would be enormously strengthened.

General Choudhri, who now heads the Southern Command, with headquarters at Poona, might be named chief of staff if Thapar retires in 1963, but he is not likely to prove any lasting impediment to Kaul. He is a stickler for British-style protocol and an opportunist who would probably back the top man in Delhi. Moreover, he has a heart condition that may prevent him from serving even one term as chief of staff.

The most powerful and important man in the Indian Army today outside Delhi is Lieutenant General Lionel Protip

("Bogey") Sen, now in charge of the Eastern Command, which includes the Nagas and the long frontier with Tibet. He is a Sandhurst product and a holder of the Distinguished Service Order. He commanded the 10th Baluch Regiment in the famous "all-Indian brigade" that smashed the Japanese at Kangaw in World War II, and led the attack in Kashmir in November 1947. He is widely regarded as a Thimayya man, essentially nonpolitical, but anti-Menon and probably anti-Kaul.

Before the Chinese offensive, the Menon-Kaul strategy seemed to be to move Sen into the job of deputy chief of the army staff, then held by Lieutenant General Mohinder Singh Wadalia, a beardless Sikh who has wanted to retire for years, and is due to leave early in 1963. This would be a comedown for Sen, but if he refused, he could then be forcibly retired and eliminated from the picture. In either case Kaul would take over the Eastern Command. I have heard talk that Sen might try to pull off a coup of his own before his position is eroded. Although his present post carries more weight than Kaul's, the CGS is closer to the levers of power in Delhi, including the Prime Minister and the Defense Minister. Kaul has exploited his central position to extend his control over every branch of the Army in a way that Sen would find difficult.

So the long finger of history always seems to swing back to Kaul when the Indian Army is discussed. He strikes me as being one of those tormented figures committed by his own inner compulsions to dominate or disappear. No middle ground or compromise is broad enough to contain his soaring ambition.

Napoleon said that he found the crown of France lying in the gutter and picked it up with his sword. Kaul may find that the crown of India will crumble when he reaches for it. The disciple of discipline could become the harbinger of dissolution. The supreme blow to preserve Indian unity could shatter the object of its desire. India could disintegrate like a crown of sand.

A successful army coup, on the other hand, might prove more stultifying than one that failed. India, like the mythical

phoenix, may always rise from the ashes of its own dismemberment, but it may never rise if it is uprooted from its past by
a military despot with alien ideas of order. A certain amount
of chaos is endemic in India; military rule is not. Chaos after
Nehru would not necessarily spell the final extinction of
India's democratic experiment; military rule probably would.
The dissolution of India, however catastrophic in the short
run, may be remediable in the long run. Modern totalitarianism often proves irreversible.

Military rule could be imposed on India while Kaul stayed
discreetly in the background. He could be a Nasser to Thapar's
Naguib or some other venerable façade. But such an arrangement would not change the real power in an Indian military
regime. Moreover, Kaul would not be an unattractive military
ruler. He could rationalize the demise of Indian democracy
as skillfully as he does his relations with Menon. His performance would certainly have more drive and polish than does
the faltering Indian democracy in the second half of a cyclonic
century of change. Kaul would do many things that now
remain undone for want of courage. He would probably make
a real attack on the awesome glut of people and animals in
the Indian countryside. He would dynamite some of the musty
catacombs of superstition and ignorance that still imprison
the mind of India. He might well succeed in streamlining the
clay-footed Indian bureaucracy and building armed forces
capable of effectively protecting the country. He would certainly be acclaimed in Washington and London, and possibly
also in Moscow. He could be the idol of all lovers of order.

But all the skill and subterfuge of this galvanic figure could
not create an orderly pattern of succession. The right of public
dissent would have disappeared from its last major foothold
on the mainland of Asia. As the rest of Asia knows, there are
few turnings from the road to dictatorship. General Kaul or
any man on horseback might soon find himself mounted on
an Indian tiger that could only follow the footsteps of the Chinese dragon.

CONCLUSION

THIS GALLERY is complete. One can agree with Schopenhauer that the hall of fame is a mixed company, and nowhere more than in India, the largest national museum of human diversity the world has ever seen.

The seven men and one woman sketched here mirror many of the contradictions of their country. At one end of the spectrum is Jayaprakash Narayan, agonizing at the sight of a lizard trapped in his bookcase; at the other extreme, Brij Mohan Kaul, dreaming of hurling his legions at the Chinese hordes. Or consider the contrast between the archpriest of arrogance, Krishna Menon, and the apostle of self-effacement, Lal Bahadur Shastri. Morarji Desai, fasting on his pallet in an airless room, and S. K. Patil, luxuriating in an air-conditioned preview theater, may share a common political outlook, but hardly a way of life. Yeshwantrao Chavan's illiterate peasant mother and Indira Gandhi's highly literate aristocratic father both contrived to educate their offspring, but by different means and with different results.

With the exception of Kaul, these persons have donned the

loose cloak of socialism in their search for a role. No ideological raiment ever concealed more fundamental differences. Senator Barry Goldwater could cheerfully acquiesce in Patil's "socialism" and might even find Desai's to his liking. Menon's socialism is not the Soviet ideal, but Nikita Khrushchev could coexist happily with it. Socialism for Narayan is the shriveled husk of a doctrine whose contents have evaporated in the heat of reality. Shastri calls himself a Gandhian socialist, demonstrating thereby the Indian gift for reconciling the irreconcilable.

Notwithstanding their differences, these eight have certain (albeit negative) things in common. None has established himself as a dominant national figure. None can lay claim to the succession as a matter of right. Each suffers from past errors and present shortcomings. All except Menon and Kaul went to jail during the freedom struggle, but none except Narayan played a major role in the movement in India. All except Kaul are or have been members of the Congress party, but all except Patil were late-starters. None of the eight except perhaps Narayan has surrounded himself with the same aura of patriotism and self-sacrifice that distinguished the old-line freedom fighters like Nehru and Pandit Pant.

It is a truism to say that none of Nehru's possible successors will inherit his vast power and prestige. At least in the beginning, none will possess his emotional rapport with the Indian masses. Foreign policy will no longer be the almost exclusive prerogative of the prime minister. For the first time, India may have a reasonable facsimile of cabinet government, with collective leadership at the top. Geographic and communal "balance" in the Union cabinet and the state governments will be increasingly necessary. The Congress parliamentary party and Parliament as a whole may become something more than a rubber stamp for the prime minister. Such prospects have led many Indians to conclude that all Nehru's possible heirs are political second-raters devoid of real ability. As I indicated in the beginning, I regard this view as dangerously mistaken. India is blessed with many capable leaders and some outstanding ones. To reproach them for not attaining giant dimensions under the Nehru banyan is to ignore political realities in independent India.

Perhaps a final word about Nehru himself is in order. No one who compares India with the rest of non-Communist Asia can disparage the service he has rendered his country. Nehru has maintained unity and continuity in the face of appalling obstacles and has resisted the temptation to abridge civil rights or the tortuous processes of representative government. He has given India an intellectual impetus that most other former colonial countries lack. Although I have always felt that he could have done more to combat caste and communal bigotry, he has at least refused to condone them. He has championed a secular India and befriended Moslems, Sikhs, Christians, and other minorities. In view of his real achievements, the Nehru cult, in which so many Indians and some foreigners engage, is the greatest possible disservice to him and to India. It ignores Nehru's warm human qualities, his admitted fallibility, and his hatred of idolatry. I consider Nehru's most serious faults his naïveté about Communism, his irrational fear of Indian and foreign private capital, his aristocratic distrust of public opinion on such a paramount issue as the struggle with China, and his egotistic refusal to prepare younger leaders for high-level responsibilities.

Nehru's long history of self-deception about the aims and methods of world Communism needs no elaboration. His proclaimed devotion to parliamentary institutions is less impressive in the light of his refusal to take Parliament into his confidence for more than four years after he knew Chinese expansionism had become a serious threat to India. His unwillingness to give free rein to the dynamic forces of Indian and foreign private capital has obliged India to rely on an overburdened, paper-bound, and partially corrupt bureaucracy to provide the primary stimulus for progress.

Nehru's passing may in fact release creative new forces stifled by the dead hand of a tired administration committed to outmoded Fabian economics. Not that I expect Nehru's successors to solve the problems that have baffled him, but a new approach may be helpful. The quality of those under the

Nehru banyan is better than the deep shadows would lead
one to believe, although it will take time before they can
provide shade of their own for the country. As practitioners
of the art of the impossible, Indian politicians can really be
compared only for their inadequacies. None, including Nehru,
has yet found a way to translate his individual capacity into
the collective competence that India needs so desperately.

There is something typically Indian in the fact that Lal
Bahadur Shastri, who insists that he could never fill the prime
minister's shoes, will probably be the first person asked to do
so. India and Congress are ready for a respite from giants.
But I doubt that Shastri has the physical or political endur-
ance to ride the Indian tiger for long. The impasse between
the Left and Right Wing factions in Congress that would be
the condition for his being named prime minister would not
last forever. As soon as one faction got the upper hand,
Shastri's days would be numbered, unless he had meanwhile
built a national following of his own. To do that he must
demonstrate a Truman-like gift for projecting himself as the
champion of the common man.

I am inclined to agree with those who contend that the
vital question in India is not "After Nehru, who?" but, "After
Nehru's successor, who?" Nehru's removal from the political
scene, either by death or incapacity, will send a shock through
Congress comparable to that which the Soviet leadership felt
when Stalin died. Of course Nehru has conducted no blood
purges, but his passing will raise the same fears about the future of the Indian republic as Stalin's demise posed for the
Soviet state.

The first step will be a converging of party leaders on Delhi
to attend Nehru's funeral or hover solicitously by his bedside
if he is disabled. Little caucuses of state and group leaders
will assemble all over the capital. Amid public tributes to
Nehru's service, top civil servants like V. Viswanathan, in the
Home Ministry, and military leaders like Kaul will be consulted on the security situation and their own views on the
succession. The Congress Right Wing will take counsel with
its big-business allies. The Leftist faction in Congress will
sound out the Communists, hoping to learn their intentions.

On every hand (except perhaps among Menon's followers and a section of the Army) there will be strong pressure for Congress unity and maintenance of an effective central government. This pressure will be particularly pronounced if Hindu-Moslem strife erupts in the aftermath of Nehru's removal from power. The Congress Working Committee will convene to choose a new chief, who will then be dutifully elected by the Congress parliamentary party as its leader and the party's nominee for prime minister. At this point India's chief of state, President Radhakrishnan, could upset the plans of the Congress bosses. He could refuse to appoint the first man proposed by the party and insist on another round of consultations. But I think such a conflict is unlikely in the immediate post-Nehru period. Powerful forces in Congress and the country will be working to close the leadership gap as quickly as possible. To avoid a prolonged factional struggle, Shastri might well be given the nod, especially because such powerful figures as Chavan and Kamaraj would have nothing to fear from him.

The situation will be entirely different when Shastri or whoever succeeds Nehru leaves the scene (probably not long after Nehru's passing) and a new prime minister must be chosen. This will be the supreme test for Indian democracy. Congress is almost certain to have split openly and officially by that time. At best it will be a two-way division on Left-Right factional lines. Otherwise the party may disintegrate into a galaxy of petty state-based groups trafficking in caste, linguistic, or regional politics for the benefit of ambitious local leaders. My own hunch is that Congress will not fragment when it splits. Each of the two principal wings is likely to pick up strength from outside Congress when the break comes.

Under Nehru the Congress party has shown a capacity for assimilation second only to Hinduism. The dilution of Congress doctrine has been almost as far-reaching. The parties that emerge from the breakup of the present Congress may begin life with a cleaner ideological slate, but their propensity for accretion will be no less. Indeed, the impulse will be stronger, because it will arise from necessity rather than from habit. Once each Congress offshoot has amalgamated whatever democratic splinters are in its orbit, further additions can come only from the extremists of Left or Right.

The Congress Right Wing will probably merge with the Swatantra party and may possibly steal the Jan Sangh's communal thunder. The Congress Leftists may coalesce with the remnants of Indian socialism, including the Praja Socialist and the Socialist parties. The question is not whether the Congress as presently stitched together can be kept from ripping apart, but whether the products of a split can save themselves from their potential allies on the far left and far right. If the party formed by the Congress Rightists is conservative without being communal, it will fill an urgently felt need in Indian politics. If, on the other hand, it becomes the tool of religious fanaticism and caste reaction, the effect would be to polarize the political field. Congress moderates would be driven to the left, and the Left would be more inclined to compromise for Communist support. The democratic alternative would have evaporated like the first monsoon shower.

Such a denouement is by no means inevitable if capable leadership is forthcoming. The Right has yet to rally around a single leader, but it is by no means leaderless. Morarji Desai commands the widest support and promises to be most effective in office. Even he, however, would have to function, at least in the early months of a conservative government, as the first among equals. The Right Wing leadership would include S. K. Patil as campaign manager and tactician-in-chief at the local level, assisted by two promising younger leaders, Dr. Ram Subhag Singh, now Patil's deputy in the Food Ministry, and C. Subramaniam, the able minister of steel and heavy industries. Patil is not likely to lead the Right unless Desai disappears before one of the younger leaders is ready to step in.

Among the Congress Left, Krishna Menon and Indira Gandhi are the only leaders who can claim any following. Each has depended on Nehru's patronage and protection. Menon is a political solipsist with an anarchist's hatred of authority. His fiery brilliance is always visible, but his charm registers infrequently. Except for the fact that he is not Jewish, Menon is a caricature of the "rootless cosmopolitan" that Stalinist propagandists lampooned after the war. India is a

rather unwelcome port of call on his restless voyage of intellectual discovery and disillusion. My guess is that he will cast
off his lines and sail away after Nehru goes unless he can
somehow quench his thirst for power in India.

Indira Gandhi is neither rootless nor anarchic. She lacks
her father's political finesse, but has infinitely more tact and
decorum than Menon has. She cannot be ignored, especially
if the Right Wing is forestalled in its first bid for supremacy
after Nehru. In that event the Congress conservatives and
moderates would certainly prefer Mrs. Gandhi to any other
Leftist in the party. The Leftists themselves would gladly
back her. I think she is a strong possibility in case of a deadlock between the rival factions either immediately after her
father or after one successor has been discarded. If she did
become prime minister, I would discount her staying power,
because the magic will soon fade from the Nehru name.

Apart from Menon and Mrs. Gandhi, the Congress Left has
no leaders worthy of the name. K. D. Malaviya, the oil minister, has made a reputation by jousting successfully with the
Western oil companies and bringing Russian petroleum products to India, but his political following is nil. He has nowhere to go but left. Bijoyananda Patnaik, the youthful millionaire businessman who retrieved Congress fortunes in
Orissa, is a more sinister figure. He could embrace extremism
of Left or Right with equal fervor. For tactical reasons he
has opted for Menon's socialism, but principles will never
interfere with his political mobility. In the summer of 1962
Desai was saying privately that he enjoyed Patnaik's support,
which must feel like the support provided by the hangman's
noose. Patnaik still lacks national stature, but he is dangerous because he combines political cunning and a certain
demagogic appeal with Menon-like drive and ambition. He
is unscrupulous and autocratic without needlessly alienating
his followers, as Menon does. He has the added advantages
of youth and good health. His most serious liabilities are his
reputation for shady business deals and his dependence on
primitive Orissa as a political base. Nevertheless, Patnaik is
a man to watch.

Jayaprakash Narayan enjoys wide popularity in parts of

India, but, as one British diplomat has observed, he is a man who likes to accumulate vast power in his hands in order to do nothing with it. I regard him as a candidate of last resort, to whom the Congress bosses would turn only if a succession of party-line premiers had brought India to the brink of ruin. Narayan still has the taste for power, but I doubt if he could absorb the shocks of office at his age and in his present state of disenchantment. No compass shows where he stands today in relation to any known political landmark. Narayan, the man whom Nehru once considered his most likely successor, has come so nearly full circle that he could say by 1962 that he agreed on "almost everything" with the Swatantra party, Nehru's bête noire. Indian revolutionaries—or prime ministers —must be made of sterner stuff than Narayan is.

A few Indians believe the stuff might be found in Ashoke Mehta, the scholarly young chairman of the Praja Socialist party and the only one of the party's four founders who still clings to it. Mehta and practically the entire PSP leadership were defeated for re-election to Parliament in 1962. The party's socialist platform has been pre-empted by the Communists on one side and Congress on the other, especially since 1955, when Congress became formally committed to a "socialist pattern of society." Mehta provides badly needed intellectual leavening for Indian politics, but he has shown little talent for organization and even less popular appeal. He spends much of his time abroad on lecture tours and other subsidized travel, which the West lavishes on articulate Indians. He may rejoin Congress in hopes of leading the Left Wing if Menon and Indira Gandhi are eliminated. But if he sticks with the moribund PSP, I think this dour and querulous figure can safely be consigned to ivy-covered lecture halls.

The most promising prime-ministerial timber I have seen in India grows in Bombay. Yeshwantrao Chavan, who, in November 1962, went to New Delhi as defense minister, is young (by the standards of Indian politics), intelligent, tireless, and infinitely adaptable. I think he is likely to prove India's most durable prime minister after Nehru and the one who most nearly approaches Nehru's stature. Chavan may not be ready to bid for the premiership before the mid-sixties at the earliest. Then I expect his political star to rise with phenomenal speed. He has the advantage of not being publicly identified with either the Desai or the Menon faction. Eventually, of course, he will have to define his position.

An army coup in India is unlikely to my way of thinking unless Congress dissolves after Nehru and allows the country to plunge into chaos. But if it were to happen, I am sure that Lieutenant General Brij Mohan Kaul, the most politically astute officer serving under Indian colors today, will be ready to step into the breach.

As I said at the beginning, the eight Indians I have dealt with are important not only because of their own political prospects, but because each represents, in my opinion, something enduring in contemporary India. They are, of course, not alone. There are many others—party bosses, dark horses, and ambitious members of the Congress rank and file—who may shoulder their way to the center of the stage or manipulate the players from the wings after Nehru.

One potential kingmaker is K. Kamaraj Nadar, a rough-hewn member of the toddy-tapping subcaste of Madras who has been that state's chief minister since 1954. Kamaraj, beetle-browed, taciturn, and impassive, looks like the captain of a pirate ship. He is generally considered the ablest chief minister in the business. A bachelor, he spends most of his time touring his state and talking with large numbers of its thirty-five million inhabitants. If he thinks a petitioner is wasting his time, Kamaraj simply murmurs the familiar Tamil phrase, *"Akaddum partpom,"* meaning "Let it be" or "We'll see," and moves on. But if he thinks something should be done, he acts at once. And more often than not, his orders are carried out, which cannot be said for most other state leaders in India. Madras is probably the best-administered state in India. Kamaraj keeps his cabinet small (unlike many other chief ministers, who try to accommodate all factions in their official family). His traveling retinue is held to a bare minimum. He is as unpretentious and direct as Chavan is. He cleaned up factionalism in the Madras Congress soon after he

came to power. His position is now so secure that he can defy
New Delhi on important matters and extract development
money from the Planning Commission with more success than
most state leaders. But he does not have to wage a running war
with the central government, as the late Dr. B. C. Roy used
to when he was chief minister of West Bengal. Kamaraj runs
a taut ship at home without resorting to the strong-arm tactics
that S. P. S. Kairon uses in the Punjab. A long-time foreign
resident of India told me, "No future government will be
able to operate in India without Kamaraj's approval, although
he could never be an all-India figure himself." This opinion
is well founded on all counts. Kamaraj could not come to
the Center with any hope of success because he speaks almost
no Hindi and little English. He is studying Hindi and under-
stands a good deal of English, but has a command of neither.
Even if he spoke both languages fluently, it would be difficult
for a Tamil to win support in north India. Moreover, as his
former protégé Subramaniam told me once, Kamaraj is the
kind of politician who prefers to stay close to the soil of his
native province and away from the pomp and protocol of
capitals. Tamil patriotism is unquenchable, and Kamaraj
knows where his political strength lies. In Delhi he would be
just another once-powerful state leader adrift in unfamiliar
waters. But as a member of the Congress Working Committee
and party boss of the most important south Indian state, his
role in choosing Nehru's successor will be comparable to that
of Governor David Lawrence, of Pennsylvania, at the 1960
Democratic National Convention.

The only threat to Congress in Madras today comes from
the Dravida Munnetra Kazhagam (DMK), or Dravidian *
Progressive Federation, a regional extremist party that is the
main opposition in the state legislature. The DMK exploits
south India's historic anti-Brahmanism and advocates secession
from the north. The party's bogy is "Hindi imperialism"—
meaning the attempt to impose Hindi, a north Indian tongue,
as the only official national language. Because Desai is a Hindi
proponent who has also said some needlessly tactless things

* The Dravidians are reputed to have been the original inhabitants of
south India.

about Kamaraj, the Chief Minister of Madras is likely to throw his support to Shastri in the immediate post-Nehru maneuvering. Shastri also favors the use of Hindi, but his approach and methods are far less autocratic than Desai's. The south feels it could live with Shastri; it is not so sure about Desai.

There are only three south Indians now conceded any chance of becoming prime minister. Menon is a maverick who might as well have been born on the moon as far as most south Indians are concerned. T. T. Krishnamachari, of Madras, former Union finance minister who is now in charge of economic and defense co-ordination in Nehru's cabinet, is a professed socialist and champion of state-owned industry. His record has not been free of scandal, and he suffers from the handicap (in south Indian eyes) of being a Brahman. TTK is a very long shot for the premiership, but he does have a certain Tamil agility of mind that would make him useful to a Left Wing Congress government. Subramaniam, who came to the Center for the first time in 1962, is another upper-caste south Indian, but he has a more attractive personality than either TTK or Menon has. He has executive ability of a high order. Everyone agrees that he is a rising figure, but he will have to establish a reputation in Delhi before he could possibly be considered for prime minister.

Kamaraj is known to dislike Menon. He has little use for TTK and is probably jealous of Chavan. I have a feeling that he would go along with Indira Gandhi if Shastri proved ephemeral.

India's sixty-five million untouchables have not yet acquired the political power of American Negroes, but they can no longer be ignored by caste Hindus. Many of the outcastes are swayed by the two members of their community who have attained most prominence in Congress: Jagjivan Ram, the rotund, Left-leaning minister of transport and communications, who has served longer in the Union cabinet than anyone except Nehru, and Damodaram Sanjivayya, who at forty-one became the first untouchable elected president of Congress. Ram's record as railways minister, before he was switched to his present post in April 1962, was marred by scandals and a series of fatal accidents. He is retained in accordance with the principle of communal "balance," which will become even more important in Delhi cabinet-making after Nehru. Anyone who knows how New York City slates are drawn up to include at least one Jew, one Irish Catholic, and one Italian can understand why Jagjivan Ram is still in Delhi. Sanjivayya was not particularly effective as chief minister of the south Indian state of Andhra, but he began to show promise after his election in June 1962 to the Congress presidency.

Neither Jagjivan Ram nor Sanjivayya can deliver the entire untouchable vote, because both the Communists and the Republican party (founded by former untouchables who have embraced Buddhism) have sizable support among the outcastes. Nevertheless, the two leading Congress untouchables will have a say when Nehru's successor is nominated. Jagjivan Ram may throw in his lot with Menon or Indira Gandhi. Sanjivayya's preferences are not widely known, but I think he might back Mrs. Gandhi or Shastri.

By rights, the chief minister of Uttar Pradesh, with some seventy-four million people in his state (the most populous in India), should exert strong influence in the selection of the next prime minister. In fact, the UP Congress party has been so riddled with factionalism and "groupism" that C. B. Gupta, the chief minister, will need several years to consolidate his own position before he can speak with authority in party councils. Whatever power he wields, his choice of a successor will be purely opportunistic, based on the tactical situation at the moment.

Bihar, India's second-most-populous state, with almost forty-seven million inhabitants, produced many leaders during the independence movement, but today its chief minister is a nonentity and the state Congress is a shambles. Bihar's most illustrious son, former President Rajendra Prasad, retired at the age of seventy-seven in May 1962 after a prolonged illness. Although his conservative Gandhian views still carry weight with many Congressmen, Rajendra Babu (as he is affectionately known in India) is obviously a declining force in national politics. Bihar's only other contributions are Narayan, Subhag Singh, and the Jan Sangh leader, A. B. Vajpayee.

West Bengal, whose capital is Calcutta, has a more sophisticated electorate than any other Indian state has. Historically Bengal has played a prominent role in India's cultural and political life. Tagore was from Bengal. Now, however, the temperamental Bengalis have virtually withdrawn from the scramble for power in Delhi. They take a kind of perverse satisfaction in their economic misery, which they blame entirely on the Center. West Bengal (whose predominantly Moslem eastern half now forms East Pakistan) regards itself as the Cinderella of India. It has produced no national leaders of importance since independence. The death on July 1, 1962, of Dr. B. C. Roy, the state's venerable chief minister, threatened to plunge the local Congress into the same factional turmoil as in Madhya Pradesh, Rajasthan, and other states where the party is divided. The only Bengali Congressman who seems to have any hope for rising in national politics is Ashoke K. Sen, the youthful Union law minister, who defeated a strong Communist bid to unseat him in the 1962 election.

India has three elder statesmen whose voices are still heard on the national scene. The founder of the Swatantra party, Chakravarti Rajagopalachari, is eighty-three and almost toothless. Although he is still mentally alert and occasionally astringent in his attacks on Congress, his importance seems to be dwindling. Acharya J. B. Kripalani, the Gandhian ex-president of Congress, now seventy-four, went into semi-retirement after failing to unseat Krishna Menon in the much-publicized North Bombay election in 1962. He had quit the PSP even before the election, and now appears headed for a political comeback if he can regain his seat in Parliament in a by-election. The third member of this aged trinity is Acharya Vinoba Bhave, Gandhi's so-called "spiritual heir" and apostle of the Bhoodan land-gift movement. Bhave is now sixty-seven and in indifferent health. He has succeeded to a large extent in keeping himself and Bhoodan out of party politics, although many of the things he says are implied criticisms of the bureaucratism that has overtaken

Congress. Vinobaji, as he is called, will probably play no political role after Nehru unless his confederate Narayan is summoned to take the helm. His orthodox Gandhism seems to be a waning attraction.

One elder statesman who will figure significantly in the political process after Nehru is India's President, Sarvepalli Radhakrishnan, who succeeded Rajendra Prasad in May 1962 for a five-year term. Radhakrishnan, who is seventy-four, is a scholar and Kantian philosopher of world renown who clearly intends to exercise much more of the executive authority vested in the president than his predecessor ever did. Under the Constitution, all executive power, including supreme command of the armed forces, is vested in the president. He appoints the prime minister, summons and dissolves Parliament, and issues executive ordinances when Parliament is not in session. The chief of state is also empowered to proclaim a state of emergency and to take over the administration of any state. Nehru's dominance reduced Prasad largely to figurehead status. After Nehru, the president will have proportionately more prestige because Nehru's successors will have less. Radhakrishnan has the added advantage of having been in Delhi's limelight as vice-president from 1952 to 1962. As Frank Moraes says, "With Nehru's withdrawal from the political scene and the growing pressure of non-Congress groups in various states, the fulcrum of power would tend to be identified with the president rather than the prime minister, since in theory all executive power of the Union of India is vested in the former, and the likelihood of his exercising it more assertively will increase in the changed circumstances."

In the event of a deadlock in the Congress hierarchy over the succession, Radhakrishnan's stand could be decisive. If the party leaders' nominee for the premiership did not suit him, he could withhold his consent and force them to reconsider. Such pressure might well tilt the balance in favor of Radhakrishnan's choice. Whomever he supports, the President is expected to uphold constitutional procedure. He is articulate, democratically minded, and suspicious of Menon and the other Congress Left Wingers. His preference would probably be for a successor from either the moderate or the Rightist group in the party.

Personalities and political ideas have dominated this book. In India personalities are tremendously important. It would be a mistake, however, to conclude without a reminder that the forces shaping India today and destined to shape it in the decade after Nehru are not primarily generated by leaders or the ideology they profess. These elemental impulses spring from the ancient soil of India. The will to worship—gods or men—is stronger than the most secular democrat in India. Caste will outlive every leader discussed here. A bicycle or a metal-tipped plow is probably a more powerful engine of change than the platforms of all the political parties in the country. The most important changes are often unnoticed by-products of the much-advertised "reforms" enacted by Parliament and promulgated by the president. For example, land reform has generally failed to achieve the goals set by its proponents, but by prompting a city-ward migration of Brahmans, it has profoundly altered the social and political structure of the Indian countryside. The reason is that land reform has expropriated absentee landlords, many of whom were Brahmans, but has not affected resident landowners (mostly of lower castes), who have been able to evade the law by making a paper division of their holdings among members of their family. The upshot is that in Maharashtra and several other states non-Brahmans now control village panchayats for the first time. The caste complexion of panchayats is infinitely more important than are their party affiliations. Such changes in the countryside have not yet stimulated any wide upsurge of initiative or prosperity, but they may eventually produce an entirely new breed of political leaders, who will supplant the upper-caste hierarchy that now assumes it will continue ruling India after Nehru. The new class of lower-caste politicians may be more egalitarian; it may also be more corrupt and less inclined to temporize with the vagaries of democracy.

Whenever I think about India's future, I am reminded of a tiny Siva temple on a hilltop in Kashmir that I visited once. I could hear the worshipers performing their devotions, but in the semidarkness I could not make them out clearly. I was conscious of motion, a kind of intensity of feeling, and the overpowering smell of incense, yet it was impossible to say who was leading the prayers, or, indeed, if there was a leader at all. So it is, too, with that most inscrutable riddle, India.

acharya: literally, "teacher"; an honorific title given elder statesmen and others supposed to possess wisdom

achkan: a long coat buttoned up to the neck

ahimsa: noninjury to animal life or nonviolence regarded as a religious principle

AICC: the All-India Congress Committee, the national committee of the Congress party, which meets twice yearly. Its membership now exceeds 500, based on a ratio of one member to every 100,000 of the population.

Anavil: literally, "without blemish." It refers to a caste in Gujarat whose members are Brahmans by birth but traditionally farmers by occupation.

anna: a coin equal to one sixteenth of a rupee; about four fifths of a cent at current exchange rates. The Indian government has legally replaced the anna with a rupee consisting of one hundred naye paise.

Ayur-Veda: the book of the ancient, indigenous Hindu system of medicine

Azad Dasta: literally, "the Freedom Brigade"; guerrilla

fighters equipped and trained in Nepal during World War II by the Indian underground for use against the British in India

bania: a member of the Vaisya or merchant-trader caste. Banias are often petty storekeepers. The term has assumed a derogatory connotation when used by non-Banias.

Bharatiya Jan Sangh   (usually referred to simply as *Jan Sangh):* the Indian People's party—the traditionalist, Right Wing Hindu party

bhoodan: literally, "land gift"; the movement started by Acharya Vinoba Bhave to collect voluntary land donations for distribution among landless laborers in the countryside

bidi: a cheap Indian cigarette in which the tobacco is rolled in leaves instead of paper. It is smoked mostly by the poor.

Center: the term used in Indian politics to denote the central government in New Delhi

charkha: a hand-operated, one-spindle spinning wheel which became the Congress party symbol after Gandhi launched his campaign to replace imported, machine-made cloth with homespun

chief minister: the highest elected official of any constituent state of the Indian republic; roughly equivalent in power to the governor of an American state

chiuda: parboiled, hand-pounded rice

communalism: the general term used in India to cover religious and caste differences, especially when exploited for political purposes. The word sometimes refers to any caste, linguistic, or regional division, but most often it is used in connection with Hindu-Moslem or Hindu-Sikh relations.

Community Development: the name of the village improvement program launched in India in 1951. It has now been widely extended throughout the country, with varying effectiveness.

Congress Working Committee: the twenty-one-member supreme executive body of the Congress party *darshana:*   literally, a "glimpse." It usually refers to spiritual communion with a god or some eminent figure.

dhoti: the diaper-like white cotton garment that many Indian men wear in place of trousers

Dravidian: the term used to describe the original inhabitants of south India before the Aryan influx from the north. It also denotes any of the indigenous languages spoken in south India today.

gosamvardhana: literally, "the development of cow wealth"; the slogan taken up by Hindu traditionalists who oppose cow slaughter on religious grounds

gram sabha: the assembly of all adults in a village which is supposed to oversee the functioning of the village panchayat, or council

gramdan: literally, "village gift"; a movement associated with bhoodan in which private ownership of all land is relinquished in favor of collective village ownership

gumashta: a revenue clerk or agent appointed by a landlord to administer a village controlled by him

Gurkha: one of the class of Nepalese mountain people who have long served with distinction as mercenaries in the British and Indian armies

Harijans: literally, "children of God," the name Gandhi bestowed on untouchables

hartal: a stoppage of all activity, usually used to exert economic or political pressure

Hindi: the most widely spoken Indian language, and mother tongue of about 40 per cent of the population. Hindi is the official language of India, but English has retained its associate status under pressure from non-Hindi-speaking areas, principally south India

ICS: the Indian Civil Service, a mixed British and Indian administrative corps that attained the status of a governing elite during British rule. The initials after an official's name are still a badge of respectability in government circles.

Jain: an adherent of Jainism, a sect of Hinduism founded about the sixth century B.C. in which the principle of nonviolence and preservation of all living creatures is carried to its most extreme lengths

jawan: a common soldier, the Indian equivalent of GI

jeevandan: dedication of one's life to a cause, usually to Bhoodan in current usage

Karma: the Hindu doctrine that holds that every deed, good or bad, entails certain consequences that may appear during successive incarnations of the soul. It is often called the doctrine of retribution.

Kashi Vidyapeeth: the so-called National University founded at Banaras as a result of Gandhi's campaign against British-supported educational institutions.

Kayastha: an intermediate caste originally composed of scribes and petty government officials who served the Moguls at a time when the Brahmans boycotted the Moslem conquerors. Kayasthas are now widely dispersed over north India.

khaddar or *khadi:*   hand-spun and hand-woven cloth popularized by Gandhi during his campaign against imported machine-made cloth. Khaddar has long been the symbol of allegiance to the Congress party.

kucheri: the place where a magistrate or other local official conducts judicial and administrative affairs in a town or larger village. The word originally referred to a court, but has come to mean any place where administration is conducted in a smaller locality.

lathi: a long metal-tipped stave used by Indian police to disperse crowds

Lok Sabha: House of the People, the lower house of India's central Parliament in New Delhi

mantra: a Hindu hymn or psalm

Maratha: the martial Hindu caste concentrated in what is now the state of Maharashtra, in western India. The most famous Maratha leader, Sivaji, established an empire in the seventeenth century, remnants of which survived into the early part of the nineteenth. The Marathas are primarily farmers and soldiers. Their language is Marathi.

maund: a measure of weight equivalent to between 25 and 82.28 lbs. depending on the district

Moslem League: the principal Moslem political party during the British period. The League's leader, the late Mohammed Ali Jinnah, is regarded as the father of Pakistan. In parts of India where the Moslem minority is politically important, the Moslem League is still active, although it disavows any links with Pakistan.

Nair: a member of the powerful administrative caste that has historically controlled government and politics in what is now the state of Kerala. The Menons are a sub-caste of the Nairs.

neem: an evergreen tree believed by many Hindus to have sacred significance

padayatra: a walking tour, usually undertaken by political campaigners

panchayat: an Indian village council originally supposed to consist of five elders

panchayat-i-raj: a system of local government under which authority is decentralized to democratically elected bodies at the village, block, and district levels

panchayat samiti: a statutory representative body elected by a number of panchayats grouped in a development "block"

Panch Sheel or *panch shila:*   the so-called "Five Principles of Coexistence" first enunciated in the preamble to the Sino-Indian treaty of 1954 on trade with Tibet. The principles are mutual respect for each other's territorial integrity and sovereignty; nonaggression; noninterference in each other's internal affairs; equality and mutual advantage, and peaceful coexistence and economic co-operation. The 1954 treaty has now lapsed.

Parsi: a descendant of Zoroastrian Persians who migrated to India as religious refugees after the Arab invasion of Persia in the eighth century A.D. The Parsis are now concentrated in Bombay and are engaged mainly in commerce and the professions.

Patri Sarkar: the movement to establish a "parallel" or insurgent government in the Satara district, southeast of Bombay, during World War II. Although the movement succeeded in challenging British authority in many parts of the district, no "parallel government" was ever established.

raj: literally, kingdom or empire; used in such expressions as the "British raj"

Rajput: a member of the high martial caste that long held sway in the arid fastnesses of what is today the state of Rajasthan. Rajputs are now found in many parts of northern India.

Rajya Sabha: the House of the Nation, the upper house of India's central Parliament

Rashtriya Swayamsevak Sangh (RSS):   the so-called National Volunteer Association, a militant organization of Hindu extremists often involved in conflict with Indian Moslems

sadhu: a holy man, usually a mendicant

sampattidan: the gift of one's wealth for community projects or village betterment

sarvodaya: literally, "the uplift of all"; the Gandhian ideal of the good life based on social uplift, with strong emphasis on village life and traditional Hindu values. The *sarvodaya* ideal is now propagated by a loosely organized movement of Gandhi's disciples and followers.

satyagraha: literally, "force of truth" or "soul force"; nonviolent civil disobedience originally used by Gandhi as a weapon against the British, now often employed for political and economic causes

Scheduled Castes and *Scheduled Tribes:*   the names used in the Indian Constitution to describe untouchables and members of backward tribes who have retained their tribal identity. These groups are guaranteed special protection under the Constitution, including reserved places in legislative bodies, educational institutions, and government offices.

sepoy: the old term for a soldier

Shanti Sena: the so-called Peace Brigade, a private voluntary organization set up to promote communal harmony and to intervene if necessary in Hindu-Moslem outbreaks

Shastri: literally, a "learned man" or "one versed in knowledge"; the honorific surname given to graduates of the so-called Shastri course at the Gandhi-sponsored Kashi Vidyapeeth (National University) at Banaras during the British period.

shramdan: voluntary donation of one's labor, usually for a community project

Sikh: literally, a "disciple"; a member of the martial religious community that grew up in the Punjab in the time of Moslem rule as a reformist monotheistic sect. The founders of Sikhism borrowed heavily from both Islam and Hinduism. Sikhs are now found in all parts of India and many foreign countries.

Siva (pronounced shee-va):   one of the supreme Hindu deities, thought to embody the powers of destruction as well as reproductive or restoring power. Siva worshipers are one of the most numerous Hindu sects.

swaraj: independence

Tamil: a member of the largest linguistic group in south India. Tamils are also found in Ceylon, Burma, and Singapore as well as in all parts of India. The word also denotes their language, the oldest and most highly developed of the south Indian Dravidian tongues.

toddy: an intoxicating drink made in south India from the flower of the coconut palm. Toddy-tappers are a caste whose members collect the palm liquor.

Urdu: the most widely spoken north Indian language after Hindi. Urdu developed as a lingua franca in army camps in Moslem times. It is now the official language of West Pakistan and one of the fourteen languages recognized for official use by the Indian Constitution.

zamindar: a hereditary revenue collector under British rule who became the *de facto* landlord of areas under his jurisdiction, often including entire villages

zila parishad: an elected council set up by law at the district level in rural areas and usually charged with administration and development

INDEX